Praise for *Faery*

"This promises to be the fairy book of the year."
—Simon Young, secretary of the Fairy Investigation Society

"A comprehensive assessment of the attributes of faerie folklore, which will provide an indispensable guide for many years … For anyone interested in how the concept of the faeries has infiltrated our culture through centuries of folklore, John Kruse's encyclopedic treatment of the subject matter is essential reading."
—Dr. Neil Rushton, archaeologist and freelance writer of mythology and faerie lore

FAERY

About the Author

John Kruse is a writer and blogger on faery themes. His professional interests are law and legal history, but in recent years he has brought his research skills to a subject that has fascinated him since his late teens. In 2016 he began to write the *British Fairies* blog on WordPress. In 2017 he published *British Fairies* with Green Magic Publishing and he has several other books on faery and faery beasts forthcoming.

To Write to the Author

If you wish to contact the author or would like more information about this book, please write to the author in care of Llewellyn Worldwide Ltd. and we will forward your request. Both the author and publisher appreciate hearing from you and learning of your enjoyment of this book and how it has helped you. Llewellyn Worldwide Ltd. cannot guarantee that every letter written to the author can be answered, but all will be forwarded. Please write to:

John T. Kruse
℅ Llewellyn Worldwide
2143 Wooddale Drive
Woodbury, MN 55125-2989

Please enclose a self-addressed stamped envelope for reply,
or $1.00 to cover costs. If outside the U.S.A., enclose
an international postal reply coupon.

Many of Llewellyn's authors have websites with additional
information and resources. For more information,
please visit our website at http://www.llewellyn.com

JOHN T. KRUSE

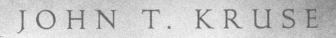

FAERY

A Guide to the Lore, Magic & World of the Good Folk

Llewellyn Publications
Woodbury, Minnesota

Foreword by Morgan Daimler

FIRST EDITION
Third Printing, 2023

Book design by Samantha Penn
Cover design by Kevin Brown
Cover illustration by Dominick Finelle
Interior illustrations by Wen Hsu

Llewellyn Publications is a registered trademark of Llewellyn Worldwide Ltd.

Library of Congress Cataloging-in-Publication Data
Names: Kruse, John T., author.
Title: Faery : a guide to the lore, magic & world of the good folk / John
    T. Kruse ; foreword by Morgan Daimler.
Description: First edition. | Woodbury, Minnesota : Llewellyn Publications,
    2020. | Includes bibliographical references and index.
Identifiers: LCCN 2019055143 (print) | LCCN 2019055144 (ebook) | ISBN
    9780738761893 (paperback) | ISBN 9780738761978 (ebook)
Subjects: LCSH: Fairies—Great Britain. | Folklore—Great Britain.
Classification: LCC GR549 .K78 2020 (print) | LCC GR549 (ebook) | DDC
    398.20941—dc23
LC record available at https://lccn.loc.gov/2019055143
LC ebook record available at https://lccn.loc.gov/2019055144

Llewellyn Publications
A Division of Llewellyn Worldwide Ltd.
2143 Wooddale Drive
Woodbury, MN 55125-2989
www.llewellyn.com

Printed in the United States of America

Other Books by John Kruse
British Fairies

For Sue, for her love and support, Rhiannon,
Fliss, and the Lady of the Elder Tree.

CONTENTS

Section 2

❧ ❧

FINDING FAERIES

Section 3

FAERY LIFE

Section 4

CONTACT WITH THE FAE

Section 5

❧ ❧

MODERN TIMES

FOREWORD
by Morgan Daimler

Fairies are a subject that has intrigued people across the world and across time. They appear in the earliest written Irish mythologies and fill the pages of modern urban fantasy; they once captivated Shakespeare's audiences and today fascinate contemporary moviegoers. Fairies cavort in early modern artwork and across the greeting cards and posters of the twenty-first century. Songs have been written about them and there are even several songs supposedly passed on from them by people who have heard fairy music firsthand. Fairies have been found in every form of human art and expression, perhaps because they are intrinsically linked to us. As foreign as they often seem to be in their actions and moods, they nonetheless are intimately tied to humanity. Yet in our fast paced and technologically modern Western world they remain shrouded in mystery.

Perhaps some of that can be put down to the slow erosion and loss of the older folklore and folk beliefs that have formed the backbone of fairy beliefs. It has been said that, since at least Chaucer's time, fairies were in retreat. While it never appeared be true, every generation claimed that fairy belief was waning and had been stronger in their grandparents' time. Yet in the twenty-first century there may be for the first time some bite in this claim. This is not because the fairies are actually leaving, but because they have been radically re-envisioned in popular culture with mainstream belief replacing the boggart of folklore with that of Harry Potter, and the human-size, ambivalent fairy folk with Disney's tiny Tinker Bell and friends. Paganism is not exempt from these newly remodeled fairies either, with many books aimed at a Pagan audience gleefully adopting the twee fairies or looking to the New Age and Victorian understandings of fairies to shape their own.

One might be tempted to think that these reimagined fairies are the sum of what fairies today have become, but this is not so; rather, they are the illusion that fairies have taken on, which obscures the older, often grimmer, culturally based folklore. However, the genuine folklore and belief does persist, but it is not as easily accessible to a wider audience, and therein lies a considerable problem for those fairy-seekers who aren't embedded in a living culture that still includes fairy belief. Certainly many older works of folklore can now be found in the public domain. But those must be taken in their context and read with an understanding of the biases with which they were written; that task can be complicated if the reader isn't aware of what the problems with the works are. It is also possible to connect to the living cultures on an individual scale, but that is also often complicated, and sometimes very difficult. And individual connections are ultimately only a short-term solution to reviving and revitalizing the fairy beliefs. The only way to bring the folklore outward to a wider audience, and for the beliefs and ideas surrounding them as they exist today to be preserved, is for them to be written about, ideally in a thoughtful manner that acknowledges their sources. I am delighted to see John Kruse taking on that effort.

To really understand who and what fairies are, we have to look beyond the current façade that has sprung up around them, the modern glamour that cloaks them in forms both friendly and harmless. To find the still-beating heart of Faery we have to dig deeper into the folklore and the living cultures that preserve the beliefs. This is a uniquely challenging quest in a world that is as full of false leads as it is of true information, but there are good resources out there to be found. This book, Kruse's *Faery: A Guide to the Lore, Magic, and World of the Good Folk*, is one of the rare few that delivers on its promises to give readers a glimpse into the otherworld and an understanding of the beings who dwell within it. It touches on the folklore but doesn't neglect the living modern beliefs either, and includes a balance of theory that is nicely delineated from established folk belief.

Kruse's *Faery: A Guide to the Lore, Magic, and World of the Good Folk* is a much needed addition to the corpus of fairy lore on the market, even more essential because the subject of British fairies has sadly been neglected in recent years. Nothing this thorough on the topic has been produced since Simpson and Roud's *Dictionary of English Folklore*—and yet, what that work lacked in depth on the subject of fairies, Kruse's work more than fulfills, going further with its inclusion of practical material and thoughtful analysis. While there is some natural crossover between fairy lore, British—and specifically English—fairies are truly an essential niche too often glossed over in favour of the more popular Celtic fairies. I am delighted to see such an in-depth and thoughtful work on the subject and readers will no doubt find themselves both intrigued and educated as they proceed on into Kruse's careful guide through faeryland and introduction to its inhabitants.

Morgan Daimler
Author of *Fairies: A Guide to the Celtic Fair Folk* and *A New Fairies Dictionary*

Section 1
INTRODUCTION

Chapter 1

MEETING THE GOOD FOLK

This book is about the centuries-old relationship between humans and faery-kind. This interaction, this dialogue, between mortal and supernatural is absolutely central to our knowledge of Faery. It is only through this relationship that we can know our faery neighbours. They come from another realm or dimension; they may visit our world but they exist mainly outside it. The faeries have almost no concern with our preoccupations with books, records, and the history of events in time; none of these have any meaning or utility to them and, as a result, we shall never have a faery account of faeryland. The sole way that we can understand the faeries is through the lens of our dealings with them—and their treatment of us.

Nearly a century ago, Welsh folklore researcher Mary Lewes wrote about what she called "the path of the faery faith." She described how it "takes us to a region where, in some strange way, we feel at home; as if something or someone in us had "once upon a time" dwelt in that serene country of faeryland, where all things happened as we wished and where the only danger lay in the knowledge and exercise of those emotions which possess and disturb our human plane."[1]

In her poem "The Fairies' Cobbler," Rosamund M. Watson describes a visit from the faeries, who sweep in with a sound like old dried leaves, their slim shapes dark in the evening light but their eyes glowing brightly. The cobbler looks up to greet them because "I felt the Good Folk near."[2] I have felt fascinated with and at home in this region for many years, researching British faery lore, immersed in the myths of Wales and Ireland and enchanted by the romances of King Arthur. In this book I want to guide others along the curious winding paths I've followed, in the hope that we may all feel the Good Folk near.

My Faery Philosophy

It might be helpful for me to begin by being explicit about my approach to the subject, to outline some of the fundamental ideas that lie behind what I've written. What are my basic preconceptions about faerykind? What assumptions and prejudices may I be carrying over into my interpretation of the folklore sources?

First, I have almost exclusively concentrated on the folklore of the British Isles, by which I mean Britain along with Orkney, Shetland, and the Isle of Man. Particularly within the mainland of Britain there's a common core of shared ideas and knowledge that has deep roots dating back at least two thousand years. Over that time, we have been in constant and evolving contact with our resident supernaturals. Every country and every people have their own conceptions and classifications of faery and I feel that to borrow examples too liberally from too many sources results in a loss of clarity and focus. This is not a book of comparative folklore, in which I try to uncover the personal and social factors that might have given rise to faery belief within a community. Instead, this book is a description of who the British faeries are, what they do, and what they want. The faery lore of the British Isles is an integrated whole: common ideas and processes can be traced through the ages and across the regions. For that reason, by eschewing a "pick and mix"

---

1. Lewes, *The Queer Side of Things*, 111.
2. Watson, "The Fairies' Cobbler," *The Poems of Rosamund Marriott Watson*.

approach and by concentrating on one consistent and coherent body of faery lore, we can understand faery temperament and conduct far more accurately and get much nearer to analysing what motivates them.[3]

The key features of my faery beliefs are quite clear. First, I see the faeries as being present amongst us here and now. For example, the Fae folk I've depicted in my novels are resident amongst their human neighbours (if, perhaps, in more marginal areas) yet, at the same time, they are not wholly of the present. Their speech and material culture are all slightly adrift from ours and this can give rise to misunderstanding on both sides as a consequence.

I see faeries as being very like humans; they are of the same stature and form—no wings, therefore—although they may be marked out by the colour of their hair or their eyes. Their life span is very different, however. Faeries are prepared to interact with humans—socially, intellectually, and, quite often, sexually. There may well be an element of exploitation by them in this—especially as, at the same time, they like to protect their privacy. The faeries will tolerate contact with humans on their terms and at the times and places of their choosing. Nonetheless, they wish to hold themselves apart from us, and resent any uninvited intrusion. The faeries are not to be antagonised or ignored—and it follows from this that trespasses into faery territory may be punished. Attracting the antipathy of faerykind is to be avoided because they are powerful; they have magical abilities and they will not hesitate to use force against offending humans.

It follows from what has already been said that I think the faeries *have their own aims, objectives, and agenda.* Interaction with humans is undertaken for their own ends. It may be pleasurable (the sex) but it serves other, greater purposes too. The faeries expect respect and compliance with their wishes.

Lastly, but very importantly, I see the faeries as a timeless part of the land. It seems natural to me to associate them with standing stones, burial mounds, and other ancient monuments of the British Isles.

That's a summary of the key themes and characteristics that I realise have united all the faery fiction that I've written, and that permeate my approach to

---

3. Morgan Daimler has recently done something very similar for the Celtic faery tradition, covering Ireland and parts of Britain, in *Fairies: A Guide to the Celtic Fair Folk.*

the great body of faery lore we have. These, then, are the prejudices I brought to writing this book! Unavoidably, they will have shaped my approach to how the text was imagined and organised.

Faeries and Culture

Whatever our views on the existence (or not) of the Good Folk and of a supernatural realm, there can be no denying the profound impact of Faery (or the idea of it) upon our art and culture. The reason for all this creativity, it seems to me, is that Faery as a subject is so rich and complex. Faeries can offer artists every emotion: sexual obsession, love, fear, jealousy, unbounded joy, mystery, and mysticism—the list is lengthy. Fae themes have been persistently rich sources of inspiration for a range of artists, whether in literature, song, or the visual arts. I'll present a few examples, though I'm sure that proof is scarcely needed for most of the readers of this book.

Faeries have been influential on the stage, whether inspiring the high art of Shakespeare or in pantomimes and popular plays such as *Peter Pan*. They have provided inspiration for novels and short stories (for both adults and children), from Charles Kingsley and George MacDonald; through Enid Blyton, Beatrix Potter, and E. Nesbit; to Tolkien, Alan Garner, and J. K. Rowling. In romance and legend, faery themes are strong, found constantly throughout many of the Arthurian myths and in related stories, including the Welsh *Mabinogion*.

The Good Folk have always provided a rich source of inspiration for poetry, from Robert Herrick and Michael Drayton through Keats and Blake to Walter de la Mare and Ivor Gurney. In the visual arts they have inspired numerous paintings, from the nightmare visions of Fuseli to Froud; in illustration, from Rossetti and Burne-Jones through Edmund Dulac, Arthur Rackham, and Henry Justice Ford to the flower faeries of Cicely Mary Barker and Margaret Tarrant. There has even been faery-inspired sculpture—for example, the puppets of Wendy Froud or the wire creations of Robin Wright. In modern times, the Fae have successfully colonised film and cartoon, so we have both fantasy films, such as Disney's *Peter Pan* or *The Dark Crystal*, as well as documentaries and "factual" stories based upon the Cottingley case. Lastly, and very powerfully, there is faery-influenced music, ranging from ballet, opera, ballads, light opera—such as Gilbert and Sullivan—to contemporary rock (Led Zeppelin or Sigur Rós).

Of course, the additional value of all of the above is that they are a supplement to the folklore evidence. As with traditional stories of faeries gathered by folklorists in the field, these various extra media give us a view of contemporary beliefs on the conduct and appearance of the Fae. These are rich resources, but there is a drawback too. The danger of the very fertile nature of faery belief is that it has created an abundance of images (in plays and stories as well as pictures) and these are often more familiar to us than the original folklore. As a result, we confuse the two, or allow the artistic representations to displace the source material: we remember Shakespeare and Peter Pan and forget our homegrown and authentic pixies and brownies. I shall return to this theme several times during the book; what we often think of as faery lore bears no resemblance to traditional thinking.

What's more, faery works have in turn inspired other faery art. For example, Shakespeare's *A Midsummer Night's Dream* has been the source for many works of art (by Paton, Dadd, Millais, and many others). In a very good example, the famous play inspired a painting by Thomas Stothard, *Oberon and Titania,* which in turn inspired a poem by Letitia Elizabeth Landon, "The Fairy Queen Sleeping." In just the same way, Louisa Anne Meredith wrote "The Enchanted Island" in 1825 in response to seeing the painting of the same name by Francis Darby; "'Tis the fairies' home," the verse declares.

I'll make a radical suggestion: even were faeries proved not to exist, their impact upon human culture would be almost undiminished. We might even propose that, even if faeries did not exist, it would have been necessary to invent them to provide ourselves with such rich and fruitful veins of imagery and ideas.

The faeries have inspired our creativity for centuries, whether the ultimate source of that inspiration is our own imaginations or is an external supernatural force. The power of this creative stimulus is expressly acknowledged by artists working in this genre. It is not just a matter of the work produced, but of the transformative impact upon the artists themselves. Interviewed by Signe Pike for her book *Faery Tale,* painter Brian Froud said that many of his readers and fans sense that with a rediscovery of their faery faith, "they feel they are coming home. They tell me they want to go away and write, or make something…" His wife agreed: "Often people have a creative response to our work." She starts her puppet workshops with meditation, within which "you do actually, genuinely, touch faeryland—you're in it, whether you realise it or not. So, when you come back, and make a figure, it's imbued with its own personality." In the act of imaginative faery creation, it would seem, there is a re-creation of the creator.[4]

In his introduction to David Riche's *Art of Faery* (2003), Brian Froud further argued that "Faeries mediate art, the mysterious moments of our creative relationship with the world." Whilst the twentieth century had emphasised our alienation from the world, the resurgence of visionary faery art in its last decades and into the new millennium suggests the reversal of this, and through that resurgence "the beginning of a spiritual journey. To paint faeries is not childish—but it could certainly be said to be childlike—in its openness to creative and emotional impulses."[5]

Our culture is richer for faeries; we are richer for faeries. In fact, I'd say it was a process of mutual enrichment that has been going on for centuries. Before looking in detail at this deep and complex relationship as it exists today, I want to spend a little time sketching out its evolution and some of its perennial concepts.

---

4. Pike, *Faery Tale* (London: Hay House, 2010).

5. Riche and Froud, *The Art of Faery*, Foreword.

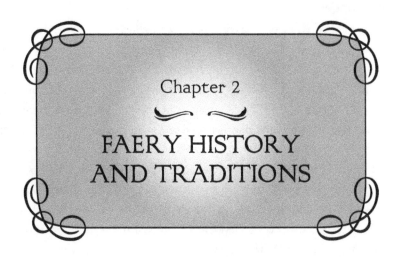

Chapter 2

FAERY HISTORY AND TRADITIONS

How humans understand their faery neighbours has evolved over the centuries—and is still evolving. In this book I draw upon the rich and extensive folklore of the whole of the British Isles to formulate as detailed a picture as possible of the Good Folk inhabiting this land.

The British view of the Good Folk is a complex amalgam of elements, the core being brought by successive invaders of these shores, to which have been added concepts derived from classical and continental culture. Our perspective and our reactions have shifted as time has passed, but there's a fundamental body of knowledge that has remained constant for at least a millennium. In this chapter, I sketch out how our understanding of the Good Folk has deepened and become richer over our many centuries of contact.

Anglo-Saxon Elves

When Saxon immigrants arrived on British shores in the sixth century, they brought with them an established body of belief on faeries and elves. Here I outline the core elements of that mythology, before it interacted with existing insular British ideas.

Saxon Sources

We get an idea of what our Saxon ancestors believed from several sources. There are their own literary productions—poems, stories and medical texts—which provide valuable information. There are contemporary Norse texts which examine the Viking pantheon. Lastly, we may compare more recent Scandinavian—especially Danish—folk beliefs with English faery stories; where they share elements, it's reasonable to suggest that these derive from an early, common mythology believed by the Saxons and Danes in their common homeland, and probably by all the continental Germanic tribes.

Viking myth is a good starting point for us, as it gives a clear statement of Northern European ideas about the elves. In the early 1200s in Iceland, scholar Snorri Sturluson compiled the so-called *Prose Edda,* a record of the Norse myths and legends. The story *Gylfaginning* describes the heavens and the many splendid places there:

> There is one place that is called *Alfheim* [the home of the elves]. There live the folk called light-elves, while the dark-elves live down in the ground. They are unlike them in appearance, and even more unlike them in nature. Light-elves are fairer than the sun to look at, but dark-elves are blacker than pitch.

The Vikings differentiated between the light elves living in the sky and the dark elves living underground. In much later British belief, we come across stories of Elfame from Lowland Scotland. It seems inescapable that this local version of an underground faeryland—the *elf-hame* or "elf-home"—is a direct remnant from the earliest English and Norse legends. As we'll see later, this place is conceived as a subterranean kingdom where the good faeries, the so-called "seelie court," reside.

As for the division of Anglo-Saxon Faery into light and dark, or good and bad, elves, there are several later references to ghostly "white fae" in later English folklore, and one echo that may be particularly significant. Being interrogated on charges of witchcraft in 1566, John Walsh of Netherbury in Dorset told his inquisitors "that there be iii kinds of faeries—white, green and black. Whereof the blacke faeries is the worst…" If the colours reflect more than mere taste in clothes, and are symbolic of their natures, there could be here another survival of the light/dark opposition. It's also worth noting the Old English term *aelfscyne* (very roughly, "elf-shining"), which was applied to women in a couple of texts. The word seems to imply something like "elf-beautiful" or even "enchantingly bright"; perhaps in this suggestion of light or radiance there is a further hint of the light and dark elf dichotomy.[6]

Elvish Ways

From the limited evidence it may be possible to sketch out a basic Anglo-Saxon mythology of an *elf-home*, divided between the good (light) elves and the bad (dark) elves. Beyond that, it's not safe to go. Luckily, although we can't be sure exactly where the Old English elves lived, we do possess some direct evidence of Saxon conceptions of their moods and behaviour.

The elves are mentioned in several medical texts as the cause of illnesses, mainly internal pains or mental disturbances. For instance, a spell to cure "the stitch" goes as follows:

> Out little spear, if herein it be …
> To them another I wish to send back …
> A flying dart against them in return …
> If it were gods' shot, or if it were elves' shot,
> Or if it were witches' shot, now I will help you-
> This is the remedy …[7]

These Saxon elves seem to be hurting people by throwing tiny spears or arrows at them. In later times "elf-shot" was a recognised cause of disease of people and cattle and it appears as a major diagnosis in the Saxon medical books. A selection of herbs was employed in treating humans and livestock afflicted with these maladies.

The Old English medical texts also refer to other "elf" illnesses such as *aelfsogetha*—which appears to be something like bronchitis or heartburn—and *aelfsidenn*, which literally means "elf-enchantment" and seems to be a

---

6. "The examination of John Walsh before Maister Thomas Williams" (London: John Awdley, 1566).

7. The charm "*Wiðfærstice*" (against stabbing pain) found in the Old English medical text known as *Lacnunga*.

night fever or nightmares. There is also a cure for the condition called *waet-eraelfaedle* (water-elf sickness) which is characterised by the patient's livid nails, watering eyes, and downcast looks. This term may indicate another key subdivision of the elves; certainly in later times in Scotland there was a clear distinction made between land (or dressed) and water faeries. Equally, though, the name of the disease might just as well be read as "watery elf-sickness" and so be more concerned with the symptoms than the identity of the agent inflicting it.[8]

Anglo-Saxon elves seem to have been imagined as being human in size and shape, but having a semi-divine nature. Scandinavian elves shared this character and were the subject of sacrifices, called *aelfblot*. For instance, in *Kormaks Saga* a wounded man was told to sacrifice a bull and then to take the beast to a mound "in which elves dwell ... and redden the outside of the mound with the bull's blood and make the elves a feast with the flesh; and you will be healed." There are records of comparable practices in Britain.

Common Traits

The attributes shared by later English faeries with those of the original English homelands in Denmark and northern Germany are extensive and include a range of traits that will become familiar as we work through this book. These common characteristics strongly suggest that this knowledge was brought over by the Anglo-Saxons when they settled in Britain.

The continental elves are to be found living under hills, which will periodically rise or open up to reveal feasting and music within. For human guests, residence with the elves under the hills is perilous, because time passes differently there and because the food is unsafe for humans.

The Scandinavian elves have a love of singing and dancing and a preference for dancing in circles in grassy places, leaving marks on the ground. There's a strong link between elves and certain trees, especially oaks. Elder trees also feature in Danish folklore, which tells of the Old Lady of the Elder Tree who must be appeased before taking any of her wood. This spirit also appears in Lincolnshire, very strongly suggesting that Danish settlers brought the belief with them to East Anglia.

---

8. John Campbell, *Popular Tales of the West Highlands,* 64.

The Danish elves love cleanliness and tidiness, for which humans are rewarded (or punished). They have an aversion to loud noises, which may drive them away. They show a decided preference for wearing green and red, especially red caps. Elves have the power to make themselves invisible, change their shape, see the future, or confer prosperity. There is magic power in their names, which must be concealed from humans. Despite all these magical abilities, though, they still need to use human midwives and they're unable to cross running water.

The elves take human children and leave faeries behind as "changelings," which may be exposed by tricks or by the threat of burning. There is also a species of faery that resides with humans, doing farm work, stealing fodder and grain from neighbours, and becoming so attached to a household that it is impossible to escape them by trying to move away. Nonetheless, if they are insulted, they will become a nuisance.

The huge number of parallels between Danish faery lore and English tales confirm that they have a common source. All this evidence indicates that a rich set of beliefs was imported to British shores, there to mingle with the mythology of the existing British population and so produce the complex and developed faery lore that this book will examine in detail.

Faeries in the *Mabinogion*

What might the British people have understood about faeries at the time the Anglo-Saxons arrived? The *Mabinogion* is a collection of early medieval Welsh stories that connects us to ancient Celtic mythology and gives us the first literary mentions of the later Romantic hero, King Arthur. Much could be written (and has been) about the connections between these stories and the better-known Arthurian stories; yet more can be said about the links between the Welsh myths and the ancient Irish myths. Here, I focus solely upon the traces of faery lore in these accounts.

It's fair to say that the *Mabinogion* is steeped in magic. Faery glamour—the use of concealment, deception, and transformation—is a theme that runs throughout the different stories. The "glamorous" quality of the tales is so fundamental to them and so subtle that we might almost overlook it. Nonetheless, the otherworldly quality of many of the stories shares a nature and a source with Faery. These are faery tales just as much as they are hero stories, pseudo-history or courtly romances.

There are several features that more clearly show the faery presence in the *Mabinogion*. In several tales, the action takes place on ancient mounds—grassy knolls are a typical faery haunt. In the stories of Pwyll and Manaw yddan, the *gorsedd* hill at Narberth has a particularly central role, as it has too in the stories of Owein and of Peredur—in the latter tale one mound is also explicitly stated to be a barrow, underlining the link between faeries and ancient sites.

Magical ointment also features in the tales. In an incident in the story of Peredur, an ointment is used to revive knights killed in combat. This quality of bestowing immortality or overcoming mortality is something we'll discuss later. There are faery hounds—at the very start of the story "Pwyll Prince of Dyfed," the eponymous hero comes across Arawn, lord of Annwfn, who is out hunting with archetypal supernatural hounds—white with red ears. This is very plainly a faery pack and Arawn appears to be the lord of faeryland.

In the story "Culhwch ac Olwen," the many members of King Arthur's court are listed. Amongst them is his messenger, Sgilti Light Foot, who can run over forests on the tops of the trees and over mountains on the tips of the reeds. This skill is directly paralleled by a faery trait recorded much more recently at Llanberis in North Wales; the Welsh faeries, the *tylwyth teg*, were said to be so light and agile that they could dance on the tips of the rushes. Characters in the *Mabinogion* tales travel with a telltale gliding motion, most notably Rhiannon in the story of Pwyll; she cannot be pursued either slowly or quickly, but always mysteriously moves ahead of those following her. This gait is distinctively faery and is a feature of the "faery rades" that are often seen.

Lastly, we must address the identity and nature of the people called *Coranyeit* or *Corannyeid* (modern Welsh *coraniaid*) who bring plague to Britain in the story of "Lludd and Llefelys." These mysterious people appear to be faeries of some description—or, at least, they're strangers with magical powers. Their name is linked to the Welsh adjective *corr* (dwarf), suggestive of diminutive faeries, and to the Breton faeries called *korriganed*. The latter closely resemble the pixies of the British southwest, but it is hard to identify any clear parallels between the *korrigans* and the *Coraniaid*. All we *do* know is that the troublesome beings of the Welsh story are said to have come from Asia.

The *Coraniaid* are classed as one of the three *gormessoedd* (foreign oppressions or invasions) of Wales; this is because they have an unfortunate gift: they can hear anything that is said, however hushed the voice, provided that the wind catches it. As a result, no one could plot against them and they could seemingly never be harmed. It's because of this skill, perhaps, that we must always refer to the faeries by pseudonyms, such as tylwyth teg, *bendith y mamau* (the mother's blessings), or "Good Neighbours," so as not to insult or antagonise them. It's still the case across Britain, from Wales to the Shetland Isles, that the faeries will be listening and that it's best to avoid words they dislike such as "faery" or "trow" and use some polite circumlocution instead.

Eventually, the *Coraniaid* are driven away by mashing insects in water and sprinkling this upon the assembled people. The humans present are unharmed by the potion but the intruders are destroyed. This detail is very puzzling and has never had any satisfactory explanation; some commentators have suggested that Spanish fly may be involved. The Welsh word used in the story (*pryfet*) is of very limited assistance in solving the mystery as it simply means "insects" in a general sense. Nothing is clear, then, but there is some parallel at least to the use of various plants like rowan or of offensive substances to repel faeries (in one case for example, stale urine was used on the Hebrides to trap faery cattle on the shore so that they could be rounded up).[9] These measures may be distasteful to humans, but they are none of them fatal.

In the *Coraniaid*'s size, their malevolence, and their supernatural senses there is plainly a good deal of faery nature. A final observation may clinch this identification. In 1779 a clergyman called Edmund Jones wrote *A Geographical, Historical, and Religious Account of the Parish of Aberystruth.*[10] He had cause to criticise (at length) his parishioners' foolish attachment to old delusions concerning the tylwyth teg. Amongst the beliefs prevalent in the area in the late eighteenth century was the idea that the faeries would always

---

9. MacPhail, "Folklore from the Hebrides II," 384.

10. Jones, *A Geographical, Historical, and Religious Account of the Parish of Aberystruth.*

know whatever was spoken out of doors, especially at night. This seems to be a direct preservation of the *Coraniaid*'s regrettable eavesdropping abilities.

Medieval Fae

As we move from Anglo-Saxon England to medieval Britain, a number of key faery lore features stay in place and in fact have persisted into the modern belief. Whilst we may have stopped talking about "elves" in preference for "faeries," the people being described, as well as their essential traits, remain the same.

The faeries continued to inhabit a parallel world as several stories illustrate. The underground realm of Faery is visited in the legends of Elidyr and King Herla whilst the Green Children of Woolpit stray into rural Suffolk from just such a place. A notable feature that is several times mentioned is the curious half-light that prevails in Faery; there is neither sun nor moon, but a dim luminosity like torchlight. Despite their separate realm, the Fae still have the ability to enter our world and kidnap children—Ralph of Coggeshall's story of "Malekin" demonstrates this. Malekin was stolen by the faeries from a cornfield where her mother was working during harvest; after which, rather like a ghost, she could contact the human world but not return to it. Given their ready access to our world, it follows that there are portals to Faery. In the account of Elidyr, he enters faeryland by a riverbank; in the story of King Herla, it is a cave in a cliff; the Green Children follow a long tunnel that leads them out of "St. Martin's Land." William of Newbury located a faery feast under a barrow, which we know is a quintessential faery locale, and Gervase of Tilbury described how a swineherd at Peak Castle in the Peak District followed a lost sow into a cavern and stumbled upon faeryland.

Equally, medieval faeries may be found living in human homes. Gervase of Tilbury tells of the "portunes" who closely resemble brownies. They work on farms, doing any work required of them, however hard; they serve the household but never injure the inhabitants and, at night, they enter the house and cook frogs on the fire. The portunes like mischief, too, riding horses at night or leading nocturnal travellers' horses into ponds; a thirteenth-century sermon speaks of "all such ben led at night with gobelyn and erreth hither and thither" (all those who've been led astray at night by goblins and who've wandered hither and thither). In another story, two faeries knock a rider from his horse for no reason and then sit by the road laughing at him impishly.

The medieval accounts also tell us that time passes differently in Faery: when King Herla returns to the human world he is warned not to step from his horse until a small dog given to him has leaped to the ground. A couple of his retinue forget this injunction and dismount from their steeds; they instantly crumble to dust, for he has been away several hundred years, although to him it seemed but hours. It is said that he and his company are still riding, waiting for the dog to jump down. The story of Malekin also has a typical feature: she has been seven years in faeryland, she says, and must remain another seven before she may return home. Seven is a common magic number in faery measurements of time. The very common delay of a year and a day between events is also seen in medieval tales. King Herla celebrates his wedding and, a year later, visits the king of Faery to celebrate his. The same commitment to meet a year later also appears in *Sir Gawain and the Green Knight*. In Gervase of Tilbury's story of the lost sow in the Peak Cavern, time in Faery was the exact reverse of time here: their winter was our summer.

Adults as well as children are abducted. In one story a farmer called Richard of Sunderland is out cutting reeds for thatching when three men dressed in green and riding on green horses appear and carry him off. He's taken to a fine mansion and offered ale in a green horn, which he wisely refuses to drink. They try to persuade him to stay with them, but he won't, so eventually he's returned home—but struck dumb as a punishment.

Beautiful faery women are a common feature of medieval romance. They dance at night and will sometimes wed humans—but always subject to conditions that in due course are inevitably broken. The story of Wild Edric epitomises the irresistible beauty of the faery bride and her unavoidable loss. In Layamon's history *The Brut*, the lovely elf queen Argante takes Arthur to Avalon after the battle of Camlann to heal and care for him. Readers may recall the *aelfscyne*, or elf-bright women, of Saxon myth that I described earlier; these faery maidens are their later incarnation. Lastly, there is evidence suggesting that the faery women could have their own independent sexuality (or be loose and lustful, to medieval minds) as well as being very beautiful. There are menacing accounts in thirteenth-century sources of elf women visiting men at night as succubi. The sister of the Green Children grew up, it was said, to have quite lax morals—an indicator, perhaps, of her faery birth.

Marriage between humans and faeries takes place, but is subject to conditions; as mentioned above, faery maids will wed human husbands, but there is always a catch. In the story of Wild Edric, the hero was warned never to mention his wife's sisters; of course, he eventually did, and she promptly left. Walter Map described the experience of Gwestin of Gwestiniog, who captured a faery wife at Llangorse Lake in the Brecon Beacons. She lived with him and raised a family, but he was told never to strike her with a bridle. Eventually, accidentally, this happened and forthwith she and all but one of the children disappeared. This is the first of many such stories from Wales, as we'll see. The inevitable result of these liaisons was children. We learn from the medieval stories another common fact of the Fae: that they often need human help, especially in childbirth. Gervase of Tilbury tells a story that features the theme of the midwife to the faeries, later a regular element in many faery tales.

Next, feasting is a major pastime of the medieval Fae, as in the story of King Herla and in the account by William of Newbury of a faery cup stolen from a banquet under a barrow. The medieval faeries have a particular liking of dairy products; in Gerald of Wales's account of Elidyr's childhood visits to faeryland, he mentions their vegetarian diet and their preference for junkets (a mixture of curds and cream, sweetened and flavoured). Also quintessentially faery is their green colour—as we've already seen in the account of Richard of Sunderland. The Green Children of Woolpit emerged into this Middle Earth green tinged and they would only eat green beans at first, although their colour faded as their diet changed.

Another pastime or habit of medieval faeries is to either bless or torment humans: according to the historian Layamon, King Arthur was blessed by elves at his birth (our earliest faery godmother account). Conversely, Gervase of Tilbury tells of a faery horn stolen by a hunter in Gloucestershire. It brings with it bad luck and the man is executed for his theft.

Some medieval faeries are of diminutive size. The portunes of Suffolk are said to be only a half-inch high (probably a mistake for half a foot, or six inches). The faeries encountered in a cavern under the High Peak are the size of "cocks and hens," according to Gervase of Tilbury in his book *Otia Imperialia*, and those in the story of King Herla are described variously as being as big as apes, pygmies, dwarves, and half human size. The faeries met by Elidyr are likewise small, but by contrast the Green Children, the faeries under the barrow seen in William of Newbury's story, and the bearers of the faery horn in Gloucestershire are all of normal proportions. Clearly the faery women who wed mortal men must approach human stature but there are some who are larger than average: the faery maidens seen dancing by Wild Edric are described as being taller than human women.

Some medieval faeries give warnings and have foreknowledge of events. This supernatural power is mentioned in the story of King Herla, and Gervase describes the "grant," a foal-like creature which warns villagers of fire. Honesty and keeping promises were vital to faerykind during the Middle Ages. This an element in King Herla's story (and in *Sir Gawain and the Green Knight*); it is also seen in the story of Elidyr, who reported that the supernatural people he met never took oaths and abhorred lying.

Medieval faeries can disappear at will (as in the story of King Herla) and generally remain invisible to normal human sight (as with the changeling Malekin). This concealment can be overcome in two ways: a person might apply a magic ointment; or it may be possible to obtain the second sight through contact with a "seer."

Summary

All these characteristics will be recognised in the more recent faery lore that will be examined later in this book. In other words, most aspects of our understanding of the nature, preferences, and dislikes of the Good Folk have been settled for a good thousand years or so. We can always learn more, of course, but most of our ideas today about our Good Neighbours would have been perfectly familiar to the writers just mentioned, and to their audiences.

The Good Folk have always been with us, therefore, but our knowledge and understanding of them have been expanded and rounded out as we have been able to share perspectives and experiences from across Britain over the last two hundred years or so. It's this fully matured and elaborated faery lore that I draw upon in the rest of this book.

Chapter 3

A FAERY PRIMER

In this chapter I discuss some of the basic elements of our knowledge about the Good Folk. Before we examine the detailed aspects of our relationship with the faeries, we need to clarify some key facts: what terms to use when talking about them, how they're grouped, what faeryland is like and, perhaps most importantly, how we might experience a faery encounter ourselves.

Naming Faeries

There are many ways of classifying British faerykind and lots of different names for them. For example, in one Tudor play a character lists the sundry names by which they're called, which include Puck, puckerel, Hob Howlard, Robin Goodfellow, pickhorne, Hob Goblin, Rawhead, Bloody Bones the Ugly, and Bugbear; this is one of the shorter of several such lists from the period.[11] Each of the faeries mentioned has its own character and preferred location. Some types of faery are found across regions, and some are very local indeed.

---

11. Gascoigne, *The Buggbears*, Act III, lines 47 & 55.

Before we look at specific terminology, it's worthwhile saying a bit about our choice of terms. We know for certain that the faeries themselves do not like the term "faery," meaning that circumlocutions are often preferred, even by declared disbelievers. As a rule, it's better to avoid references to them that may draw their attention to you and, if the faeries must be mentioned, euphemisms that are complimentary seem to be preferable. Some of the labels chosen are merely descriptive, whether of the appearance of the supernatural being or of the location in which they are found, and this neutral approach may well be safest. For example, in the far north of Britain where Gaelic is spoken, *sidh* or *sith* is the preferred term; this name for the Good Folk is generally believed to refer to the fact that they live under hills, although it may be a euphemistic name denoting "people of peace." This kind of complimentary name is certainly very popular. Mary Lewes noted the possibly significant fact that there are no Welsh place names in Wales that involve faery references, indicating the cautious respect shown by the Welsh to the supernatural people they call the tylwyth teg (the fair family).[12]

In this connection, it's also worth emphasising that there is power in personal names. There's a string of stories we'll examine later in which faeries who help women complete impossible spinning tasks will also conceal their names from them as a way of gaining mastery over the women. For humans too, keeping back your own name from the faeries is just as important as avoiding insults and addressing them correctly. This is something that's very well illustrated by the *"ainsel"* series of stories, such as that of Meg Moulach: a faery child meets a human and asks his name, to which he replies "my ainsel" (myself). Later the faery child is injured during a game and runs to its parent to complain. When asked for the name of whoever had inflicted the injury, the answer "my ainsel" provokes the response that, if it had been anyone else, they would have suffered for it. Faeries withhold their names from us to stop us getting power over them and the reverse is just as true; put simply, if they have a grievance against you, it's harder for them to find you if they don't have your name! Nonetheless, I've always felt rather uncomfortable about this strand of thought about the Fae. On the one hand, it seems to suggest that humans are cleverer than their Good Neighbours, and that a

---

12. Terrell, *The Wee Folk of Menteith*, 48; Lewes, *The Queer Side*, 117.

bit of cunning can outwit them or can trick them into betraying their names themselves. At the same time, it introduces an element of deceit into the relationship, a want of openness and honesty that runs directly counter to other precepts on promoting good relations with faeries.

Types of Faery

There is a tendency to generalise on faery types and characteristics (of which, of course, I will be guilty in this book) but many faeries were very restricted in their distribution, very individual in their behaviour, and very local in their interests and preoccupations. We must always keep these personal and regional differences in mind, but we can still set out some broad categories of faery. The most common and widespread types we'll be discussing are as follows:

Faeries

Throughout this book I will use this term (varied with the Fae) as a general catch-all category for all supernatural beings of a generally humanoid description. These may take animal form from time to time, but their basic form is very close to our own, albeit with differences in size, look, and abilities.

"Faery" is interchangeable with names like pixy or brownie, and many faeries have special personal names which I'll use, but the term is also a convenient label for the mass of supernaturals who are lacking some familiar individual name, or who don't readily fall into some regional category. As a general rule, faeries inhabit Faery, although we'll soon see it's more complicated than that.

Elves

Before the British adopted the French word "fairy," they called their indigenous supernatural beings "elves." There is essentially no difference between the two in British folklore. Elf was borrowed into Welsh to give the word *ellyll*, indicating that the same family of faeries was found dwelling across the whole of the British Isles. Our tendency now is to distinguish between elves and faeries, but this isn't anything to do with traditional folklore. In recent centuries, faeries have tended to shrink down into little girls with wings, whilst the influence of Norse myths, through the stories of J. R. R. Tolkien, have preserved the elves for us as tall, warrior-like figures. These are inspiring stories, but forget them for the purposes of investigating the actual folk accounts. They're unhelpful and misleading.

Pixies

The pixies, or piskies, or pisgies, are the faery folk of South West England. There's a fairly consistent perception of them as being small and dressed in green with red caps and having a mischievous disposition. All the same, they are far from being the only supernatural inhabitants of the region—there we'll find mermaids and the *bucca* too.

We'll also hear from time to time of *spriggans*, but these don't appear to be an entirely different type of faery, just a permanently bad-tempered and nasty pixy. They are described as dour and ugly; their particular role seems to be protecting other faeries from intrusions or insults by humankind (see the stories of "The Miser on the Faery Gump" or "The Faeries on the Eastern Green," both from Penwith in West Cornwall). They are very closely linked to ancient sites, such as hill-forts, where they guard buried gold. In this the spriggans seem to be linked to the Redshanks or Danes of Somerset. The localisation of spriggans on distinctive sites in the region is especially notable.

There are also some reports of domestic pixies, who live in people's homes and perform household tasks for them. These individuals begin to shade into "brownies."

Brownies

A major and very well-known type of British faery is the "brownie," a domestic sprite who cohabits helpfully with people in farms and houses. Brownies can be found from Lincolnshire all the way north into the Scottish Lowlands, sometimes being called "dobbies" as well as "broonies" in the most northerly areas.

The older names of Puck and Hobgoblin, signifying other domestic spirits, have been largely absorbed into this normally friendly creature. Brownies are distinct from most of the Good Folk described in this book. The latter may be characterised as reserved and self-interested. In contrast, brownies are attached and subservient to humans; they are devoted to their duties and extremely diligent in their performance. They are very close to their human families and will even migrate with them in some cases. Brownies are faithful and reliable and can be trusted with valuable items and tasks such as guarding treasure or children and fetching a midwife. Nonetheless, they can tend to mischief, they may be easily offended and overreact, and they are very fussy about the reward they get for their dedicated service. They will accept some food in recompense but won't accept clothes (or, at least, certain types of clothes). These domestic spirits live on farms, or very near to them; the rest of the Good Folk will live in faeryland, or "Faery."

Trows

The trows are the faery beings that inhabit the Orkney and Shetland Islands, north of Scotland. They are a generally secretive and unfriendly family of the Fae who are small, ugly, and live under hills. The name is related to the Norse "troll," reminding us of the long Viking heritage of these islands. Generally, the trows are described as sullen and morose, although one local expert believes they have been feared and disliked more than they deserved. They can't abide humans using the word "trow" and will disappear the instant it's pronounced—which is why they're also often called "the grey folk."[13]

Derricks

These are a kind of elf or pixie, and they only occur along the south coast of England. The Hampshire derricks are apparently friendlier and more helpful than those of Dorset. They may guard buried treasure.

Orchard Sprites

The orchards and other fruit groves of England are inhabited by various faery spirits, such as Old Goggy, who exist to guard them from thieves and children. These faeries are a good example of those members of the faery species who seem to have just the one role to perform (at least as far as human society's concerned).

---

13. Saxby, *Shetland Traditional Lore*, 132; Marwick, *The Folklore of Orkney and Shetland*, 36.

The Lincolnshire Fens

This unique region is home to the Tiddy Ones, also called the Yarthkins, the Strangers, and the Greencoaties. They are rooted in the local soil and act as fertility spirits, helping the growth and ripening of plant life; as such, they receive tribute or offerings from the local people—the first fruits and the first taste of any meal or drink. If neglected, these beings may be vindictive, affecting harvests, yields, and even the birth rate. They have been described as being a span high with thin limbs and oversized hands, feet, and heads. They have long noses and wide mouths, and they make odd noises. They dance on large, flat stones in the moonlight.

One particular Fenland spirit, the Tiddy Mun, seemed to control the floodwaters in the days before the Fens were drained. From time to time, he appeared from pools at night and might drag victims back into them, but generally he was sympathetic to local people. His close ties to the management of water levels emphasise his local nature and function.

East Anglian Faeries

In Norfolk and Suffolk, people spoke of the *feriers*, *frairies*, or *farisees*. These local faeries were known to be very small and very secretive. They lived underground and were seldom seen. This was perhaps fortunate as, above ground, they could be dangerous to humans; certainly, they rode cattle and horses at night.

Two Tribes

There are many types of faery creature and a number of ways of grouping them over and above the regional or family types such as pixy and brownie. They can be categorised according to whether they live together in groups or not, or on the basis of their attitudes to humanity.

What we conventionally imagine when we think of faeries are what have been called the communal, mound, or sometimes trooping faeries. Folklore suggests that these communal faeries may generally be favourable, or at least not actively hostile, toward humans, although their moods can be changeable. Many of the rest of the faeries, who are frequently solitary, tend by nature to be antagonistic to humans—if not downright fatal.

This distinction into "good" and "bad" faeries can be traced back to the earliest times. As we've already seen, the Vikings distinguished between the fair or light elves and the dark elves. In much later Scottish faery lore, there survives a very clear and marked distinction between what are called the *seelie* and *unseelie* courts (the names come from the Anglo-Saxon *sælig*, meaning "blessed" or "happy"). The seelie court comprises the kindly, benevolent faeries who help the elderly and the poor, assist the hard working, comfort the distressed, and reward good deeds. These "guidfaeries" can nonetheless act vindictively against humans if they feel that they have been slighted.

Secondly, there is the unseelie court, which is made up of the host of the unsanctified dead. They are consistently inimical toward humankind. They capture stray individuals and make them fire elf shots at other people or at cattle. These "wicked wichts" inflict harm unprovoked and will carry off unbaptised children. They might harshly shave men they've caught, and they particularly resent those who dress in the faery colour of green. Some of the solitary and deadly Scottish faery beasts, like the kelpie and the njugl, seem to be numbered amongst the unseelie court.

In Wales a dichotomy may also be found: the tylwyth teg can be both good and bad. In the area around Nant y Bettws the faeries "were thieves without their like." They would steal milk, cheese, and butter from farms and would pick pockets at the local markets, according to witnesses. Alongside them, though, there lived another branch of the "fair family" who were distinctly more beautiful and who always treated their human neighbours with honesty and goodness.[14]

In England there is some small trace of a tradition of good and bad faery tribes, though it is only to be found in a couple of allusions in literature. Writing in *A Treatise Concerning the Original of Unbelief* in 1625, the Reverend Thomas Jackson made such a claim (although he ascribed all such tales to satanic delusion):

---

14. Rhys, *Celtic Folklore*, 83

Thus are Fayries, from difference of events ascribed to them, divided into good and bad, when as it is but one and the same malignant fiend that meddles in both ...[15]

This indication of two differing temperaments is also reflected in George Gascoigne's play *The Buggbears,* published in 1565, which mentions

... the white and read fearye ... some lovely and amyable, some felowly and friendly, some constant, some mutable, of hylls, wodes and dales, of waters and brookes; we coonyng in that art can ken them by their lookes.[16]

The tendency of us humans to divide faeries into good and bad camps seems to be long-standing and widespread. However, there's probably a lot of wishful thinking involved on our part. It's wiser to stress that *all* faeries are potentially mischievous or malicious. Some only act in this manner; others will be well-disposed most of the time but may be swift to be offended or irritated. At the heart of our dealings with the Good Folk must be the awareness that they're changeable and unpredictable.

Contrary Faeries

One thing that anyone interested in faery lore will soon notice is that Faery is a place where contradictions are rife. A present-day faery authority has recently said that "when it comes to Faery the only generality we can make is that we can't easily make any generalities."[17]

Inconsistency and uncertainty seem par for the course in faery studies. There's a distinct lack of consensus as to the appearance of the Fae (their height, their facial features, the presence or absence of wings) or regarding their dress. Of course, one might fairly observe that a nonhuman, presented with a selection of humans of varying age and ethnicity, who are each dressed in their own traditional, indigenous costume, might be equally puzzled to

---

15. Jackson, *A Treatise Concerning the Originals of Unbelief,* 178.

16. Gascoigne, *The Buggbears,* line 47.

17. Daimler, *Fairies: A Guide to the Celtic Fair Folk,* 173.

determine what the "typical" human looks like. There are many sorts of faeries, so the lack of consistency in reports need not trouble us too much.

Non-believers will say that inconsistency in accounts is hardly remarkable, given that we're discussing a wholly imaginary set of beings. The believer, in contrast, may explain the contradictions by pointing to the variety of faery forms, their magical abilities, and their well-known sense of mischief. Janet Bord argues as much in her book *Fairies:* discrepancies in descriptions of faeries' height may all be put down to their use of glamour and illusion.[18] Undoubtedly, the biggest problem in any attempt to rationalise or generalise faery behaviour is the existence of downright irreconcilable differences between descriptions. I'll highlight just a few here to demonstrate my point.

As we'll see later, human midwives are very frequently taken into faeryland to assist with births. Accounts of such incidents are extremely common. Given this apparent inability to handle deliveries, it's odd that Queen Mab has a reputation as a faery midwife and that, from Baslow in Derbyshire, there comes the tradition of faeries dancing in a ring in a field around a small blindfolded woman called "the midwife." When any local woman is about to give birth, the faeries will bring to the house a little hooded woman who helps with the delivery before being taken away again.[19]

We'll also see later that the Good Folk can be insistent upon their code of behaviour and impose it upon humans—and yet act in ways we find objectionable. They love the virtues of cleanliness, justice, kindness, and chastity. In Fife it's said that they pulled down a house in which a murder was committed, presumably because it offended their sensibilities so much. Mrs. Bray suggested (perhaps not entirely seriously) that turning your clothes works to free you from pixy enchantment because they cannot bear disorder in dress. The faeries hate greed in particular. One Cornish pixy was so vexed by a farmer who rushed and bullied his family and his labourers to get their work done that he chastened him with a trick in order to reform his behaviour. Hurrying to market one day in his horse and cart, the farmer constantly saw a vision of the church tower ahead of him, but drive as hard as he might throughout the

---

18. Bord, *Fairies: Real Encounters With Little People.*

19. Addy, *Household Tales*, 134.

day, he never got any nearer, leaving him and his horse exhausted and sorry by evening. The faeries will chasten us and teach us lessons then—but it won't prevent their own pranks, their occasional viciousness, nor their thievery.[20]

The faeries are secretive, but they show no reservations about invading human homes and purloining human buildings and property. They are proud and independent, but then sometimes seem very dependent upon human aid, in that they cannot apparently carry out simple repairs to their property or deal with basic health matters such as childbirth. Of a piece with this contrariety is the fact that there is always evidence to the contrary: we've just seen it with midwives; another example comes from Worcestershire. There are numerous stories of faeries seeking help to mend broken seats and baking peels; sometimes, though, the help is reversed. At Osebury on the River Teme the tradition is that a broken baking peel left in a faery's cave will be mended for you. In the Northern Isles it was believed that if a spinning wheel was not working well, leaving it out overnight on a faery mound would fix it. This willingness to lend a hand is again contrary: in the main, the faeries are selfish in the extreme, but we must also accommodate with this the domestic faeries like the brownies who have been called "industrious, attentive, and willing to serve." They show "unparalleled fidelity" and are always promoting their masters' interests.[21]

Here's another puzzle. Iron is known as a material that repels faeries. A child in a cradle can be protected by scissors hung over it; shears placed in a chimney prevent faery incursions by that route and wise travellers will carry metal with them, even something as small as a pin, as a defence against supernatural encounters and to evade being pixy-led. Tales are often told of rescues of abducted spouses from faery hills in which the rescuer will place his knife or a nail at the threshold in order to stop the entrance to the hill reclosing and trapping him (sometimes it will be necessary to equip yourself with as many metal implements as there will be people escaping from the hill—otherwise someone may end up stranded). This list could be extended considerably, but the principle is very well established and consistent looking. However, how do we explain faeries using metal tools—which they often

---

20. *County Folklore,* vol. 7, 33; Harris, *Cornish Saints and Sinners,* 20.

21. Roy Palmer, *Folklore of Worcestershire,* 180; Marwick, *The Folklore of Orkney,* 41; Crofton Croker, *Fairy Legends & Traditions,* 48.

do, as evidenced in the stories of human help being sought to repair damaged pails, pickaxes, and the like? Even more aberrant, perhaps, there is a Shetland story of an abducted boy who returns home skilled in making scythes, a craft he has learned whilst living with the trows. The faeries are said to be expert smiths and metal workers whilst simultaneously being repelled by iron ...[22]

It may reassure readers to discover that long acquaintance with the Fae doesn't necessarily make them any more predictable or comprehensible. Brian Froud, renowned faery artist, was interviewed by Signe Pike for her book *Faery Tale*. He described to her his reaction to his first investigations into Faery and to the contradictions he found: "It's very typical of faery, actually. In one way it simplified everything for me, and at the same time, it suddenly made everything very complicated."[23]

Faeries are often regarded as being creatures of the "betwixt and between." If this is so, it's only fitting that our knowledge about them should, in the same way, be indeterminate and unsettled. It's typical, too, of the faeries to want to withhold something from us—whether it's their name or full knowledge of their personalities. I'll conclude this brief survey of contrariety with some very fitting words from another recent faery book. Noting the conflicting descriptions of faeries, the author states, "None of them are wrong, and none of them are exactly right either, and that's your first lesson about Faery: it is in all ways and always a contradiction."[24]

Faeries and Faeryland

Faeryland, also termed Faery or Faerie, or even Elfame, is the place where the faeries live and where they originate. The problem for us is to define its nature and to fit it into the human world we know. This problem has become greater in recent centuries as our knowledge of and control over our physical surroundings have expanded.

---

22. See for example Simon Young & Ceri Houlbrook, *Magical Folk*, 38, 133 & 135.

23. Pike, *Faery Tale*, 86.

24. Daimler, *Fairies*, 12.

Where Is Faeryland Found?

The faeries' "natural environment," as we might call it today, has always been a concern of humankind—primarily so that we can be on our guard and avoid it. These precautions are compounded by the fact that the faeries inhabit both parts of the everyday world surrounding us and, at the same time, have their own sphere largely exclusive to them.

All isolated, inaccessible, uninhabited, and unspoiled locations have been regarded as Fae places. The faery otherworld has very often been thought of as being below ground; this might mean that prominent hills are inhabited or that the entrance to Faery might be found through caves and the like, under lakes, or at the bottom of wells. For instance, on Dartmoor, the area around Lustleigh was a warren of rabbit holes which were believed also to serve as "pixy holes": places where pixies would hide from humans if they could not escape to their hidden lairs. Ancient sites—stone circles, burial mounds, and such like—also have strong faery associations, and faeries may reach their underground homes from entrances beneath standing stones, or may actually live inside tumuli.[25]

Nowadays, the association between faeries and the natural world seems obvious and fundamental to their character. In fact, this belief is relatively new, and it derives from several sources. First, humans have become increasingly urban, separating themselves from the rural world and making it look more uniquely faery. At the same time, over the last century or so, faeries have come more and more to be seen as nature spirits, beings whose primary or sole purpose is to motivate and to shape the processes of nature, most especially the growth of plants. As such, it might be added, they tend to lose some of their individual personality and become incorporated into those natural systems themselves, so that—for instance—it can be a bit unclear whether they live in trees or are in fact the spirits of those trees.

The other origin of our idea of "nature faeries" is a great deal older and looks back beyond our recent flight to the cities. Human representations of faerykind have always tended to mirror our own society, hence to medieval people it seemed obvious that the Fae would live in a world much like their own, with the same organisation and occupations. There were faery kings

---

25. See chapter 4 of my *British Fairies*.

and queens, and the faery court went out hunting deer with hounds. In the Middle Ages, too, we all lived much closer to nature, far more in contact with the cycles of growth, with the seasons, and with woods and wildlife. The faeries accordingly were imagined no differently—and whilst human society has since then rapidly developed, our perceptions of Faery have tended to remain fixed by the descriptions in those old stories.

Be that as it may, it seems right and proper to us that faeries should live in forests and be intimately associated with the blossoms, foliage, and springs. That link with woodland has grown especially strong in recent centuries.

How Is Faeryland Reached?

Some locations are habitually frequented by the Fae; others are liminal places, "portals," where we may meet them and where we may gain access to Faery. The folklore and traditional ballads suggest that the most likely spots tend to be singular or noticeable in some way. Distinct and solitary hills are preeminent sites, as mentioned already, but others to watch out for will include lone trees (especially thorns and apples), wells, and verdant banks, most notably those where daisies grow. Experience suggests that faery encounters often take place in such spots and that it's from them that the journey to Faery commonly begins.

Who Is Found in Faeryland?

It seems an unnecessary question to wonder who lives in faeryland, but as I've already implied, the Fae themselves aren't the only residents. Various humans will be found there too, nearly all of them arriving more or less unwillingly.

One of the theories of faery origins is that they are the spirits of ancestral dead—the departed who have been transformed into immortal beings. In other words, faeryland is the realm of deceased humans. For example, in the West Country pixies have been believed to be the souls of unbaptised children or of virtuous Druids and other non-Christians. The association of the pixies with standing stones, long barrows, and stone circles naturally reinforces this particular idea. Others have argued that the faery preference for green is symbolic of death and decay, rather than indicating vibrant and vigorous growth, as is most commonly supposed. When they were initially found, the so-called Green Children of Woolpit ate only green beans, which Katharine Briggs suggested might further link them with death.

If on no other grounds, it is very likely that part of the reason for asso- ciating the faeries with the dead is the belief that faeryland is underground. Describing Dartmoor, it's been said that "Pixyland is a shadowy realm some- where beneath the bogs, down which the pixies vanish at the approach of dawn." Like corpses, they are hidden beneath the turf; like ghosts, they disap- pear when daylight comes.[26]

The evidence isn't completely consistent, but overall it doesn't actually seem to indicate that faeryland is identical with either hell or purgatory. The Scottish belief was that faeryland was a "Middle Earth" partway between the land of living men and that of the dead. There is one Scottish tale in which dead neighbours are seen reaping corn and picking fruit in Faery, apparently as a consequence of their evil deeds in life, but this doesn't necessarily mean they are suffering eternal punishment. Death may have been the cover for their abduction to faeryland and, once there, they are treated very much like slave labour. Nonetheless, in some parts of Britain the distinction between faeries and ghosts has become very blurred indeed. A story from Lancashire illustrates how the ancestors, the unsettled dead, and the Fae have all merged into one: a boggart haunted a prehistoric tumulus near to Over Darwen and, as late as the 1860s, children passing by would take off their shoes and clogs for fear of awakening the dreaded being within the burial mound.[27]

In the surviving folklore, then, the faeries don't actually seem to be our departed ancestors: whilst the dead are definitely present in faeryland, these deceased persons aren't faeries and, in fact, they may not actually be dead at all. The faeries themselves certainly aren't dead and they aren't ghosts. Rather, they might better be thought of as the keepers of the dead. In the Cornish story of "Cherry of Zennor," there are some dark details, one of which is a group of apparently dead people in a room from which housemaid Cherry is excluded by her faery master. One day she spies on him in the room through the keyhole. She sees him release a woman from a coffin-like box whilst all the "dead" statues come to life and dance.

---

26. Page, *An Exploration of Dartmoor and its Antiquities*, 37.

27. Hardwick, *Traditions, Superstitions and Folklore (Chiefly of Lancashire and the North of England)*, 141; Aitken, *Forgotten Heritage*, 14 & 5.

Furthermore, stories tell us that only certain groups of deceased people end up in Faery. In the Middle English poem "Sir Orfeo," the knight visits the castle of the faery king in search of his abducted wife. There he sees many people "thought dead, and yet not." Some of these were headless, some lacked limbs, some were badly wounded, mad, drowned, burned, had choked on food, or had died in childbirth. Of all of them, the poet states, "Eche was thus in this world ynome / With fairi thither ycome" ("Each was thus taken from this world and had come into faeryland by enchantment").It seems from this story that Faery is not the land of the dead as a whole. Those taken there are those who have died early, by violence or in circumstances involving some mystery—especially the suspicion of preternatural intervention. Similar stories come from the Scottish witch trials: we hear of denizens of Faery who are there because they died in battle or at the magical hour of sunset. Faery authority Katharine Briggs said it well when she wrote that "on the whole one might say that those of the Dead who inhabit Fairyland are people who have no right to be dead at all."[28]

So, there are various humans in Faery who have been taken there unwillingly: there are those taken to perform general chores, and those wanted for a particular skill or quality. They have been stolen away from their own world by several means: by the semblance of death, or by being lured into a faery dance, for example. For these involuntary guests, Faery is a kind of prison. They become trapped in the supernatural realm by consuming the food and drink there. For example, in the Cornish story of the "Fairy Dwelling on Silena Moor," a farmer called Noy gets lost on the moor and comes upon a party in a house. There is a girl serving the guests who turns out to be his former fiancée, someone who had apparently died three or four years previously. His lost love warns Noy not to eat the food at the feast—she herself has done so and has as a result been rendered into a state in which she appeared to be dead to the human world, when in fact a sham body (a stock) was left behind whilst she had been kidnapped and taken to serve the pixies. Comparable to this is the case of Katherine Fordyce of Unst on Shetland, who was believed to have died in childbirth but who had really been taken to act as a nursemaid to the trows. Katherine ate faery food and so became

28. Briggs, "The Fairies and the Realms of the Dead," *Folklore*, vol. 81 (1970), 96.

trapped with them. All these individuals have been stolen away from their earthly homes and have been set to work serving the Fae.[29]

Fortunately, the permanent state of earthly death need not apply to all those abducted to Faery, because people can escape; the faery enchantment can be overcome. An account from Skye reveals that simply wetting your left eye with spit will dispel the faery glamour and defeat the captivity. The woman in this story returns home, but it must be confessed that she is uniquely lucky and her escape very easy.

Magic rituals can sometimes reverse the seeming state of death, under cover of which people have been kidnapped. In the ballad of Childe Rowland and Burd Ellen, the faery king abducts Ellen; her brothers are killed trying to free her but finally Rowland succeeds. The faery king then releases Ellen from the spell she is under and resurrects the brothers by touching their eyes, ears, lips, nostrils, and fingertips with a blood red liquid. In Milton's poem "Comus," two brothers seek their abducted sister Delia and eventually Sabrina, faery of the River Severn, frees her by touching her breast, lips, and fingertips with drops from a magic fountain. There seems to be some idea here that the state of death associated with being "taken" to faeryland is only an illusion or spell and can be cancelled by application of a magic liquid (and later, too, we'll discuss magic faery wells in detail).[30]

Faery Encounters

British faery tradition tells us a great deal about faery society and behaviour *and* about the way in which they interact with humankind. Accepting that contacts between faery- and humankind have taken place for centuries—and that they continue today—it's only proper to talk about how you might experience it if you are lucky enough to encounter one of the Good Folk.

What it feels like to meet a faery is at the heart of much folk tradition, but we also have the up-to-date evidence of the *Fairy Census 2014–2017*. Based in particular upon these contemporary reports from witnesses across the

---

29. See too Gwyndaf in Narvaez's *The Good People: New Fairylore Essays*, 160; Bruford in Narvaez *Good People*, 131; Campbell, *Popular Tales of the West Highlands,* vol. 2, 65, "The Tacksman of Auchriachan."

30. Bett, *English Myths and Traditions*, 25–28.

world, we can say that the experience is much more likely to be positive than not, although some people report feeling mixed emotions.

The accounts described in the *Census* suggest that an encounter is twice as likely to be a positive, pleasant experience as not. Witnesses refer to feelings of happiness, love, amazement, calmness, and peace as a result of meetings with kindly, smiling, playful faeries. This is not, nonetheless, to downplay the fact that quite a few of the encounters were unpleasant, involving fear, alarm, panic, and a sense of hostility or malevolence from the faery. Opposite reactions can be felt at one and the same time: an encounter with the supernatural can bring joyfulness and revelation combined with shock, or at least profound surprise, at seeing a supernatural entity. For example, one witness summarised his feelings as "totally shocked but filled with wonderment." Many of the reports echo this, or are tempered by an awareness that faeries can show animosity as well as amity.[31]

If you are lucky enough to have an encounter, how many faeries might you expect to see? By far the majority of sightings have been of a single faery; many, in any case, are solitary in habit. Occasionally parties of as many as five or six may be seen; when this does happen, it's not infrequently because the Fae have gathered to dance together. Larger groups of faeries are seen very rarely indeed. In the British Isles, the best chance of coming across such an assembly seems to be on the Isle of Man. The Manx Fae seemingly enjoy processing in considerable numbers: one time a "small army" of them was reported; on another occasion a man came across between one and two thousand faeries like small girls, all singing.[32]

If a meeting does take place, how should you behave? Faery lore expert Katharine Briggs once gave some wise advice on dealing with the Fae: You need dexterity and presence of mind when you meet them, otherwise you may never escape. You must avoid falsehood—but also eschew direct answers to their questions. It's better to describe things than to name them outright. Avoid directly refusing a faery something—and always have the last word.

Faeries don't always want to be seen; faeries aren't always happy. Faeries can be very curious about humans, but this quite commonly manifests itself

31. *Fairy Census* no. 131.
32. *Yn Lioar Manninagh*, vol. III.

as mischievousness, so that an encounter can be a source of wonder, but also of annoyance if the faery's playing pranks. Janet Bord proposed that people are more likely to see faeries if they're slightly distracted or detached; but if it does happen, be alert and be careful![33]

Summary

People have been in contact with the Good Folk for at least the last two thousand years. In the course of that enduring relationship, we have come to know intimately the ways and wishes of our near neighbours—how they live, how they think, what pleases them, and what antagonises them. It's that accumulated practical knowledge, the fruit of good and bad experiences, that I shall explore in the following chapters.

---

33. Bord, *Fairies*, 35.

Section 2
FINDING FAERIES

Chapter 4

IDENTIFYING FAERIES

Regardless of more poetic or mystical conceptions, traditional folk belief does not doubt that faeries are actual solid presences in our world, beings with whom we can interact just as with any human. Accepting this physical reality, we need to discuss the intimate elements of our relationship. How do we recognise the Good Folk? How do they smell? How can we communicate with them? How do they respond to us?

How Big Are Faeries?

This is a question without a definite resolution because, as I discussed in the last chapter, there seem to be many different types of faeries. The answer therefore seems to depend upon the type of faery being discussed.

The tylwyth teg in Wales have been described as being like men and women in their appearance and behaviour—but having the stature of six-year-olds. Another Welsh witness confirmed their height, but stressed their distinctive complexions: they had lovely white skin, but combined alarmingly with white hair and eyes too.[34]

The pixies of Dartmoor, in contrast, are described as little creatures much smaller than children, who can get into flower bells and many other places where girls and boys cannot creep, meaning that they can't be excluded from any place or container. However, they can change their size; the average height of a pixie is eighteen inches high, but their size can vary between twelve inches to three feet. Because of their small size, they're often said to look like dolls.[35]

Much farther north, the trows of Orkney are also described as small—and ugly too (we'll return to the issue of good looks later in this chapter). The Lowland Scottish faeries living under hillocks have been said to be child-size faeries—although one source described them vividly but unhelpfully as being no larger than a bottle. These diminutive Fae can be found alongside Fae who are just the same height and form as adult humans.[36]

To add to this confusion, some faeries can change their size and some can even change their shape. This is a particular trait of Cornish faeries. The spriggans are known to be able to swell themselves up to the size of a giant and the same ability is seen in the story of "Cherry of Zennor." The English hobgoblin Puck is especially renowned for his ability to transform not only into a range of different people but also into livestock, wild animals, amphibians, and birds. Whilst Puck can turn into whatever he likes, most other faeries are strictly limited in what they can become. The Scottish kelpie may appear either as a handsome man or in horse form. The East Anglian hyter sprite can take the shape of a sand martin, and the Cornish pixies can metamorphose into goats (so as to steal away the best milkers from human flocks) and into a variety of small birds such as redbreasts, yellowhammers, and

---

34. Robin Gwyndaf, "Fairylore: Memorates and Legends from Welsh Oral Tradition," in Narvaez, *Good People*; J. Simpson, *Folklore of the Welsh Border*, 73; Lewes, *Stranger than Fiction*, 160; Jones, *Parish of Aberystruth*, 84 & 75.

35. Bray, *Peeps on Pixies*, 11; Page, *Dartmoor*, 39; Bottrell, *Traditions and Hearthside Stories* vol. 1, 77.

36. Bruford, "Trolls, Hillfolk, Finns and Picts," in Narvaez, *Good People*; Aitken, *Forgotten Heritage* 1; Bennett, "Balquhidder revisited" in Narvaez, *Good People*; John Campbell, *Waifs & Strays of Celtic Tradition* vol. 5, 86; *County Folklore* vol. 4, 14; Coxhead, *Devon Traditions & Fairy Tales*, 49.

wagtails. There's a catch to the Cornish pixies' ability to transform, though. It seems each transformation shrinks them, so that eventually they dwindle away to virtually nothing, being no bigger than an ant.

In summary, it may be best to anticipate that if you ever have the luck to meet one of the Good Folk, it will be quite tiny—and very fast. As we've seen, comparisons are often made with dolls, and even if they can't take on the form of them, it's also not unusual for witnesses to liken faeries to some small, swift animals, such as squirrels, or flocks of birds such as partridges or sparrows. This may prepare you for what might only be a fleeting glimpse of something anxious to evade you.[37]

Smell

Even if your encounter is only very brief, traces of the faeries may remain behind to verify what you saw. When the question is raised, it seems obvious to ask what a faery smells like. If we are in close contact with other living beings, we will be aware of their odour. We recognise horses or goats by their distinctive scent, so it follows, reasonably, to enquire whether or not the faeries similarly have their own particular smell by which they're known. Whilst it is not the subject of vast amounts of discussion, there is still evidence scattered across sources which answers this question in the affirmative. Nor should this surprise us: it's a faery characteristic that is acknowledged worldwide. In the Philippines, for example, it is said that the smell of damp earth on a hot day, as if there had just been a downpour, is a sign of the presence of supernaturals. In Tagalog this is called *maalimuom* or *masangsang*.[38]

The Good Folk have their telltale aromas, then. The accounts suggest that we may find these either pleasant or repulsive.

Pixie Perfume

English writer John Aubrey, in his *Miscellanies* (1695), has the following record for 1670:

---

37. Bord, *Fairies*, 34.

38. Licauco, *Dwarves and Other Nature Spirits*, 8.

> Not far from Cirencester was an apparition. Being demanded
> whether a good spirit or a bad, returned no answer, but disap-
> peared with a curious perfume—and a most melodious twang.
> M. W. Lilly believes it was a fairie.

Aubrey's account implies (I think) that the smell was not unpleasant. One
Cornish tale, of the Miser on the Gump at St. Just, seems to confirm this. It
describes how the appearance of spriggans was accompanied by the odour
of blooms filling the air. The faeries meanwhile scattered flowers, which
instantly took root. At Staining Hall in Lancashire there is a spot haunted
by a boggart who is said to be the ghost of a murdered Scotsman. The sweet
odour of thyme lingers there.[39]

The twentieth-century link that has been forged between the Fae and
flowers has definitely consolidated the idea that floral perfume is wafted
from fluttering beings: in the verse "What the Toys Do at Night," for example, the faeries emerge from opening blossoms and "fly upon their scented
wings." Faery writer Geoffrey Hodson, who saw faeries as nature spirits helping plants and flowers grow and reproduce, certainly experienced the scent
of blossoms on their presence; in fact, he displayed what appears to be syn-
aesthesia, perceiving the smell of flowers as akin to musical chords—a statement echoing that of John Aubrey.

It's certainly believed that sweet scents will attract spirits. The Renais-
sance philosopher and magician Cornelius Agrippa described in his book
The Occult Philosophy how to summon such beings as nymphs, satyrs, dryads, hobgoblins, and the faeries of rivers, woods, fountains, fields, and meadows. He recommended the use of "odoriferous perfumes with sweet sounds
and instruments of music" in combination with magic circles, incantations,
and offerings of food and drink.[40]

Much more recent evidence also suggests that faeries may, from time to
time at least, be detected by their perfume. A report of an encounter with a
winged faery who was washing her wings in a woodland stream in Maine in
the US records that a smell of cinnamon pervaded the air. A teenaged girl

---

39. Hunt, *Popular Romances of the West of England*, 85; Thornber, *A Historical and Descriptive
Account of Blackpool and its Neighbourhood*, 38.
40. Book III chs. 16, 19 & 32; Book IV.

living in New Jersey in the 1980s also reported meeting a tiny female faery called Goldenrod. "I wasn't afraid and the room smelled good," she recalled.[41]

Fetid Faeries

Despite the pleasant encounters just described, the bulk of reports suggest that the scent left behind by the Fae folk is not altogether pleasing. It may be a natural plant smell or it may be something downright noisome.

As I just noted, over the last century and a half the role of the Fae as nature sprites has been increasingly emphasised. In keeping with this trend are the frequent incidents in which a dank odour of vegetation or soil is detected. We read of a "strange earthy smell" associated with gnome-like beings—or odours like fungus.[42] A "dark aroma" was given off by one black, winged faery and a "strong smell of decay" was associated with a tree-like being. On Dartmoor in Devon some horses were said to be able to "smell a pixy," meaning they could detect the rank, dank smell of the bogs under which they lived.[43]

A creature that resembled a cat standing on its hind legs, seen in Indiana, gave off "an unpleasant odour."[44] This introduces us to the last group of encounters. A young woman in late Victorian Yorkshire told the Reverend M. C. F. Morris that "She'd never seen the faeries but she'd smelt them. What was the odour? If you have ever been a very crowded place of worship where the people have been congregated for some time, then you knew the smell."[45]

At best, therefore, the faeries smell of damp and decay; at worst, they smell unwashed (despite the widespread accounts of them requiring water to be left out at night for bathing). The stink might be even more offensive than that though. To the English, the drake is reputed to smell of rotten eggs or a dirty hen coop. On the Isle of Man, the upper parts of glens on the isle are the best places to see, hear, *and smell* the faeries. What you will encounter is a stale, sour smell, apparently. The nature of this unpleasant odour may be explained by an Irish tale. Biddy Mannion was abducted to act as nurse

---

41. *Fairy Census*, numbers 290 and 336.

42. Johnson, *Seeing Fairies*, 186, 33 & 36.

43. *Fairy Census*, nos. 53 & 54; *Transactions of Devonshire Association*, vol. 49, 1917, 65.

44. Johnson, *Seeing Fairies*, 214.

45. Morris, *Yorkshire Folk Talk*, 1892, c. XI "Customs and Superstitions."

to the sickly infant of the king and queen of Faery. After successfully caring for the child she was permitted to return home—but not before an ointment was rubbed on her eyes. This revealed that she was in a frightful cave full of dead men's bones, which had "a terribly musty smell." This seems to be a vivid demonstration of the association between faeries and the dead.[46]

The evidence is sparse, but what little there is certainly gives us a new and intriguing perspective on the denizens of Faery. We may tentatively propose that winged faery types are more likely to smell pleasant than pixies and gnomes. What we can say is that, for some at least, the experience of encountering supernaturals is not solely a visual and aural impression; if you encounter an inexplicable scent in the air, it could very well indicate the very recent presence of the Good Folk.

Lastly, and in fairness, it should be added that *we* too have a distinctive smell that the faeries for their part don't much like. In one Manx story a man was hidden in a house when faery visitors arrived. His presence inside a barrel was easily exposed, though, by the faeries' sensitive noses.[47]

Faery Beauty

For centuries humans have found the physical charms of faery men and women irresistible. Whether it is the many alluring faery queens who feature in medieval romances, the Irish *leanan sidhe* and her male counterpart the *geancanach,* or long-haired mermaids on the shore, all are so desirable that we would abandon all we know to be with a faery lover. Throughout history, faery beauty has been extolled above that of humans—this is the case with the elf-wife of Wild Edric in the twelfth-century story of his fate; the same was so in Wales in the accounts of the lake maidens and the girls of the tylwyth teg (the fair family) who lured men into their dances.[48]

Whilst it's not clear whether there's really a division of the Fae into good and bad, seelie and unseelie, opinion seems to be agreed that there are two physical types: those that are attractive and those that aren't. The majority of elves and faeries are at least unremarkable or normal in their features but

---

46. *Yn Lioar Manninagh,* vol. 4, 161.

47. *Yn Lioar Manninagh,* vol. III.

48. Rhys, *Celtic Folklore,* 3, 23 & 44 and 85–6 & 90 respectively.

some, quite frequently, will surpass human looks, with "faces strangely fair." Whilst the Fae might be shorter in stature than us, they are certainly not regarded as any less comely. In Wales the tylwyth teg were "fair of complexion beyond everybody," and there used to be certain families in the north whose renowned good looks were the legacy of a famous faery ancestress. Another Welsh story informs us that the tylwyth teg ideal of beauty is red-haired and long-nosed.[49]

Faeries' eyes are often the most noticeable thing about them. For example, one Scottish witness recalled "their wild unearthly eyes, all of one bright sparkling blue..." Another wrote that "their eyes sparkle like diamonds," in addition to which "their lips are coral, their teeth ivory..." Faery eyes are distinctive: they may be very brilliant—but they may also be very small or oddly coloured.[50]

Secondly, there are certain types of faery that are renowned for being ugly or deformed—amongst those that spring to mind are the hairy hobs and brownies, the notoriously small and ugly trows of Shetland, and the spinner Habetrot, with her distended bottom lip (misshapen through years of pulling thread). Mentions of some repulsive feature—an extra-long tooth or a malformed nose—are quite common, but do not seem to include pointed ears. Some Manx faeries were seen that had over-sized ears "like wine bottles" and others have been seen with feathers growing in their hair (or even with feathers *instead* of hair).[51]

Where then did the standard pointed ears come from? The source is visual art. Popular depictions of faeries date back to the sixteenth century and certain conventions were fixed very early on. One consistent faery type is the hairy Puck-like creature, also known as Robin Goodfellow. He derives substantially from classical images of the satyr, often with the horns and pointed ears of a goat. Contrasted to these goblins, naked young females derived from classical nymphs came to be accepted as the standard image of the elf or faery.

---

49. Walter de la Mare, *The Unfinished Dream*, 1922; Rhys, *Celtic Folklore* 86 & 96; E. Owen, *Welsh Folklore*, 15.

50. Hogg, "Odd Characters," in *Shepherd's Calendar*, vol. 2.150; Crofton Croker, *Fairy Legends*, 14; Gill, *Second Manx Scrapbook*, c. VI.

51. Gill, *Second Manx Scrapbook*, c. VI; Dathen, *Somerset Fairies and Pixies*, 30.

Also largely absent from the folklore of Britain is the combination of beauty and deformity that is found in the Danish elle-maids, who may have gorgeous faces but hollow backs or cows' tails. There are very few British examples of this type: one is the Highland *glaistig,* a lovely woman who purposely wears a long green dress that conceals her hooves. Some faeries once seen on the Isle of Man were like pretty little girls—except that they had scaly, fish-like hands.[52]

Whilst there's a clear dichotomy between lovely faeries and ugly ones, certain faery types can have both lovely *and* hideous members—just like their human neighbours. Some of the Devonshire pixies have been said to be "dainty beings…of exceeding beauty; others are of strange, uncouth and fantastic figure and visage." One of the distinguishing features of the pixies is said to be their pronounced squint.[53]

Very occasionally, there are reports of faeries that describe features that are not just unattractive but frightening. I mentioned a little earlier a description of white eyed and white haired tylwyth teg. From earlier in the Victorian period comes the story of John Jones, a farm labourer from near Aberystwyth. Walking home across Rhosrhydd Moor one moonlit night, he realised two boys were following him. Although it was late, he at first assumed they were just local youths messing around. However, Jones then saw the boys quit the road and start dancing in an "unearthly" manner, at which point he realised that they were both "perfectly white." Just as sinister was a lost faery child found at Middleton-in-Teesdale who had green clothes and red eyes. Compare with this a report that Shetland faeries are of a yellow complexion, with red eyes and green teeth.

Mostly, though, what strikes you in reading the older folktales is how rarely a physical feature (other than height) is remarked upon as identifying an individual as a faery. What tends to indicate that a person is Fae is their clothing—and then not the style, but the colour. A man or woman dressed in green will be implicitly understood to be a faery; on Shetland, it's grey. Red caps are another regular indicator of Fae nature.

---

52. Jenkinson, *Practical Guide to the Isle of Man,* 75.

53. Bray, *Peeps on Pixies,* 12; Worthy, *Devonshire Parishes,* 28; Page, *Dartmoor,* 38.

It can be very hard for us to set aside the preconceptions we've derived from books and films, but the traditional material indicates that many of the Good Folk will be noticeably good-looking, although some too may seem distinctly sallow, pinched, and wizened. Either way, for good or ill, there may well be something in their looks to set them apart from human kind.

Airy Faeries?

In spite of what has been mentioned about the possibility of sexual relationships with the Fae, there is nevertheless a body of opinion that faeries have no fixed physical form at all and that, when they appear to us, they shape themselves to our expectations. It's for this reason that I've referred to the way our preconceptions have been shaped by art.

There seems very little doubt about the physical reality of the Good Folk in the overwhelming majority of the folklore reports. Almost the only exceptions are a case where some little folk, seen dancing in a meadow near Stowmarket in Suffolk, were described as "light and shadowy, not solid" and an incident from Wales when a girl put her hand right through a tylwyth teg woman walking beside her.

The notion of physical mutability first seems to be mentioned in a faery context by W. B. Yeats in his introduction to *Faery and Folk Tales of the Irish Peasantry* of 1888. Many generations of mystics and occult writers have acknowledged the existence of spiritual beings, he wrote—beings "who have no inherent form but change according to their whim, or the mind that sees them."[54]

Thought Forms

Yeats did not originate the idea of the mutable spirit body. Victorian Theosophists formulated the concept of "thought forms." Mahatma Koot Hoomi, one of Madame Blavatsky's mentors and inspirations, wrote that "thoughts are things ... they are real entities." This idea was elaborated by Charles Leadbeater and Annie Besant in a book, *Thought Forms,* in 1905; they asserted that thoughts produced a radiating vibration conveying their emotion and also had a floating form. In due course, this idea was applied to nature spirits

---

54. Yeats, *Faery and Folk Tales of the Irish Peasantry*, 2.

and elementals. To become visible, they are said to assume etheric bodies, which are shaped by folklore stories and human imaginations. Robert Ogilvie Crombie of the Findhorn Community explained that, although its natural form is a swirl of light, an elemental "can put on any of these thought forms and then appear personified as that particular being...elf, gnome, faun, faery and so on." Edward Gardner had a related but different conception. He believed that Elsie and Frances at Cottingley had abilities akin to those of mediums. They could materialise the faeries they photographed through ectoplasm, which was the explanation for the contemporary appearance of the beings they snapped.[55]

The idea of faeries as thought forms was developed further by Geoffrey Hodson in his 1929 book *Angels and the New Race.* He declared that faeries have no physical body but are formed of light, albeit along the "same model" as humans. In *The Kingdom of the Gods* in 1952 Hodson elaborated on these ideas even more: he proposed that the archetype for the faery form was the human body and that their appearance was further determined by our expectations as to what we might see.

These ideas have become embedded in much of the thinking about faeries today. In Signe Pike's 2009 book *Faery Tale* she interviewed artist Brian Froud, who told her

> it's often thought that faeries use our own thought patterns to manifest themselves. For example, when a faery appears to a person, it will typically look quite similar to the creatures you see in storybooks. This is because if you were to see a ball of energy, would you really know it was a faery? No. So, they try to "speak" our visual language. We see wings, and flowing dresses, and heads and eyes.[56]

There are, of course, many sceptics who dismiss faeries as entirely illusory and imaginary, but this is for quite different reasons. All of that said, if faeries *are* but mutable forms responding to our own thoughts, it could explain their

---

55. Besant & Leadbeater, *Thought-Forms,* 21; Crombie, *Encounters with Nature Spirits,* Prologue.

56. Pike, *Faery Tale,* 91; see too Bord, *Fairies,* 12; Dathen, *Somerset Fairies and Pixies,* 14, 16 & 31.

evolution in recent centuries, whereby they have acquired wands and wings and come to look like the leprechauns and flower faeries that contemporary books and paintings have taught us to expect.

Solid or See-Through Illusions?

I doubt that faeries only look how we expect them to look. If so, what was the starting point for these expectations in the first place? There are compelling reports of "faeries" that look nothing like our expectations (see the next section) which challenge any suggestion that they're purely subjective. If they only ever appeared as we expect them to, it would be impossible for witnesses to see beings that challenge all our preconceptions of the supernatural.

Most importantly, the theory is hard to square with cases which appear to be accounts of genuine encounters with solid and physical faeries. If faeries are solely balls of energy it's difficult to reconcile this with the cases where their physical presence was either central to an incident or appeared already to be established before the human encountered them. I am thinking here of the cases where humans and faeries have entered into sexual relationships and where children have been born of these pairings—children who often must be physically delivered by human midwives attending a faery knoll. I also am thinking of cases where faery celebrations have been stumbled upon accidentally by people—the many cases where the faeries have been found dancing and have then lured in human partners, or the stories of faery feasts discovered under faery hills. In one story told by William of Newburgh, readers may recall, the man who discovered the celebration also managed to make off with a gold cup. These are all very solid incidents where the human form of the faeries was central to the incident and was also, as I've suggested, already established independently of any Schrödinger-like observation. Traditional faeries, too, are very concerned with taking and consuming human food—a fleshly pleasure that's very hard to reconcile with some of the ideas of an insubstantial and spiritual nature.

Our forebears definitely conceived of the Fae as real and tangible—and so consistent in their appearance that classification into standard groups was possible and remained applicable over hundreds of years. Any mutability in their looks was purely of their own making, the result of their magic and glamour. Accordingly, in this book I accept that they have a fixed and physical

form and that we can interact with them as beings who are constant and predictable in their bodies—and in their characters.

Furry Faeries: Alternative Physicalities

Throughout this book, the fundamental assumption is that the faeries we are
discussing are solid human-like beings, closely resembling us in form and,
sometimes, size. There is, nonetheless, a body of sightings that within themselves are consistent and that challenge our conventional ideas. All faeries
have adapted to their environments; some resemble gnomes or goblins much
more than the archetypal girly flower faery, and some, apparently, do not
look like faeries at all.[57]

Sharp and Skinny

Amongst the recorded sightings over the last century or so there are some
which, whilst very small in number, are nonetheless striking for the fact that
they contrast so strongly with our conventional image of the pretty, femi-
nine Fae. We are used now to the idea of pointy ears, even on the child-like,
appealing Fae, but sharply pointed faces and noticeably disproportionate
bodies are much less anticipated. All the same, these features appear consistently enough to require us to revise our preconceptions about faeries (or, at
least, pixies).

A good example comes from Worcestershire in 2006. Two drinkers at a
country pub saw a small creature, about the size of a toddler but with gangly
limbs, climb over a fence at the bottom of the beer garden and disappear into
the field beyond. It was brown-skinned and naked. On its own this sighting might seem aberrant, but it is not alone. Quite a few of the witnesses
in Marjorie Johnson's book *Seeing Fairies* remarked upon how "slight" and
"slender" were the creatures they had seen. Such descriptions are even more
common in the 2017 *Fairy Census*, in which witnesses describe such features
as "arms … just a little too long and the fingers [that] came to sharp points"
or "spindly" limbs.[58]

---

57. For some uglier examples see Dathen *Somerset Fairies and Pixies* 15, 30, 61–62 & 70.

58. Young & Houlbrook, *Magical Folk* 41; Johnson, *Seeing Fairies*, 71, 85, 115, 182 & 243; *Census* nos. 61, 97, 109, 129, 147, 181, 350, 354, 428 & 456; see too Bord, *Fairies*, 55 & 65.

It's also noticeable how several Somerset pixies are reported to have spindly limbs, especially long, twig-like fingers, perhaps appearing to have an extra joint. The impression of extra joints is also remarked upon in the *Fairy Census*. The resemblance of the digits to sticks connects us too to the category of "ent-like" sightings we'll consider a little later.[59] The other notable feature that is identified is the sharpness of faces and noses, making them appear bird- or beak-like; this seems especially pronounced amongst pixies.[60]

These beings, humanoid in form but distinctly different from us—gangly and with caricatured features—are both familiar and alien. They do not resemble the elegant, artistic faeries, but they do look very like some of the more grotesque images depicted by Brian Froud and others. As Froud is a resident of Dartmoor, perhaps many of his images have been informed by sightings of just such pixies.

Small Animals

It is not unusual to hear of faeries and pixies being described as particularly hirsute and shaggy, with dark and unkempt hair, but a small number of encounters have been with mammalian beings that display human-like characteristics. Some faeries seen on Man in the early nineteenth century were reported to be like small dogs running about—except that they wore red caps.[61]

Some faeries are feline rather than canine. During the summer of 1920, faery seer Tom Charman spent nine weeks in the New Forest and repeatedly met with small cat-like creatures. Similar beings were described to Marjorie Johnson by witnesses from around Britain, but she also received a comparable report from Indiana—of a cat standing on its hind legs and wearing brown trousers. When disturbed, though, it bounded away "like a rabbit."[62]

This "leporid" comparison is also quite common. Jon Dathen interviewed a Somerset farmer who recounted a sighting from his childhood, some seventy years earlier. Late at night he had sneaked downstairs to find a small

---

59. Dathen *Somerset Fairies and Pixies* 30 & 61; *Census* nos 68 & 327.

60. Dathen *Somerset Fairies and Pixies* 14, 30, 61 & 70; Johnson, *Seeing Fairies*, 121; *Census* nos. 325, 345, 354 & 470.

61. Jenkinson, *Practical Guide to the Isle of Man*, 39.

62. Johnson, *Seeing Fairies*, 213–214.

person "like a hare done up in clothes" sitting in front of the farmhouse fire. He had long ears, whiskers, and buck teeth, but he could speak; he explained that he had come in to escape the cold. Later in his life, the farmer had heard of other sightings of hare-type pixies, whilst other witnesses described the Somerset "oak-men" as being hairy with long noses and tails; the witnesses compared the pixies to little goats or hedgehogs (again, Brian Froud seems to have been aware of such sightings when he illustrated the book *Faeries* in 1978). A Welsh witness in Victorian times once saw some mysterious creatures the size of guinea pigs, covered with red and white spots.[63]

Furry Shapes

A handful of reports take furriness even further. A woman on holiday in mid-Cornwall during the 1930s described how she regularly met a pair of cliff-dwelling pixies, both of which were about two feet in height. The male was a small human with some distinctive features but the female was covered in short dark brown hair with yellow rings on her body and arms, somewhat like a bee.[64]

Two other accounts are even more surprising. During the early 1940s a woman on a country walk in Kent saw a furry tennis ball rolling up a slope toward her. It briefly opened when it drew close to where she was sitting, to reveal a pixie within—and then it disappeared. Returning to Cornwall in the 1930s, a final witness on a coastal walk sighted a pisky who then changed into "a long furry black roll, which gambolled about on the grass and then disappeared." Odd as these modern reports sound, such descriptions are not wholly unknown in the older sources. Devon pixies have been said to move around like "balls of fern or heather, swept before the wind," and a Welsh brownie called the *pwcca* looks like a handful of grass blowing along.[65]

"Ent Fae"

Over the last one hundred fifty years the identification of faeries with the environment and natural processes has become more and more common-

---

63. Dathen *Somerset Fairies and Pixies*, 103–104, 21 & 68; Rhys, *Celtic Folklore*, 215.

64. Johnson, *Seeing Fairies*, 53.

65. Johnson, *Seeing Fairies*, 28 & 236; *Choice Notes & Queries*, 35; R. King, "Folklore of Devonshire," *Fraser's Magazine*, vol. 8, 781.

place. Some faeries are seen dressed in garments made from leaves and flowers, but it may not be especially surprising to find that supernatural beings
are met with who appear to be more vegetative than animal. These are creatures whose bodies seem to be composed of vegetable matter; they may perhaps be subdivided into "ents," i.e., walking trees, and smaller hybrid entities.[66]

The tree-beings can be tall, seven feet high or more, perhaps with faces
showing in the bark of their "bodies." The smaller vegetation faeries appear
to be far more mixed in their appearance. Some have bodies made of animated leaves and sticks, some are composed of a mixture of plant and insect
elements, some are tiny leaf-like creatures.[67] With more evidence it may very
likely become possible to analyse these types further.

Monsters

Last of all, there is a collection of witness accounts that tests our conceptions
of faeries to the limits. There are strange hybrid creatures: a dragonfly-fish, a
frog-sparrow, or a butterfly-bird. There are also semi-human forms: beings
that are part human and part insect, reptile, dog, spider, or frog, as well as
faeries that seem to have a combination of traditional faery and mermaid
features. One type of faery has appeared as a huge tadpole, another as an ape
dressed in leaves.[68]

Some Other Forms

There are various other classes of sighting which, whilst fitting within the
conventional imagery of the Fae, still display some unique features. Some
faeries look like our conventional ideas of aliens. The boundaries between
"aliens" and "faeries" are increasingly uncertain and permeable, it seems.
In *Seeing Fairies,* a tiny number of witnesses mentioned beings with pronounced pointed faces or slit-like black eyes. Reports of this type of being are

---

66. Johnson, *Seeing Fairies,* 48 & 95; Dathen *Somerset Fairies and Pixies,* 29

67. Trees: *Fairy Census,* numbers 39, 54, 57, 97, 276 & 390; Sticks: *Fairy Census* no. 324; Johnson *Seeing Fairies,* 24; Insects: *Fairy Census* numbers 129, 228, 244 & 428; Leaves: *Fairy
Census* no. 175.

68. Hybrids: *Fairy Census* numbers 69, 74 & 271; Johnson, *Seeing Fairies* 54; Semi-human:
Fairy Census numbers 293, 116, 191 & 359; Johnson, *Seeing Fairies* 125; Faery-mermaid:
Fairy Census numbers 234 & 261; Monsters: Johnson, *Seeing Fairies,* 54, 94 & 125.

distinctly higher in the *Census,* suggesting that the now-standard concept of a "grey alien" may be shaping faery experiences.[69]

Some faeries are simply pure light. The luminosity of faeries is often mentioned, but the last transformation is the eradication of the body altogether: the faery is reduced to a point of light, which is often seen darting about. Johnson's witnesses experienced this only a handful of times. In the *Census* 14 per cent of cases were sightings of bright lights, of which nearly three-quarters were moving. We may suspect here the influence of Tinker Bell in the minds of those having the experience and it is probably strong, but these ideas aren't entirely without traditional precedent. On Dartmoor in 1876, pixies were said sometimes to be seen as white spots moving about in the dark. Faeries seen in houses in Stowmarket in Suffolk in the mid-nineteenth century would flee the occupants' arrival, but their recent presence was betrayed by the fact that, if you climbed the stairs, sparks of fire as bright as stars appeared around your feet. This may in some cases have been residual glamour, but not always: if the Shetland trows' fire went out, they'd simply steal some from a human hearth, a theft that would be disclosed by the trail of sparks seen crossing the room.[70]

It's noticeable throughout the recent *Fairy Census* how contemporary imagery shapes people's descriptions of their experiences. The beings sighted are quite often compared to Disney faeries (Tinker Bell), to the artwork of Brian Froud, and, in one case, to Gollum in the film version of *Lord of the Rings.* We must be alert to how our expectations and interpretation might be shaped by what we already know. At the same time, though, the reports described here diverge so markedly from the conventional imagery as to lend them increased authenticity. People may be less likely to make up something which so little resembles what we're told a faery is like.

On their own, many of these reports are so anomalous as to make no sense, but grouped together some sort of pattern does start to emerge, and it's possible to begin to identify certain "species" that are regularly sighted. Perhaps they are so different from the standard idea of a faery to demand a

---

69. Johnson, *Seeing Fairies,* 120, 121 & 240; see for example *Census* numbers 154, 267 & 361.

70. Johnson, *Seeing Fairies* 37, 51, 226, 266 & 313; *Transactions of Devonshire Association,* vol. 8, 57; *County Folklore Printed Extracts* vol. 2, 36; Marwick, *The Folklore of Orkney,* 35.

new name, but at present "faery" is the only category to which we may assign them.

This survey of faery physicality may have raised more questions for readers than it has answered. If so, you must remind yourself to beware of the powerful influence of pervasive images derived from books, films, and paintings. Our definitions of "faery" may be far too narrow, and the variety of form amongst the Good Folk may be much wider, than most of us can possibly imagine.

Faery Language and Speech

To interact with the faeries, we have to be able in some manner to communicate with them. Unfortunately, their speech turns out to be an area of some doubt and dispute. Very much like faery music, which we'll examine later, speech is a point of contact between the human and faery worlds, but transmission of sound between the two appears to be subject to interruptions and distortions, which naturally inhibit a free flow of information. We need to consider two separate aspects of faery speech here: the words used and the way they speak.

"Hidden Tongues"

The typical treatment of the matter of faery speech in the literature is either to use it as a source of humour or to regard it as an area so obscure and insoluble that little meaningful can be said. The two extremes are illustrated by the following authorities. Ben Jonson in *The Alchemist* opted for the frivolous and mocking approach. His elves enter crying "Titi, titi, titi…" which allegedly means "Pinch him or he will never confess." Dapper, the dupe of this scene, declares that he has told the truth, to which the elves respond "Ti, ti, ti, ti, to, ta"—"he does equivocate." Similar nonsense is spouted by the faeries in Thomas Randolph's *Amyntas* of 1632. You wonder whether this is all just a play on the name Titania; it certainly doesn't help us talk to real faeries. It's also been observed (more or less seriously) that if you go by a lot of the folklore sources, faeries always tend to speak in rhyme.[71]

---

71. Halliwell, *Popular Rhymes and Nursery Tales*, 190.

The other view of faery language may be represented by the Reverend Edmund Jones, in his discussion of contemporary faery beliefs in Gwent in the 1770s. His description is typical of many of the Welsh texts and accounts of around that time: he states that the faeries are often talking together "but the words are seldom heard." This is either because they were indistinct, or because they were spoken in neither Welsh nor English. Similar communication problems were experienced much farther north, with the trows on Shetland. For example, a girl once saw a "grey woman" wandering and "making a noise like scolding" in a "hidden tongue." The speech reported was both harsh to hear as well as incomprehensible.[72]

Sometimes there's a complete language barrier and no communication at all is possible. Luckily, more often the Fae seem quite at home in the local tongue, whether that's English, Welsh, or whatever. A few recent reports also suggest that Old Irish or some non-local, but known, language like Danish or Swedish might be heard.[73]

On the nature of faery language, we are lucky to have the detailed testimony of Irish seer and poet Ella Young.[74] She heard both faery song as well as music and tried to record the words she heard. If her account provides a half-accurate transcription of actual speech, we have the most tantalising evidence we possess for the language of the Irish *sidhe* folk (at least). Young kept an account in her diary for the summer of 1917 in which she described what she had heard in the far northwest of Ireland. On August 28 she heard "a great litany of chants and responses with words in an unknown language: abaktha … nyetho … wyehoo." On September 1, a chorus sang the word "Beeya" repeatedly; this was followed on October 9 by voices chanting "Balaclóo … Beeya …" and it culminated on October 17 with an extended "Gregorian chant" of which she recorded what she could: "Hy bermillu, hydramel, heroó, wyehóobilik, kyeyóubilik, wyehóo, balalóo …"

This may of course all be the product of a deluded mind: on September 8 Young wrote quite frankly that "my head has been for several days quite normal" as a consequence of which she had heard neither music nor song

72. Jones, *Aberystruth*, 69; Saxby, *Shetland Traditional Lore*, 149–150; see too Dathen, *Somerset Fairies and Pixies*, 69; and Hunt, *Popular Romances of the West of England*, 85.

73. *Fairy Census* numbers 238 & 310.

74. Young, *At the Gates of Dawn*, 2011.

from the *sidhe* people. All we can say is that, if it is genuine, it is untainted testimony of faery speech. Young's experiences predate Tolkien and his confection of elvish languages from Welsh and Finnish; there could be no imitation of his pervasive influence nor, for that matter, does Gaelic appear to have shaped what she heard. If her snatches of verse resemble anything at all, it's an Algonquian tongue from New England. It's worth recording that Young was not alone in her claims to have met and conversed with faeries. As respected a figure as poet William Butler Yeats made the same claims at around the same time.

Sadly, even if they're authentic, the words transcribed by Young may, in practical terms, remain complete nonsense: without a "Rosetta stone" to give us a key to translation, they might as well be gobbledegook. Nevertheless, as the poet Philip Dayre hoped in his verse "An Invocation," if we could relearn the forgotten faery speech we might be able to recover our close links to nature. Restoration of this lost unity might be the reward awaiting the person who finds that key to faery speech.

Silvery Voices

Still, regardless of the words spoken, the faeries' speech will be distinctive for its tone: repeatedly, faery voices are reported to be "high pitched," "bell-like," "plangent," "clipped and very quick," and "tinkling." They are often compared to children's voices, shrill and gabbling. A Miss Eva Longbottom told Sir Arthur Conan Doyle about her meetings with some faeries who had "dulcet silvery voices"; they spoke and sang, she said, more in sound than with distinct words, and in a language of their own. This chirping, squeaking, ringing nature might in itself cause problems of comprehension. Faery voices have been said to be too high to distinguish all the words—or even to hear.[75]

The Vikings thought that elves spoke in low tones, making a whispering sound like the wind. Scottish brownies are "a' rough but the mouth"—that is, they may be very hairy to look at, but they speak softly. Several modern cases

---

75. Doyle, *The Coming of the Fairies*, 168; Johnson, *Seeing Fairies*, 34, 35, 279, and 44, 51, 59 & 255; see too Dathen, *Somerset Fairies and Pixies*, 133; and *Fairy Census* no. 350—"like little bells" or no. 355—"chittering, moaning, jabbering."

also report soft hissing voices that sounded like the sighing wind or "gurgling low whispers."[76]

Sometimes the comparison made is with an animal call, such as a bird: the Serbian *vila* is said to sound like a woodpecker, and in his poem "The Ruin," Walter de la Mare described bands of faeries "chattering like grass-hoppers." Witnesses have used such words as "twittering," "like a scolding squirrel," and "chirping." A Somerset farmer often heard the pixies when he was a boy early last century and his description was of "voices sort of near, sort of far, laughing, jesting, squabbling, even singing some strange songs in some queer language, like birds." Another time, the same man overheard the pixies threshing grain in his barn, singing as they worked in "croaky bird-like voices." Lastly, one of the witnesses in the *Fairy Census* memorably describes that the small figures he met made a sound that "was similar but not exactly like the sound of kittens when they mew at each other."[77]

The problems of comprehension may not just be matters of pitch. One of the witnesses in the *Fairy Census* described her encounter in Lancashire in these words: "Her voice was almost like it was phasing in and out of our reality." This wave-like effect is also described by those who've heard faery music; comparable too is the difficulty focussing on the speech experienced by a witness in Kentucky who was listening to "voices that seemed to be close to me, just beyond my reach, and also very far from me, all at the same time ... fading in and out of the distance ... the voices faded and twisted and changed, like they were coming to me on the wind." Similar perhaps is an experience in which their sing-song voices were perceived all at once by a man from New York State, "in a kind of cascading aural waterfall effect."[78]

There seem to be lots of barriers to communications with the Good Folk, but there are two reasons for readers not to despair. First, a lot of contemporary reports indicate that spoken communication is unnecessary. Many faeries seem to communicate by telepathy rather than by words and their

---

76. Crofton Croker, *Fairy Legends*, 85; *County Folklore* vol. 3, 25; *Census* numbers 127 & 286; see too Hogg, "Odd characters," in *Shepherd's Calendar*, vol. 2, 150.

77. *Somerset Fairies and Pixies*, 101 & 106; *Census* no. 78; in *Fairies at Work and Play* Hodson describes nature spirits he calls "grass creatures" making a "curious chattering sound" (chapter III).

78. *Fairy Census* nos. 70, 286 & 337.

meaning is understood perfectly by witnesses. Conversations may very well be held in this way, thereby overcoming all problems of language.[79]

Secondly, we may just have to accept that we live in a different dimension to the faeries and that communication between us may simply not be possible. Twentieth-century spiritualist Edward Gardner had something to say on these matters. He took the theosophical view of the nature of faeries and stated that they have no language as such (or none that mortal ears can hear, anyway). Gardner's colleague Geoffrey Hodson supported this; he described seeing mannikins, faeries, and brownies whose mouths were moving, as if they were singing or shouting, yet he heard nothing. Instead of words, Gardner's supernaturals communicated by means of music—so perhaps when some witnesses have assumed the sounds they heard came from instruments, they actually came from the faery beings themselves.[80]

To finish, it's worth adding that when faery voices are reported, it's regularly said that they seem to be laughing. This is a reassuring detail, implying that most encounters may be friendly and playful. Traditionally, in Cornwall, the saying was "to laugh like a pixy." Recent reports seem to support this idea of a normally happy temperament.

Faery Intelligence and Moods

If we hope to interact happily and safely with our Good Neighbours, it is important to have some understanding of how they think and react. Whilst there's a risk in over-generalising, there are also risks in taking too benign a view of them, or in assuming that they may be just like us.

Faery Intelligence

All the evidence indicates that the Good Folk are, as a rule, just as wily and clever as any human. Nonetheless, the traditions also suggest that the domestic faeries, the brownies and dobbies, may be amongst the slower witted of the species. For example, there is a Scottish creature called Brownie Clod. His name may partly derive from a habit of throwing clods of earth at passersby, but he is also known for having made a very disadvantageous bargain

---

79. *Fairy Census* numbers 55, 78, 164, 181, 211 & 361 out of many examples.

80. Conan Doyle *The Coming of the Fairies*, c. VIII; Hodson, *Fairies at Work and Play*, c. III, and *The Kingdom of Faerie*, cc. IV & VI; see too *Census* number 154.

with some men that exploited his kind's propensity for unremitting hard work for little reward. Various boggarts too seem slow on the uptake: there is a well-known story of a farmer whose field was claimed by a boggart. They reached a settlement of their dispute whereby, in alternate years, they agreed to halve what grew above and below ground. In the first year the boggart chose to take the "bottoms" of the crops—and the farmer planted wheat. In the following year, the bogart was entitled to the tops, and the farmer planted turnips.

Some faeries, at the very least, are rather gullible. Several versions exist of the ballad "Lady Isabel and the Elf Knight." The knight woos the young woman solely for the purpose of murdering her, as he has killed seven maidens before. However, in each telling of the story Isabel tricks the elf and kills him instead. In one, she asks for a final kiss before he plunges her in a well—and then topples him in; in others his plan is to drown her in the sea and the lady asks him to look away whilst she undresses—a fatal error of courtly manners. I mentioned earlier the "ainsel" stories that play on the same guileless tendency.

Lastly, whilst not necessarily indicative of dimness, there is a story that indicates that these spirits are rather simple and literal. A Lake District farmer with fields full of ripened grain ready for reaping wished to himself that his crop was in the barn before the good weather changed. The farm hobthrush heard the wish and laboured all night to get the harvest in. The next day it turned out to be sunny after all, and the famer wished to himself that his crops had got another day's ripening in the field and that the over-enthusiastic hobthrush was in the mill-pond. His grain was dumped in the pond instead.[81]

Faery Temperament

It appears that it's extremely hard for us humans truly to comprehend how the Good Folk think and feel and the result of this is that some writers have gone to extremes in describing their temperament. Welsh writer Mary Lewes felt that the story of the Myddfai lake maiden who cried at a wedding and laughed at a funeral disclosed the faery's complete absence of recognisable

---

81. Briggs, *Remains of John Briggs*, 224.

emotions and her total inability to empathise with normal human senti-ments. On the other hand, a Scottish account portrayed the faeries as being entirely free of many human faults: they are "not limited like we are with such weaknesses as envy, hatred, spite, falsehood or intemperance." Rather they are a "Guid Little People," mischievous, perhaps, but not in the least irritable and, on the whole, "benign, good-natured, lovable, jolly Lilliputians..."[82]

In Herefordshire the belief is that *all* supernaturals are tetchy by nature, so that the old saying used to be that people from Knighton were quarrel-some—"just like the faeries." More correctly, it seems that temperament varies between the faery families. In Shetland, it's said that the local faeries are more gentle, gossamer, and harmless than the trows. The former group are consistently and uniformly cheerful, whereas trows tend to the morose, but are changeable according to their treatment by humans. There's a good deal of evidence that the household spirits like brownies can be touchy and temperamental; it seems their feelings are easily injured and they can quickly take offence at slights—perceived or real—and respond peevishly. For instance, the boggart of Syke Lumb farm near Blackburn would smash the cream pots, set the cattle loose, overturn carts, and pull off the bedclothes whenever he was irritated. The domestic faeries are especially sensitive to scolding or criticism of their work. In the famous story of the brownie of Cranshaws in Berwickshire, the faery took umbrage at criticism of his mow-ing and threw the whole hay harvest off a cliff. A very similar falling-out on a farm near Levenshulme in Lancashire ended with the crops back in the fields and the boggart gone forever.[83]

Faery Joy?

Faery moods can be changeable, but we'll end this part of the book with what might sound like a strange question: Are the faeries happy?

Some would argue that they are not: there are frequent accounts of faer-ies agonising over their ultimate Christian salvation and this certainly sug-gests a deep dissatisfaction with their state, as they lack immortal souls. In a

---

82. Lewes, *The Queer Side*, 126; Terrell, *Wee Folk of Menteith*, 48 & 51.

83. Leather, *Folklore of Herefordshire*, 43; Hardwick, *Traditions, Superstitions and Folklore*, 125; Henderson, *Notes on the Folklore of the Northern Counties of England and the Borders*, 250; Bowker, *Goblin Tales of Lancashire*, 52; Nicholson, *Folklore of East Yorkshire*, 79.

description of Perthshire in 1810, Scottish author Patrick Graham portrayed the faeries as

> a peevish, repairing race of beings who, possessing themselves of but a scanty portion of happiness, are supposed to envy mankind their more complete and substantial enjoyments. They are supposed to enjoy, in their subterranean recesses, a sort of shadowy happiness, a tinsel grandeur, which however they would willingly change for the more solid joys of mortals.[84]

I'm mistrustful of the idea of faeries as being envious of humans and constantly trying to imitate us. From a Christian perspective, the Fae do indeed live a sort of miserable, marginal half-life. Trows in particular have been described as "melancholy and morbid." It's not at all clear, though, that they themselves see it the same way. For example, another Scot who actually met the faeries recalled how they had whispered about him, with now and then "the repetition of his name, which was always done with a strain of pity."[85] Perhaps it is we mortals who should feel sorry for ourselves: our lives are full of worries and woes whilst the faeries live a carefree existence, filled instead with dancing and music.

A further Scottish writer describes the Fae as "a sociable people, passionately given to festive amusements and jocund hilarity." Without doubt, this is what most people believe and what you'll find described again and again in poems and stories celebrating the "frolicsome faeries" and how, for "jocund elves… In mirthful glee the hours unheeded roll." Sir Walter Scott put it most attractively: "Tis merry, tis merry in Fairyland, When Fairy birds are singing…" There is too the Cornish saying "laughing like a pixie"—although we ought to admit that this may refer to the fun to be had in "pixy-leading" some hapless person at night.[86]

In conclusion, perhaps the best view is more balanced and realistic. Faeries' lives are in many ways much like those of humans and they have,

---

84. Graham, *Sketches Descriptive of Picturesque Scenery,* 103.

85. Edmondston, *A view of the Zetland Isles,* 189; Hogg, "Odd Characters," 150.

86. Stewart, *The Popular Superstitions and Festive Amusements of the Highlanders of Scotland,* 90; George Meredith, *The Poetry of Shakespeare;* Charlotte Dacre, *Will o' Wisp;* Scott, *Alice Brand.*

of course, a variety of dispositions: some are good and some are wicked; some are cheery and some are sad. Their thieving has been ascribed to their "naturally spiteful" nature, but it's probably less clear-cut than this. Famous authority Crofton Croker has described the faery temperament as being "a strange combination of good and evil, duplicity and sincerity… they may be generous and obliging or malicious. They like teasing and mockery—but they won't be mocked. They are faithful and keep their vows; they are subtle and cunning."[87]

Summary

In the south west of Scotland this advice on the Good Folk was recorded: "The faeries are unchancy people. If they don't like you, then your life can be made a misery. If they like you, then things can be so much better for you, or worse…"[88]

As I stressed in the previous chapter, there are many different regional types of faery and they can seem quite contrary in their behaviour. Although more recent attitudes have undergone a change, in the past people viewed the Fae with a good measure of caution and apprehensive respect. In light of what's just been said on the faery temperament (and although it may seem to be lacking in the deference I just mentioned), I'd suggest that the folklore paints a picture of a folk who are quite child-like in their disposition. They can be capricious; they may bear grudges; they veer from amity to enmity with little warning or provocation. They can be very playful, yet at the same time they will remain very conscious of the regard they feel to be due to them.

Clearly, the Good Folk are a people who should be approached warily—tentatively even. Yet—as we've just seen—they may not always look like we think faeries ought to look. This being so, the more information we can gather about where we may find them and what we may find them doing, the better.

---

87. MacGregor, *Peat Fire Flame,* 1; Lewes, *Queer Side,* 11; Crofton Croker, *Fairy Legends,* 35 & 99.
88. Browning, *Dumfries & Galloway Folk Tales,* 52.

Chapter 5

FAERY-FAVOURED SPACES

The Fae inhabit two spheres: faeryland and the human world. We've already discussed what and where Faery may be; in this chapter we examine the places in this world that can be frequented by faeries, but also consider how everyday elements of the human environment can be imbued with faery glamour. This can mean that parallel forms may exist in the otherworld, or that ordinary plants and animals may take on special significance and powers or be filled with the faery presence.

Faery Plants

A range of plants have faery associations, both good and bad. If you're concerned to contact the Good Folk, but wish to do so respectfully, or if you're worried about faery influence and seek protection from it, these links are very important.

Trees

Later I'll talk about the link between faeries and woodland, but certain species of trees are known to have strong links to faeries. The commonest trees with which faeries are associated are as follows:

- **Hawthorn:** These trees are considered to be magical throughout Britain and Ireland. For instance, Northumbrian faeries are said particularly to prefer dancing around thorns. From across the border comes a Scottish story of a man ploughing a field who made a special effort to protect an old hawthorn, known to be a faery meeting place, by leaving an unploughed circle of turf around it; he was rewarded with a faery banquet and a lifetime's luck and wisdom in consequence.

- **Elder:** I mentioned the Old Lady of the Elder Tree earlier on. The tree was believed to have general magical properties. In Scotland it was thought to protect against evil, so that an elder cross would be placed in byres and stables to safeguard the livestock against faeries. So powerful was the elder, though, that on the Scottish island of Sanday, stepping over the elder tree growing in the church yard was said to ensure death within a year. On the Isle of Man, the faeries' particular home is in elders, and in Ireland elder sap is believed to grant a second sight of the faery rade.[89]

- **Oaks:** That oak trees have a special status as places for faery dancing, or even as their homes, is widely known. In *The Discovery of Witchcraft* of 1584 Reginald Scot listed the many different types of faeries with which mothers would scare their children. He included "the man in the oke," a supernatural whose characteristics and habits are now almost entirely lost to us, although a modern witness in Somerset has described them as small furry creatures with tails. Faeries have certainly been seen dancing under oaks in Lancashire, East Yorkshire, and in Mid- and South Wales. In the grounds of Downing House near Whiteford, North Wales, there is a large "faery oak." When a child suddenly becomes peevish and is suspected of being a changeling, if it is left out overnight beneath the tree's boughs, the faeries will have returned the human infant by the next morning. Cutting down oak trees can lead to faery retribution, either death or "a strange aching pain which admitted no remedy." In South Wales the faeries liked to dance under crab apple trees as well as under oaks.[90]

---

89. Dathen, *Somerset Fairies and Pixies*, 54; Dalyell, *The Darker Superstitions of Scotland*, 401.

90. Scot, Book VII, chapter XV; Dathen, *Somerset Fairies and Pixies*, 21; Nicholson, *Folklore of East Yorkshire*, 82; Pennant, *The History of the Parishes of Whiteford & Holywell*, 5–6; Jones, *Appearance* no. 116 & 117.

- **Walnuts:** A walnut tree used to grow at Llandyn Hall, near to Llangollen in Wales, around which the faeries would assemble at night to hold their wedding ceremonies. It was cut down in the nineteenth century, sadly, although the faeries took their revenge for this, it was believed: one of the workmen involved in the felling was killed by a falling branch.

- **Rowan or mountain ash:** Rowan trees, in contrast, repel faeries. In this book, rowan will repeatedly be seen being used to guard against faeries and their depredations. Set over your door, it will allow you to watch the faery rade riding past without being drawn into their procession. A rowan cross worn about your person will prevent the faeries seizing you, and a rowan branch can be used to rescue a person trapped in a faery dance. The aversion of the Fae to rowan is amply demonstrated by one Scottish method of expelling a changeling, which involved putting the suspected faery infant in a sieve and holding it over a fire made of rowan wood.[91] The protective power of rowan is demonstrated very clearly in a story from Middridge in Northumberland. There was an old quarry outside the village and it was said that riding around it nine times would put you in the faeries' power. One reckless young man dared to do this and found himself pursued relentlessly by the faery who was conjured up. The boy only escaped because he had taken the precaution of filling his pockets with rowan bark. He strewed this behind him as he fled and the faery was slowed down by the fact that he had to pause to pick up all the handfuls of scattered bark. The dual role of the rowan—a spray of foliage can act as a charm against faery intrusion but also as a means of seeing the Good Neighbours passing—is another good example of the "contrary" nature of many faery things.[92]

- **Gorse and holly:** Both these thorny shrubs act as protective barriers to faeries around a home, although it has to be confessed that they keep out humans just as well! Conversely, faeries have been reported to shelter under holly and mistletoe leaves in the winter. In the west

---

91. Aitken, *Forgotten Heritage*, 12; given the contrary nature of the Fae, there are those who believe rowan to be a faery tree—see for instance Dathen, *Somerset Fairies and Pixies*, 41.

92. Grice, *Folk Tales of the North Country—Drawn from Northumberland and Durham*, c. 17.

of Scotland mistletoe has been hung over doors during frosts deliberately to provide faeries with shelter from the cold. Showing good
will toward the Good Folk may explain a curious custom from Herefordshire. In the villages of Kingstone and Thruxton, the practice
used to be to put out trays of moss on May Eve, so that the faeries
could dance on them. This custom is a little hard to explain: it may
be that part of the intention was to provide an alternative for the Fae
so that they didn't invade the home, which—as we'll see later—was
very likely to happen otherwise.[93]

A variety of other timbers including elm, hazel, and birch protect against
faeries. For example, birch hung over a doorway on May Eve will guard the
household and stables from the faeries at one of the times of year when they
are at their most powerful. Throughout the year, sprays or crosses of birch
put over a stable door will prevent the faeries entering at night and interfering with the horses, which is a particular pastime of theirs.

A final interesting account relates to the Cornish faery that haunts the
rock outcrop known as the Newlyn Tolcarne. The manner in which this spirit
was summoned was to pronounce a charm whilst holding three dried leaves
in your hand. These were one each from an ash, an oak, and a thorn. Now,
as some readers will know, these are the trees invoked by Rudyard Kipling's
Puck in *Puck of Pook's Hill*. We seem to have two entirely separate traditions
here, one from Sussex, where Kipling wrote, and the other from the far west
of Cornwall. If so, Kipling's "right of Oak, Ash, and Thorn" may be a great
deal older than has been suspected. Kipling's faeries are "the people of the
hills" and the Newlyn being lives under a cairn near the beach, so that what
we have seems to be an affinity with these trees rather than residency within
them. Interestingly, ash sap was once given to children as a protective against
malign faery influence.[94]

Flowers and Herbs

The faeries are especially linked with yellow blossoms, flowers such as cowslips, broom, and primroses. Our difficulty is that there's no consistency

---

93. Napier, *Folklore or Superstitious Beliefs in the West of Scotland Within this Century*, 124 & 150.
94. Evans-Wentz, *The Fairy Faith in Celtic Countries*, 176; Kipling, *Puck of Pook's Hill,* 1906,
    chapter "Weland's Forge" & "Tree song."

about whether they like, or hate, yellow blooms. For instance, ragwort stems are used for flight, rather like witches' broomsticks. Conversely, on the Isle of Man homes are protected from faery intrusions with yellow flowers on Midsummer's Eve. Gorse flowers are yellow and this—as well as their spikes— may be the reason they're so effective as a barrier against the Fae.

The primary protective plant against faeries is the (yellow) St. John's Wort, which is hung around houses on Midsummer's Eve (St. John's Eve). Again, though, folk beliefs prove contradictory. On the Isle of Man, it's said that if you picked the flower after sunset on this festival, a faery horse would appear and carry you away.

White flowers also have supernatural connections. Daisies have been said to be faery flowers and picking the greater stitchwort is a sure way to end up being pixy-led. The mugwort, with creamy-white blossoms, protected you from faerie harm, so that Manx farmers garlanded themselves and their cattle with these flowers at Midsummer. Vervain, with pinky-white florets, would be sewn into babies' clothes and adults would make a tea from its leaves to protect themselves. Across the British Isles four- and five-leaf clovers can dispel glamour and enable you to see the Fae. In Scotland several plants, including both *mothan* (pearlwort) and clover, were used as protection against the Fae; the only stipulation was that these herbs only had potency if they were discovered *"gun iarraid"* (without searching). In other words, you had to come upon them as you walked without making deliberate efforts to find and collect them.[95]

Bluebells are protected by faeries, and lone children picking them in woods risk being abducted. Heather, with its purply-blue colouring, is another ambiguous plant. The faeries use it to make ale—but it also seems to work as a protective against them.

The faeries are said particularly to favour red blooms. Foxgloves are known in Wales as *menyg ellyllon,* elves' gloves, and their particular faery association is confirmed in one Perthshire tale in which two men are waylaid by a pair of lovely but sinister young faery women dressed in green and with foxgloves in their hair. Conversely, foxglove juice can expel a changeling and cure a child who is suffering from "the feyry"—that is, one who has been elf-struck.

---

95. *Denham Tracts, Folklore Society,* vol. 35, 142; Harland, *Lancashire Legends & Traditions,* 110; MacGregor, *Peat Fire Flame,* 274.

Other red faery flowers include roses, campion, forget-me-not, scabious, wild thyme, and, more unusually, tulips. A strange tale from Devon describes how pixies near Tavistock loved to spend their nights in an old woman's tulip bed and the flowers thrived from their beneficial presence. When she died her flowerbed was converted by the next residents of the cottage to growing parsley and the aggrieved pixies blighted it.[96]

Fungi

The linking of fungi with goblins and elves is known and of long standing. Perhaps the pairing derives in part from the dual nature of mushrooms—they may be edible or poisonous. Thus, in Wales, elf food (bwyd ellyllon) is the popular name for a poisonous toadstool. Fungi are, of course, linked to faery rings and indicate where the elves have been dancing. One type of faery fungi is the Faery Cake Hebeloma, which is poisonous; another is the highly edible Faery Ring Champignon. In Breconshire the belief is that gifts of bread by the tylwyth teg, if not eaten immediately and in darkness, will prove to be toadstools in the daylight.

Faery butter is a concept found across Britain. In Wales, the butter (y menyntylwyth teg) is an agreeable-smelling fungus found deep underground in limestone crevices. In Northumberland, faery butter is a soft orange fungus found around the roots of old trees. A slightly different species with the same name is also found growing on furze and broom.

It's said that the faeries like to throw the butter at windows, doors, and gates during the night, trying to make it stick on them, and this nuisance was experienced very commonly in the North of England in North Yorkshire and Cleveland. If this is done at your home, it's said to be a portent of good fortune. In the Lake District, unpalatable as it sounds, it was eating the fungus butter that was believed to bring luck; in Wales, the faery butter was rubbed on the body to treat rheumatism.[97]

---

96. Murray, *Tales from Highland Perthshire*, nos. 190 & 173; Sutherland, *Folklore Gleanings & Character Sketches from the Far North*, 23.

97. Wright, *Rustic Speech and Folklore*, 208; *County Folklore* vol. 2, 130; Atkinson, *Forty Years in a Moorland Parish*, 53; Roberts *Folklore of Yorkshire*, 67; Rowling, *Folklore of the Lake District*, 32; Bord, *Fairies*, 27.

The sudden appearance of toadstools may seem magical and mysterious and may partly explain the faery association. Their red colouring (notably the traditionally red and white spotted fly agaric toadstool) may link them to red faery clothes. Puffballs have been called "Puck's fist" and, in his *Faery Mythology*, Thomas Keightley suggested that "Elf's fist" was an old Anglo-Saxon name for the mushrooms found in rings.

The diminutive size of many fungi may also explain the association. Robert Herrick in his poem "Oberon's Feast" imagines "a little mushroom table spread" for the tiny faery diners. In Sussex the red-cup moss is known as "faeries' baths" and it's said in Welsh folklore that the parasol mushrooms act as umbrellas to keep the faeries' dance-sites dry.[98]

The most interesting faery use of fungi involves both magic and treasure and comes from the Isle of Wight on the English south coast. A man called John saw a strange light in Puckaster Cove and, on investigating, discovered child-size people dancing on the beach. They gave him a brown powder to inhale, which resembled snuff but which may well have been mushroom dust; certainly, it shrank him to their size so that he could join in with the dancing. After a while John sat down to rest on a puffball mushroom that burst, showering gold dust everywhere. The faeries gave him some of this dust and then restored him to his normal height.

So close is the link between faeries, dancing, and the phenomenon called faery rings that I'll discuss them in detail separately. This association only serves to reinforce one undeniable fact: faeries and mushrooms or toadstools have become an inseparable pairing in the popular imagination. The earliest published picture I've found is an illustration from the 1734 edition of *Round About Our Coal Fire*, which incorporates all the key elements of the imagery (dancers, fly agaric, faery knoll, moonlight). Little has changed since, although arguably the connection has been strengthened considerably, first in children's faery poetry and then during the middle of the last century when (it seemed) almost every children's illustrator produced some variation on the theme.

Faery Rings

Faery rings are linked to faery dancing. If you read a lot of the British faery poetry, especially that of the nineteenth century, you would get the impression

---

98. Gwyndaf in Narvaez, *Good People*, 180.

that dancing in rings is, in fact, pretty much all that faeries do; it's their defining characteristic, their main habit, their primary purpose or occupation even. They come out at night—especially when the moon is bright—and dance in circles in grassy places. These are then marked by mushrooms springing up.

Usually it's said that it's the passing of faery feet that makes the tracks that are seen by people the next day. In Somerset the circles are called "gallitraps" and they are said to be made by the Fae riding colts in circles in the fields at night. Whether they're dancing or racing, the faery presence can easily be proved: set up a stick in a ring overnight and it will be found knocked down by the Fae the next morning.[99]

The rings used to be much more widespread than today, and much more noticeable: it was said that every piece of common land had at least one fairy ring. They appeared in all types of fields except those sown with corn. Modern farming practices, with increased cultivation and use of fertilisers and pesticides, have drastically reduced the evidence, but we can get an idea of what our predecessors would have seen from the writings of naturalist Robert Plot. Discussing the English Midlands in the late seventeenth century, he described rings that were forty or fifty yards in diameter, often encircled by a rim between a foot and a yard wide. These rims might be bare, or might have a russet, singed colour. The grass within could also be brown but was more often dark green. Plot sought to explain the rings scientifically, blaming moles or penned cattle, but given their size and distinctness, it is unsurprising that others would readily suspect supernatural causation.[100]

A variety of faery beliefs attached to the rings. Charming as the sight of faeries tripping all in a circle might be, the rings themselves are places of danger. To sleep in one is especially risky—you are in considerable danger of being "taken" by the faeries. One Cornishman who crossed a faery ring without first turning his pockets inside out as protection experienced a curious punishment. The pixies caught him, pinched him, bound his limbs with threads of gossamer, and then touched his eyes with their green ointment.

---

99. Tongue, *Somerset Folklore*, 115; Burne, *Shropshire Folklore*, Part III, 638; but see Daimler, *Fairies*, 133, where she suggests the faeries are drawn to dance by the mushrooms.

100. Plot, *The Natural History of Staffordshire*, paras. 17–27.

This meant he could see the feasting and revelry going on around him, but was powerless to join in—or escape.[101]

For people to spy on the dances in the rings, or join in with them, will definitely be perilous. These circles may even be traps, deliberately set to lure in humans and to abduct them for extended periods—or forever. Step into one completely and you will be in the faeries' power; put one foot inside and you will be able to see the dancing but will still be able to escape. We must also recall here the disparity in the passage in time between Faery and the mortal world; the captive dancer spins at a different rate to the human globe and may quit the ring to find their old life has long passed.[102]

It was widely believed that the rings should never be damaged and should never be cultivated. Grazing them and, even more importantly, ploughing them, was strongly discouraged by those familiar with the phenomena: a traditional Scottish rhyme warned that

> He wha tills the faeries' green
> Nae luck shall hae;
> And he wha spills the faries' ring
> Betide him want and wae;
> For weirdless days and weary nights
> Are his 'til his deein' day![103]

Anyone foolish enough to ignore such advice would find their cattle struck down with disease. In one Welsh story, even though the farmer realised his error and restored the damaged rings, a curse had been pronounced by the faeries—and was eventually visited upon his descendants one hundred years later.[104]

In any case, it was also widely believed that any attempt to eradicate the rings would fail. Ploughing could not remove them and they would return immediately, as was said to have happened with two rings in the churchyard

---

101. Richardson, *Local Historian's Table Book*, vol. 2, 134; Harris, *Cornish Saints and Sinners* c. 19 (the same story is told of a Welsh farmer from Ffridd; W. Jenkyn Thomas, *Welsh Fairy Book*, "The adventures of three farmers").

102. Tongue, *Somerset Folklore* 114–5.

103. Chambers, *Popular Rhymes of Scotland*, 324.

104. W. Jenkyn Thomas, *Welsh Fairy Book*, "The curse of Pantannas."

at Pulverbatch in Shropshire. Just as those who interfere with rings will suffer, it was believed that those that cared for them would be rewarded: as the Scottish rhyme promised, "an easy death shall dee."[105]

An aura of magic and danger attaches itself to faery rings, therefore. Mostly the tendency is to avoid them: for example, at Market Drayton in Shropshire people used to be reluctant to use those parts of the church graveyard marked with rings.[106]

Nonetheless, there's some good news as well—first, May Day dew collected from a faery ring is said to be excellent for preserving youthful skin. Secondly, it's said that dancing three times around a ring will make a wish come true within the year and that, if you can run around a ring nine times without drawing breath, you will be rewarded by the Fae. Given the huge circumference of the rings just described, this would be no mean feat and entirely deserving of reward. Lastly, and despite what was said a little earlier, in some places in England it's thought that building a house in a place marked with rings will prove fortunate for the inhabitants.[107]

To conclude, faery rings are the commonest and most immediate and tangible intrusion of Faery into the human world. They are a physical and permanent presence of the supernatural in the mortal sphere and as such rank alongside changelings and the household sprites for the light they can shed upon our relationship with the Good Folk.

Faery Animals

A number of domesticated beasts are associated with faeries, showing how often their society is seen as imitating or paralleling our own. This livestock may be imagined as being its normal size, so as to match human-size faeries; on other occasions the creatures are diminutive, just like their supernatural owners. Sometimes the creatures are larger than their counterparts in the human world, enhancing the fear associated with their unearthly origins.

---

105. MacGregor, *The Peat Fire Flame*, 2; Addy, *Household Tales*, 134; Burne, *Shropshire Folklore*, Part III, 638; J. McPherson, *Primitive Beliefs in the North East of Scotland*, 97; Chambers, *Popular Rhymes*, 324.

106. Burne, *Shropshire folklore*, Part I, 56.

107. Napier, *Folklore* 157; J. Udal, *Dorsetshire Folklore*, 260 & 330; *Chamber's Edinburgh Journal*, 1845, vol. 12, 10.

As we'll see, there's almost always something distinctive about faery animals, helping you to spot when you may be in the presence of the Good Folk.

Faery Goats

In the west of Britain, goats are often seen as mysterious faery beasts. For example, William Bottrell recorded that wherever goats preferred to graze would be certain to be places frequented by the Cornish pixies. In both Cornwall and the Perthshire Highlands, it's believed that the faeries—and especially their babies and changelings—live on goats' milk. Animals that were good milkers would be enticed away from a human herd by the appearance of mysterious billy-goats, who were actually pixies and faeries in disguise.

Some of the best evidence for the association of faeries and goats is from Wales. The bad-natured female faeries, the *gwyllion,* are closely linked with goats, which are themselves esteemed for their occult knowledge and powers. The tylwyth teg comb goats' beards every Friday so as to make them presentable on Sunday (a curious notion that perhaps says more about Welsh religiosity than the faith of the faeries). In the tale of "Cadwaladr's goat," Jenny the goat turned out to be a faery maiden in disguise, who led Cadwaladr to the court of the faery goat king. The Highland tale of the "Tacksman of Auchriachan" is a story of faery theft. The tacksman (tenant farmer) overhears the faeries in their knoll planning to pilfer his farm whilst he's absent. The faeries feel safe in their thievery as they know that he's been led out on the moors, far away from his home, "in search of our allies, the goats."[108]

Faery Steeds

The faeries like hunting and parading and, for these pastimes, horses are nearly essential. In the poem "Sir Orfeo" the faery king arrives to seduce the knight's wife with his ladies and retainers, "Al on snowe white stedes." In the Scottish poem "Young Tamlane" the faeries process on black, brown, and white mounts whilst in "Thomas of Erceldoune" the faery queen appears astride a "palfrey." We also hear of Welsh faeries hunting on grey horses and—from an old woman in the Vale of Neath in 1827—an account of faeries seen riding white horses "no bigger than dogs." These Welsh faeries were said to ride in the air, never coming to ground. Appropriately, faery horses were renowned for their

---

108. Sikes, *British Goblins*, c. 4.

swiftness. In contrast to these generally small and pale-hued steeds, a horse that collected a midwife to attend a faery labour near Tavistock was coal black with eyes "like balls of fire."

It's been suggested that the faery horses might not be real at all, but just enchanted ragweed stems, which faeries very often use like broomsticks to fly through the air. This might indeed have been the case in the north of Scotland, at least, where the belief in this type of faery transport originates. On the whole, though, the faery horses seem real enough. A Manx man found himself surrounded one night by a herd of vicious faery steeds; he had to fend them off for hours with his knife until dawn came and they vanished.[109]

The faeries have their own horses, it's clear, but they also like to take ours and to ride them, at the same time knotting their manes into "pixy rings" or tangling them with burdock seed pods. Undoing the knots can prove a considerable nuisance as they can be so entwined it takes half a day to unravel them. It should be noted in fairness that these "elf-knots" do not seem to be created out of pure mischief just to annoy the owners. The semi-wild ponies grazing Bodmin Moor in central Cornwall that were gathered in once a year for the Summercourt Fair would also be found to have badly tangled manes. The knots seem to function in part as stirrups and bridles; at the same time, they seem distinctively fae—a sign of faery presence. A Perthshire man taken from his garden by the faeries was returned three days later with his hair all in knots—visible, physical proof of his story of abduction to faeryland.[110]

Lastly, be warned: if the faeries want to go out riding and there are no suitable steeds to hand, they can use us instead. Especially on the Isle of Man, people have been known to be taken and ridden all night. They feel no weight on their backs during the experience, but they become tired for loss of sleep and thin and weak from their exertions. Wearing a flower or herb to scare off the faeries should be enough to prevent this.[111]

---

109. John Campbell, *Superstitions of the Highlands and Islands; Yn Lioar Manninagh,* vol. III.

110. Leather, *Folklore of Herefordshire,* 18; Deane & Shaw, *Folklore of Cornwall,* 91; Murray, *Tales from Highland Perthshire* no. 219; Palmer, *Folklore of Radnorshire,* 225.

111. Roeder, *Manx Folk Tales,* 11–12.

Faery Herds

Given their liking for dairy produce, it's unsurprising that the Good Folk keep their own herds for milking as well as other livestock.

In the Highlands faeries were especially associated with the red deer and, indeed, it was believed by some that they were their only cattle. It was also alleged that faery women could transform themselves into deer and might be captured in this guise. A few Fae women certainly herded deer just like cattle, but the faeries had their own conventional livestock as well.

Irish faery cattle are identified by their distinctive appearance: they are white with red ears. In Britain, though, such distinctive characteristics are not so regularly recorded, although in Wales the "comely milk white kine" were definitely famed and there's also reference to *y fuwchfrech*—a magical freckled cow. Most famous are the *gwartheg y llyn*, the "lake cattle," that were frequently brought to marriages with human males by the beautiful and mesmerising lake maidens. Alternatively, the beasts might mingle and interbreed naturally with human herds (and so are clearly envisaged as being of normal proportions and appearance). If (when) the faery wife was later rejected or insulted by her human spouse, her departure would also inevitably mean the departure of the faery beasts from her husband's herd. The same is bound to occur if the human farmer tries to slaughter the faery cattle, as this too will be interpreted as demonstrating a lack of respect for the cows' true owners and their gifts. In the Scottish Highlands faery cattle typically were dun coloured and hornless, but on Skye they were red speckled and could cross the sea.

The faeries of the Isle of Man also keep pigs and sheep. The faery pig is identifiable by the fact that it's white with a feathery tail rather like a fan, and has long, loppy ears and burning red eyes. Faery lambs are generally more appealing. Their fleeces are red and they might be equipped with a red saddle and bridle. Sometimes one will appear in a farm's flock. When they do so they bring good luck, increasing the health and fertility of the normal sheep. It has been said that the Welsh faeries may appear in the shape of sheep, poultry, and pigs. It is not wholly clear from this whether these are faery animals or faeries in the form of animals. Whatever the exact situation, these creatures were often reported as being seen flying or rising from pastures up into the sky.[112]

---

112. Sikes, *British Goblins*.

Pixie Pets

The faeries also have their own versions of our domestic pets, although the descriptions given of them hardly make them sound like friendly beasts.

For the faeries' great sport of hunting, hounds are required. Searching to recover his abducted wife, Sir Orfeo meets the king of faery riding out "with hundes berkyng." Likewise, in the ballad "Thomas of Erceldoune," the faery queen is met with "hir greye hundes" and "hir raches." The latter are "rachets"—specially bred hunting dogs. The *Cwn Annwn* (roughly, the hounds of hell) of Welsh legend were bandogs employed for the pursuit of the souls of those who had died either unbaptised or unshriven. They dashed through the air on stormy nights, terrifying the mortals below. Daintier, perhaps, were the "milk white hounds" that accompanied the elfin ladies of the lakes.

The "people of peace" of the Scottish Highlands possessed terrifying dogs the size of bullocks, which were dark green (though paling toward their feet). These hounds' tails either curled tightly on their backs or appeared flat, even plaited. Because of their look and their very loud barks, they were kept as ferocious watchdogs for the faery knolls and were said to move by gliding in straight lines. The unpleasant tempers of these dogs are found too in the faery dogs of the Isle of Man. Packs of them will chase people, and contact with them can leave you ill for months.

The Welsh faery dogs in contrast sound considerably less hostile. A woman in Denbighshire became very friendly with the local tylwyth teg and recalled that often, when she was out gathering rushes, one of their dogs would bound up and join her, just for the pleasure of her company. Sometimes the appearance of the faery dogs will foretell a death, especially if they're seen in a churchyard.[113]

If you do come across a stray faery hound, the Welsh experience indicates that you should always take good care of it. A man who treated one badly was abducted by the Fae and carried through the air in punishment. A relative of his learned from his mistake and, when she found a stray, fed and cared for it well. She was generously rewarded by its faery owners when they came to retrieve it. They asked her if she'd prefer a clean or dirty farmyard.

---

113. Owen, "Rambles over the Denbighshire Hills," *Archaeologia Cambrensis,* vol. iii, 5th series, no.9, 73; Owen, *Welsh Folklore,* 124.

She chose dirty—and they doubled the number of cows she owned, giving her the best milk herd in the district.[114]

In Scotland, there are also faery felines, which were apparently the size of human dogs, black with a white spot on their chests, their backs constantly arched and their fur bristled.

In summary, there seem to be a number of common features to faery animals. They are very commonly pure white—a sure sign of supernatural nature—and quite frequently airborne (another obvious indication of their enchanted state). Although in many respects, their behaviour is identical with that of normal farm beasts, they are prone to appear and disappear unpredictably. As with all faery gifts, poor treatment of them guarantees their loss.

Woodlands

Today many people, if asked, would imagine elves and faeries gambolling in a woodland setting. This appears to have become a very strong convention within our popular visual culture, yet it is not traditional to British faery lore (despite the regular links between faeries and particular species of tree that have been described). How did this prevalent image come about?

Although the faery king Oberon is met in a forest in the thirteenth century romance *Huon of Bordeaux*, the primary source of our close modern association between faeries and forests is Shakespeare, both the "wood near Athens" that features in *A Midsummer Night's Dream* and in which Titania, Oberon, Puck, and the other faeries make their home; and the open woodland of Windsor Great Park that features in *The Merry Wives of Windsor* and that is the setting of Falstaff's believed encounter with the faery queen and her train. Whilst their ultimate roots may lie with the dryads and hamadryads of classical myth, it was these theatrical presentations of faeries that first really fixed the woodland-dwelling elf in the English-speaking public's imagination. Much subsequent literature and visual art has cemented the pairing to the extent that it appears inevitable, even though there is little trace of it in older sources or in British folklore. It might be added that this is, as well, a very English convention; in much of the rest of Britain there weren't many wooded areas anyway.

As I described earlier, faeries tend to be linked in folk traditions to individual trees rather than to bodies of trees. The securest traditional association

---

114. Jenkyn Thomas, *Welsh Fairy Book,* "A fairy dog."

between faeries and stands of trees actually involves the Good Folk in helping humans. Orchards are haunted by Old Goggy, a sprite whose main role is
to bring life to the fruit trees and to protect the crop from thefts by children.
Other names for the spirit include Lazy Lawrence, the Grig, and the Apple Tree
Man. At harvest time a few apples should always be left behind for the faeries—an offering called the "pixy-word" (or hoard)—and, if this is done, they
will bless the crop. Somerset pixies are believed to love apple trees and orchards
above all places. There are also faeries who protect other fruit, such as the "nut-
nans" of Lancashire, who live in cobnut groves, and the Gooseberry Wife on
the Isle of Wight, who takes the form of a large green caterpillar.[115]

The British faery, according to older writers, could be found in a variety of locations. They frequented mountains, caverns, meadows and fields,
fountains, heaths and greens, the southerly side of hills and downland, as
well as groves and woods. Generally, they were more likely to be found in
"wild places." Woods feature in these sources, it's perfectly true, but they
are far from the most commonly mentioned locations. For example, one
fourteenth-century source tells us that elves are seen, "by daye much in
wodes…and bi nightes ope heighe dounes…"—in other words, they frequent woody places in daytime (presumably for concealment from human
eyes) but resort to open hilltops at night for their revelries.[116]

A particularly informative source is the Welsh minister, the Reverend
Edmund Jones. In his 1780 history of the superstitions of Aberystruth parish
he recorded the contemporary local views on the most likely locations for
seeing faeries. They do not like stony, plain, or marshy places, he reported,
but prefer for their dancing those sites that are open, dry, and clean and that
are near to or shaded by the spreading branches of trees, particularly those
of hazel and female oak trees. They also like to have easy access to adja-
cent hedges for hiding. Wirt Sikes also located the Welsh elves (*ellyllon*) in
groves and valleys. In Wales at least, then, an open wooded landscape was
believed in popular tradition to be the faeries' preferred habitat and would
be your best bet as a place for meeting them. Given the faeries' predilection

---

115. Dathen, *Somerset Fairies and Pixies*,15, 28 & 114; Tongue, *Somerset Folklore*, 119; Palmer,
    Worcestershire, 180.
116. *South English Legendary* (13th–14th century), line 256.

for dances, and for playing football and hurling, it only makes sense that they will prefer open to very enclosed locations.[117]

The Good Folk like to spend time in woodlands, definitely, and groves and glades may be excellent places for encountering them. All the same, they may not actually live in these areas and may be just as likely to be met elsewhere, as the rest of this chapter goes on to show.

Faery Islands

Throughout Britain, faeryland has been conceived as a separate, usually subterranean, country, with its own landscape, rivers, agriculture, buildings, and climate. This belief was especially strong in England and Wales during the Middle Ages (see for example the stories of "Elidyr and the Golden Ball" or of "The Green Children of Woolpit" mentioned earlier). Steadily, as human cultivation and industry expanded, the faeries' realm has tended to shrink, until they have been squeezed into the corners of our world. In some parts of Wales, though, the idea of a separate faeryland has persisted in slightly altered form: Faery moved off-shore, so that it has remained credible and occasionally visible, albeit rarely accessible.

Magical islands have a long-established pedigree in Wales. Gerald of Wales described a lake atop Snowdon which was notable for a floating islet that blew from shore to shore. In a later account of this, a faery dimension was added. A maiden of the tylwyth teg had to separate from her human husband, yet she still contrived to see him from time to time, sitting on a buoyant turf whilst he sat on the shore of Llyn y Dywarchen.[118]

Floating islands are not unique to Welsh inland waters. In 1896 a sea captain reported seeing an unmarked isle, just below the waves, near to Grassholm in the Bristol Channel. He said he had heard tell from old people of just such a land, that rose and fell periodically. These supernatural islands are called "Green Spots of the Floods" and the "Green Meadows of the Sea" or "*Gwerddonau Llion*." There's a similar belief from across the channel in Somerset; there the mysterious isles are called "The Green Lands of Enchantment." Their exact location isn't fixed and it's unclear how many enchanted isles are thought to exist between St. Davids and the Llyn Peninsula, but there

---

117. Jones, *Aberystruth,* 74 & 84 or *Appearance,* no. 57 & 116.

118. Gerald of Wales, Book II, c. 9; Rhys, *Celtic Folklore,* 93.

are consistent reports of sightings of verdant lands which have appeared and disappeared from time to time.[119]

One account stated that a faery island off Milford Haven was reached by a tunnel. The faeries used this passageway to attend the markets at Laugharne and Milford. Comparable is the description of a lake island at Llyn Cwm Llwch in the Brecon Beacons, which could be reached by a passage leading from a shoreline rock. However, this rock only opened once a year whilst the "garden of the faeries" amidst the waves was invisible unless you stood in the correct spot. It might be noted too that little clumps of flowers growing in inaccessible spots on the cliffs near Land's End were known as the "sea piskies' gardens."[120]

Returning to the coastal isles, they too may only be seen by standing on a particular piece of turf taken from either St. David's churchyard or from Cemmes parish. As soon as contact with the sod is broken, the vision is lost, so that the only sure way of reaching the islands is to sail with a piece of the turf on board; otherwise, the islands will be invisible to the boatmen. Such voyages are dangerous, though, as faery time notoriously passes much more slowly than on land. Generations might elapse in what seemed like mere days for the island visitors.[121]

The residents of these elusive islands are the tylwyth teg, more specifically the *Plant Rhys Dwfn*—the children of Rhys the Deep. His wisdom lay in protecting his land with magic herbs and in the strict moral code of honesty and good faith observed by his descendants.[122]

Magical islands are not uniquely a Welsh notion: the Reverend Robert Kirk in chapter four of his *Secret Commonwealth* remarks that Faery may be "unperceavable ... like Rachland and other enchanted isles." Rachland was believed to lie off the northwest coast of Scotland; its inhabitants were either faeries or the descendants of Vikings but, either way, it only became visible once every seven years (a typically magical period of time). Despite these problems of accessibility, some early navigation charts included the island's longitude and latitude, in case you happened to be in the right place at the right time!

---

119. Rhys, *Celtic Folklore*, 171–172.

120. Sikes, *British Goblins*, 9 & 10; Rhys, *Celtic Folklore*, 161 & 20–22.

121. Rhys, *Celtic Folklore*, 161–72; Evans-Wentz, *Fairy Faith*, 147.

122. Rhys, *Celtic Folklore*, 158–160.

The motif of the enchanted isle is ideal for faeryland: it is a place that is periodically visible, familiar but enticing, near but always out of reach. Only the very fortunate or clever may be able to see it, so that its reality or illusory quality are very hard to prove.

Seaside Faeries

It's generally (perfectly correctly) our assumption that faeries and elves prefer to frequent meadows and groves. They may from time to time be seen out on rough moorland (pixies and spriggans in South West England especially), or even in human homes and farm buildings (brownies), but we very rarely imagine them at the seaside. This is mistaken; from time to time they have been sighted on beaches and here I offer the scattered evidence for this.

Although in classical mythology the *nereids* and *oceanids* were marine nymphs, and although mermaids, selkies, and certain Scottish saltwater beasts will naturally be encountered near the tideline, there is only a little traditional British material locating supernaturals on the seashore. It was most probably Shakespeare, in *The Tempest,* who first created the association in the popular mind. Ariel famously sings

> Come unto these yellow sands,
> And then take hands:
> Curtsied when you have, and kiss'd
> The wild waves whist,
> Foot it featly here and there[123]

Here we have the conventional faery circle dance transposed from a glade or other grassy place, where a faery ring springs up, to the strand—a novelty that appears to be almost entirely the playwright's invention. Milton seems to have imitated this scene in *Comus:* "And on the Tawny Sands and Shelves, Trip the pert Faeries and the dapper Elves." Without doubt, Shakespeare's song has provided inspiration to painters ever since (for example Richard Dadd and Robert Huskisson), and it seems to have created a lasting acceptance that faeries might quite properly be encountered so far from their normal haunts. Scenes from *The Tempest* and, of course, from *A Midsummer*

---

123. William Shakespeare, *The Tempest* (1611), Act 1, scene 2.

Night's Dream were standard fare for Victorian faery artists, but we also find seashore sprites unconnected with these famous plays.[124]

From the early nineteenth century, we have the painting *Faeries on the Seashore* by Henry Howard. What exactly this tropical scene illustrates is uncertain; it may be his own idea, or it may be drawn from literature. Ann Radcliffe in *The Mysteries of Udolpho* (1794) wrote some lines about a sea nymph, who sings "Come when red sunset tints the wave, To the still sands, where faeries play…" Around the same time Letitia Elizabeth Landon wrote an entire poem entitled "Fairies on the Sea Shore," which features flower, rainbow, and music faeries as well as a sea faery riding inside a nautilus shell in the moonlight.

It seems likely that W. B. Yeats drew upon native Irish tradition, rather than any English literary or artistic works, when in 1889 he wrote his famous poem "The Stolen Child." It is voiced by faeries who are abducting a human infant and they tempt the child to accompany them to where the moon shines on "the dim grey sands" where they dance all night. The scene of this verse is Rosses Sands in County Sligo, a place known as a "very noted fairy locality" according to Yeats himself. It would be easy enough to assume that these lines were simply the work of a great poetic imagination, but this would be mistaken. Yeats, like his friends George William Russell (who wrote under the pseudonym "AE") and Ella Young, actually met faeries. In his collected letters Yeats tells of an encounter at the Rosses that took place about the time that the poem was composed, when he met and conversed with the queen of Faery and her troop. What's more, faeries weren't just to be found at this one spot on the Irish coast. There's a story from Rossport, County Mayo, concerning a man called Patch Gallagher who met with a crowd of faeries heading for a hurling match. They recruited him to their team and the game turned out to encompass a huge length of the coastline.[125]

These poetic examples have been all about the faeries playing and dancing on the sand, very much like modern holidaymakers. The links could be much closer than this, though. The Cornish *bucca* was to be found living on the strand itself, for example, and in a story of a boy's magical flight with the Polperro faeries, beaches are amongst the places they visit in their journeying.

124. John Milton, *Comus*, lines 116–117.

125. Yeats, *Fairy and Folk Tales of the Irish Peasantry*, note to "The Stolen Child," 59.

Some faeries will be found on the seashore for purely practical purposes—they are fishermen and they will be hauling in their boats or sorting their catch.[126]

Although many of the references given so far have come from literature, in the twentieth century we have actual sightings of faeries on the beach recorded, incidents which appear to replicate exactly the images of verse and art. In July 1921 Geoffrey Hodson saw some "little elf-like forms" playing on the beach at Blackpool. They had elvish faces, large heads and ears, little round bodies, short thin legs with webbed feet, and were three to six inches tall. They played amongst the seaweed and stones, but did not go in the water; they seemed unconcerned by the nearby presence of human holiday-makers. In Arthur Conan Doyle's *The Coming of the Fairies*, published in the same year, he reproduced an account by Mrs. Ethel Wilson of Worthing, who saw faeries on the beach on sunny days; they were like little dolls with beautiful bright hair, she told him. Unlike Hodson's elves, these beings played in the sea and rode on the waves, constantly moving and dancing about. These are fascinating sightings, though it is inescapable that the Fae seem to have travelled to the coast very much in tandem with British day-trippers.[127]

Part of the reason for the paucity of seaside sightings may be the fact that at least some of the Good Folk are unable to gain access to the shore. In the same way that some faeries can't cross rivers—as we'll see soon—some find the beach a barrier. In a story from the Scottish Highlands, a man called Luran stole a goblet from the *sith* and had to make an urgent escape from his angry pursuers. They were gaining on him and his prospects looked gloomy until he thought to make for the shore: once he had crossed the high-tide line, he was safe from the crowd chasing him. The Cornish tale "The Fairies of the Eastern Green" involves a related theme. One night some smugglers landed their illicit cargo of brandy at Longrock Beach, on Mount's Bay between Penzance and Marazion. One of the crew went ashore to investigate some mysterious sounds, fearing it was the excise men lying in wait. Instead he stumbled upon a large number of spriggans, dressed in red and green and enjoying a dance in the sand dunes. As soon as they realised that they had been discovered, the crowd of dancers turned nasty and chased the smuggler with spears, slings, and bows.

---

126. Courtney, *Cornish Feasts & Folklore*, 129; Thomas Quiller-Couch, "The Folklore of a Cornish Village," *Notes & Queries*, no. 11, 398.

127. Hodson, *Fairies at Work and Play*, c. 1; Doyle, *The Coming of the Fairies*, c. 7.

He raced back to his boat, calling on his companions to put out to sea again. The spriggans swarmed angrily onto the beach but could not harm the boat on the waves because "none of the faery tribe dare touch salt water."

To conclude, the evidence is patchy, and most of it is literary rather than from folklore, but the indication is that faeries might be found in any natural scene, from the seashore to the mountaintop. If we conceive of them as nature spirits, this would of course be exactly what we would expect.

Faeries and Water

One curious aspect of faery lore is the contrary relationship that faeries have with water. They all seem to need it, just like humans, but, in some circumstances, they may have a deep antipathy for it, whilst others use it to achieve their magical aims.

Faeries, like humans, require water for their basic necessities. It's pretty certain that they drink it; they are reputed to drink dew at the very least. Without doubt they use water for bathing: there are numerous folklore records of faeries expecting householders to leave out bowls of fresh water for them at night so that they and their children may wash. There's also a story of faeries surprised one morning in a bathing spa in Ilkley.[128]

As well as human supplies of bathing water, the Fae will make use of natural sources. In Northamptonshire certain "faery pools" are known where the faeries swim at night; at Brington bathing faeries were seen by witnesses as recently as 1840. Other springs are identified where they wash their clothes and even their butter. A very special faery link with water is found in the Scottish *bean-nighe* (the washer woman) and the related Caointeach (the keener). Both foretell deaths by washing clothes or winding sheets at fords or in streams; plainly they are not in the least averse to contact with running fresh water. Moreover, it's said that power can be gained over the *bean-nighe* if you are able to come between her and the stream, indicating that her magic potential in some way derives from the watercourse itself.[129]

Finally, it hardly needs to be said that certain faeries live in water and plainly cannot have any objection to their natural environment. Bodies of

---

128. Crofton Croker, *Fairy Legends,* 86; plenty of examples of bathing are in Rhys, *Celtic Folklore,* 56, 110, 151, 198, 221 & 240.

129. Sternberg, *Dialect and Folklore of Northamptonshire,* 136; Hill, *Folklore of Northamptonshire,* 149; Roberts, *Folklore of Yorkshire,* 64; *County Folklore,* vol. 2, 130.

both fresh and salt water are inhabited. For instance, the queen of the Craven faeries apparently lives behind the waterfall at Janet's Foss near Malham. Water itself is plainly not a problem.

Faeries and Flowing Water

Nevertheless, there is also evidence of faeries objecting to water that is flowing. There are many such stories, but one dramatic example of this aversion comes from North Yorkshire: in Mulgrave Wood near Whitby lived a bogle by the name of Jeanie. One day she chased a farmer who was riding by. He galloped desperately for the nearest brook to escape her; just as she caught up with him and lashed out with her wand, his steed leapt the river. Jeanie sliced the horse in half. The front part, bearing the rider, fell on the far side and was safe, whilst Jeanie had to make do with the hind legs and haunches. In a related case from Perthshire, a man was out hunting when a woman in a green gown accosted him. She tried to attract his attention and lure him near her by whistling, but given the colour of her dress he paid no attention and made haste to get away. She chased him until he leapt over a burn. She could not follow, but she had grabbed hold of his plaid, which she proceeded to shred into a powder. If she had caught him, she warned, there wouldn't have been a sieve that would have held him.[130]

Any flowing watercourse will form an insurmountable barrier, it seems, but even more antithetical to the Fae is water that flows in a southerly direction. This is shown from a couple of accounts. In the North East of Scotland, one way of expelling a changeling and recovering a human child from the Fae was to wash the infant's clothes in a south-draining spring and then lay them to dry in the sun; if the clothes disappeared it meant that the faeries had accepted them and the stolen child would have been restored. This technique was practised during the 1620s by Scottish witchcraft suspect Stein Maltman, from Leckie near Stirling, who advised the father of a sick boy to bathe him in a south-flowing well after they'd prayed over him. Maltman also treated a poorly woman by having her drink water taken from a southerly-running stream in which he had boiled an elf-arrow. Additionally, as we'll see later, faery-inflicted illnesses were diagnosed by "girdle-measuring." One practitioner of this, called

---

130. Evans-Wentz, *Fairy Faith in Celtic Countries*, 38; Campbell, *Popular Tales of the West Highlands* vol. 2, 69; Murray, *Tales from Highland Perthshire*, nos. 127 & 202.

Jennet Pearson, would wash the girdle in a south-flowing stream as part of the treatment she administered.

It may be the case that only bad faeries are obstructed by streams, whilst well-intentioned ones may pass over unhindered. Certainly, in one Scottish story a devoted brownie came and went daily to and from the home of the family he served by crossing a river on stepping stones.[131]

Sometimes, too, it appears that even plain water can repel our Good Neighbours. There's a folktale from the Isle of Uist in the Scottish Highlands in which the faeries call at the door of a house for an oatcake to come out to join them; the inmates throw water on the cake, and it replies, "I can't go, I am undone." Perhaps the water in the house had been blessed; we can be certain, all the same, that at times of dire need a river or stream will provide an effective barrier between you and supernatural harm.[132]

Faery Water Magic

We have seen that faeries have an aversion to running water. In contrast, though, still water can have strong faery and magical properties. Bogles have been banished into wells and faeries have used them as a way of trying to abduct humans. Well water can have magical properties. On Dartmoor, near Princetown, you will find Fitz's Well, the water of which is reputed to have the properties of dispelling faery glamour and enabling those who are pixy-led to find their ways again. In the ballad "Tam Lin," well water is used as part of the magical release of a faery captive.[133]

I mentioned south-flowing streams in the last section and there's also something particularly magical about wells whose waters run out toward the south. On the Isle of Anglesey, it's said that such wells are "cursing wells." The one at Penrhos could both inflict or cure cancer. Other directions might also have powerful properties, all the same. From Shetland there's the story of a faery cup that was discovered as the result of a dream. It had curative proper-

---

131. Campbell, *Superstitions of the Highlands*, 50; Simpson, *Folklore in Lowland Scotland*, 107.

132. Henderson, *Survivals of Belief Amongst the Celts*, 219.

133. Aitken, *Forgotten Heritage* 18; Crossing, *Tales of Dartmoor Pixies*, c. 9; Nicholson, *Folklore of East Yorkshire*, 79.

ties if a complicated ritual was followed, central to which was water scooped from an easterly-flowing well.[134]

The goodwill of the faeries at wells might be invoked by showing them respect. Offerings of pins are made at Bradwell in Derbyshire on Easter Sunday, and at Wooler in Northumberland, whenever a person wants a wish to come true. At various sites in Scotland, buttons, small coins, and pins may be left for the "faery of the well," perhaps the most famous of these being the so-called "Cheese Well" on top of Minchmuir, Peeblesshire, into which locals throw pieces of cheese for the guardian faeries.[135]

The wishes made at wells might be for wealth and love, but they can be for something as prosaic as simply ensuring a good water supply. In late 1971 *Countryman* magazine featured a letter that described how pixies had restored and maintained the water levels in the well of a remote Cornish cottage, all in return for the corners of Cornish pasties, broken off and laid around the well head on the night of a new moon. Unfortunately, when the owner went away and left the property in the hands of caretakers, they failed to keep up the offerings and the well dried up again.[136]

As well as granting wishes, many wells have health-giving properties, too. If a child has gone into a decline and is no longer thriving (it's "shargie" and has been afflicted by "the faery"), one old remedy was leaving the infant overnight near a well. At Wooler, too, sickly children would be dipped in the well's waters and bread and cheese left as an offering. If it was suspected that the child had in fact been substituted for a faery changeling, well water might form part of the remedy. At Chapel Euny in West Cornwall, the way to expel a changeling and restore a human child was to dip the suspect infant in the well on the first three Wednesdays in May. The days and the time of year are both particularly Fae, as will be described next.[137]

---

134. Edmondston, *A view of the Zetland Isles*, 215.

135. Addy, *Household Tales*, 115; *Denham Tracts*, 151; Gregor, *Notes on the Folklore of the North East of Scotland*, 59; Richardson, *Table Book*, 132; Grant, *Myth, Tradition and Story from Western Argyll*, 34.

136. Bord, *Fairies*, 18.

137. Dalyell, *The Darker Superstitions of Scotland*, 538; *Denham Tracts*, 151; Courtney, *Cornish Feasts*, 126.

You might even meet a helpful faery near a well. For example, a young woman visited the "faery well" at Crowle in Worcestershire, where she encountered a woman who told her how to keep her face ever young. The technique is to get up nine successive mornings before the new moon and wash your face in dew that has not yet been touched by the sun.[138]

Given the supernatural properties of well water, it is unsurprising that it should be used to imbue the human children abducted by the faeries with Fae properties. This is mainly evidenced in literature rather than folklore, but an excellent example is in the Scottish verse "Kilmeny" by James Hogg. Kilmeny is dipped in the waters of life to ensure that her youth and beauty never fade. Although it's not explained, this property of faery wells also seems to lie behind a Welsh story concerning a shepherd boy from Frenni Fawr in Pembrokeshire, who was lured into a dance and then taken to faeryland. He lived in the royal faery palace but was warned never to try to drink the water from a well in the palace garden. Eventually his curiosity overcame him and he scooped up some of the forbidden water—at which point the entire vision of Faery vanished about him and he found himself back on the moors with his sheep, at the very moment at which he'd been abducted.[139]

Summary

Faeryland cannot be easily described in human terms. It can be an anomalous location which doesn't necessarily comply with our rules of time and space. For this reason—as well as a wish for privacy—Faery is kept apart from this world and the two only rarely intersect.

When there is contact between the supernatural and the human world, something that occurs at particular faery-frequented places in our world, the meeting of magical and non-magic realms, as well as the clash of cultures, may prove unexpected and unpredictable. This happens because faery versions of familiar animals don't behave as we anticipate and because ordinary plants, trees, and landscape features become imbued with unanticipated faery powers. Even such basic qualities of our world as time and the weather may be affected—as we explore in the next chapter.

---

138. Palmer, *Worcestershire*, 180.

139. Davies, *Folklore of West and Mid-Wales*, 105; see too the references to well-dipping in c. 16 of my *British Fairies*.

Chapter 6

FAERY TIME

Having discussed the places *where* we're most likely to encounter faeries, we should consider *when* we're most likely to make contact. Some times and seasons are more propitious than others; at certain points in the day and in the year, even the most ordinary places may be transformed.

Faery Days

Folk tradition is insistent upon the fact that there are certain days of the week when faeries are more likely to be abroad in the world. We can be certain, then, that there are more auspicious days for seeing our Good Neighbours—the practical problem for us is the absence of consensus over *which* days these might be.

The earliest account we have is from Wales, written by John Penry in his polemic *The Aequity of an Humble Supplication* in 1587. He asserts that certain soothsayers and enchanters claim "to walk on Tuesday and Thursday at night with the faeries, of which they brag themselves to have their knowledge." Friday is the faeries' day in South Wales and it is also when they have their special influence over the weather.[140]

---

140. Sikes, *British Goblins*, 268; see also Jones, *The Appearance of Evil—Apparitions of Spirits in Wales*, para. 116.

In Scotland, Friday was also identified as the day when misfortune was in the air and faeries roamed the human world at their most powerful. To speak of them could attract them, as Sir Walter Scott, a Highlander, described in *Minstrelsy of the Scottish Border.*

> Will on a Friday morn look pale,
> If asked to tell a faery tale.[141]

In fact, so great was the fear engendered by the superstition that even naming the day was to be avoided. Accordingly, Fridays were only mentioned as "the day of yonder town" and knives would never be sharpened on this day for fear of antagonising the *sith*. By way of contrast, it was believed that the faery folk could do no harm on Thursdays.

From Ireland comes evidence to confuse us if we believed some sort of pattern had been emerging from our evidence. One Irish researcher was told to avoid mention of the faeries on Mondays. Lady Wilde, though, was advised not to mention the *sidhe* folk on Wednesdays and Fridays, with the latter day being especially perilous. There's a lot less evidence for England, but a collection of folklore from Northumberland and the Scottish borders records that Wednesday is "the faeries' Sabbath or holiday."[142]

So, there we are: be on your guard for the Good Folk on Monday, Tuesday, Wednesday, Thursday, and/or Friday, but most especially on the latter day. We might add that, on Shetland if not elsewhere, Saturdays were also regarded as unfavourable as this was the day when the trows emerged and entered people's homes. It seems like the only day on which you're definitely safe is Sunday.

Faery Times of Day

Not only do the faeries have favourite days on which to venture forth, they also seem to favour certain times of day. Examined on suspicion of witchcraft in August 1566, Dorset healer John Walsh admitted that he had made contact with the local pixies by visiting the hills in which they dwelled "between

---

141. Scott, *Marmion,* Introduction to Canto IV.
142. Leland Duncan, writing of Leitrim in *Folklore*, vol. 7, 174; *Ancient Legends of Ireland*, 72; *Denham Tracts*, 86 & 115.

the hours of twelve and one noon or at midnight." Scottish sources confirm that faery influence is greatest at the hours of noon and midnight.[143]

It's known to be hazardous to sleep on faery hills and this is doubly the case if you choose to slumber in the middle of the day. Here's a salutary tale from Shetland:

> A young woman was dangerously ill. She had a fever, caught by falling asleep at midday on top of a little hill. She died and her father insisted that the faeries had possessed her and left a stock in her place. He could not be convinced otherwise and smiled at the foolishness of those who denied the faeries.

It's fair to add that another Scottish source records how a child who slept on a *sithbruaich* (faery hill) was not taken but was instead endowed with the second sight.[144]

In South Wales, the Reverend Edmund Jones's account of the faery beliefs he found in Aberystruth parish in the 1770s echoed the English and Scottish evidence—to some extent. The faeries had been encountered by parishioners at all hours of the night and day, he recollected, but more at night than in the daytime and more in the morning and evening than at noon. The link between faeries and the nighttime is especially strong and well established, invoking as it does our fear of the dark as well as more benign images of faeries skipping in rings by moonlight.[145]

Faery Time and Human Time

The passing of time has always been a significant feature of many stories of faeryland, as I mentioned in chapter 2. It's known that time in Faery can pass at a different rate to time in the mortal world. A night spent under a faery knoll may turn out to have been a year, or ten, or a century in the "real" world.

As might be imagined, the consequences of this for the returning visitor can be disastrous and tragic. Family, friends, and familiar places may all have disappeared. And yet—this is not always a problem. Some visitors are able to

---

143. Dalyell, *The Darker Superstitions of Scotland*, 534.

144. Edmondston, *A View of the Ancient and Present State of the Zetland Isles*, 77; J. MacDougall & G. Calder, *Folk Tales and Fairy Lore in Gaelic and English*, 183.

145. Jones, *Aberystruth*, 69; on nighttime, see my *British Fairies*, c. 17.

come and go without ill effects: a midwife may be taken to attend a faery birth and return home the same night; a husband may go to rescue his wife from beneath the faery hill and will do so in "real time." The faeries themselves may come and go from our world without difficulty. Faery time is flexible, we must conclude, with the faeries bending it largely for their convenience.

Faery Festivals

There are also certain times of the year when the Good Folk are more likely to be abroad in the mortal world, and when encounters are more likely—whether for good or ill. The faery festivals are generally significant dates in the human calendar as well, the reason for this being that these have long been recognised as times of year when we need to be on our guard and boost our magical protection.

Evidence

The bulk of the evidence on festivals and seasons comes from Scotland and Ireland. There is a little from the Isle of Man, plus a couple of odd instances from England and Cornwall. From Wales all we really know is that there were three "spirit nights," the *teir nos ysprydnos,* when it was believed that supernatural beings of all descriptions were abroad (these were May Day, Midsummer Eve, and Halloween). The faeries were especially busy stealing children on Midsummer Eve.[146]

Despite any deficiencies, the accounts are nonetheless consistent. Two festivals stand out across Britain and Ireland—these are May Day and Halloween.

May Day

On May Day, fires were lit to scare away the faeries. This was done in Ireland, Scotland, and on Man, where it was expressly the gorse that was burned. Both in Ireland and Man it was believed to be unlucky to give fire away to a neighbour on May Day—perhaps because the protection it gave against faeries was being dissipated. On Man, too, rowan, primroses, and green boughs were gathered and laid before the doors of houses, stables, and cattle sheds to exclude the faeries.

The reason for all these precautions seems to have been that this festival was the time when the faeries re-emerged after winter and held their first

---

146. Owen, *Welsh Folklore,* 52 & 90.

dances of the year. As they were freshly abroad in the world again, they were deemed particularly dangerous. It was said to be unwise to draw water from a well for a drink after sunset on May Eve. In Ireland, it was believed too that the *sidhe* would try to steal butter at this time of year, whilst in Scotland, they stole milk from the cows. Also, in Ireland, it was considered that cutting blackthorn at this season would attract ill fortune. In the worst cases, a sudden death would be regarded as an indicator of an abduction.

Halloween

It is at Halloween (Samhain) that supernatural forces again become particularity dangerous. This is the season of the year when "they were privileged, on that day and night, to do what seemed good in their eyes."[147]

On this night the faery folk are abroad on their last major excursion of the year and mortals have to take precautions. In Ireland it's thought that the *sidhe* move home on this night, whilst in Scotland the faery court enjoys its last processional ride (or "rade"). The only way that a faery rade can be seen by a mortal without peril is to have rowan hung at their door. In Ireland offerings of food are left out near raths and other faery sites in order to deflect the *sidhe* folk's enmity. Conversely, it's said that this is the best time of year to rescue those abducted, as the doors of the faery hills will be open.

In the Outer Hebrides the season is said to be even more perilous as it's the time of year when the faery hosts fight amongst themselves, whilst in England this is the season when the Wild Hunt rides through the nighttime skies of the South West. A person out on Halloween is in grave danger of being swept up with the faery throng.

Even if you don't encounter the faeries, the countryside can be tainted. For this reason, in Cornwall and in Ireland the advice is not to eat brambles after the end of October. As in May, cutting blackthorn is discouraged in November. As at the start of the growing year, so at the end, torches are lit in the Highlands to keep the *sidhe* folk away.

Other Festivals

Other dates with faery links are Whitsuntide, when holy water was sprinkled inside Irish homes to ward off the *sidhe,* and Christmas Eve, when the faeries were invited into homes in Gloucestershire. The fire was banked up and

---

147. Hogg, "Odd Characters," 151.

water was left out for their annual bath and, it was believed, if this was done good luck would follow for the next twelve months.[148]

Midsummer (Beltane) was a particularly significant festival on the Isle of Man. Protective fires were lit and other measures, such as wearing certain plants and flowers, were employed to safeguard people and livestock from the island Fae.

Faery Seasons

There are other times in the human calendar, turning points of the year, which also seem to have faery significance and at which the boundaries between our two worlds are more porous.

Yule

During the whole season of Yule (Christmas and the New Year) on Shetland it was believed that the trows were granted special privileges to wander the islands and enter human homes. To counteract this, special measures had to be taken by the inhabitants to safeguard themselves and their property.

The Yule festivities began seven days before Christmas on Tulya's Eve. Households would pluck two straws from their stacks and lay them in a cross shape at the entrance to their farmyard. A hair from the tail of each cow or horse would be plaited and hung over the byre door and a blazing peat would then be carried around all the outhouses. This "sained" or protected the farm's stock.

On Yule Eve every person in a household washed and put on fresh (and ideally new) clothes to sleep in. They cleaned their hands and feet in water into which three pieces of burning peat had been dropped. This protected their limbs from being "taken" or paralysed by the trows. A steel blade would be placed conspicuously outside the door of the house to warn off approaching trows and any joints of meat in the larder would be left with a knife stuck in them to prevent theft. On the last night of the Yule season, Up-Helly-Aa, large fires would be lit to drive the trows back underground again for another year.[149]

---

148. Palmer, *Gloucestershire*, 145.
149. Saxby, *Shetland Traditional Lore*, 79–86.

Other Times of the Year

In fact, all the traditional quarter days of the year (Candlemas, May Day, Lammas, and Halloween) might be regarded as risky times when there was faery danger imminent. The Reverend Robert Kirk during the late seventeenth century recorded that the last night of every quarter was a time when the faeries danced; they were also abroad and dangerous on the last night of the year.

The period of seventeen days around the spring equinox and the feast of the Annunciation were believed in Scotland to be a vulnerable time when the spirits travelled about in whirls of dust, stopping the plants growing. To protect themselves people had to approach the eddies backward with their eyes and mouths closed whilst repeating a protective verse. People found sleeping in the tracks of these whirlwinds might be carried along for a short distance, though seemingly without other ill effects.[150]

Whereas the evidence on days and times of day was rather less conclusive, it is possible with some certainty to point to festivals and seasons of the year, liminal turning points in the calendar, during which the portals to the supernatural open, or at least become more porous, allowing far greater access from one side to the other. Although, as we'll see, the evidence on the nature of the faeries' religion (if they have any) is uncertain or compromised, it is unarguable that they have ceremonies and observances associated with the major solar and lunar events and transitions of the natural year.

Faery Weather

Throughout this and the last chapter, the basic assumption has been that if you go to the right places at the right times you will have a much-improved chance of finding a faery. This all assumes that you can actually see them—and the Good Folk are very good at arranging the climatic conditions so that this is either difficult or impossible.

Whether we see them as rural dwellers, or as elemental beings and nature spirits, it is universally accepted that faeries live close to nature and the environment. Intimately bound up with this is an ability to affect the weather—a power of intervention in our world that is recognised the length of Britain. For example, in South Wales

---

150. Grieve, 202; Stewart, 'Twixt Ben Nevis and Glencoe, 212; MacPhail, "Folklore from the Hebrides I," *Folklore*, vol. 7, 402.

Friday is the faeries' day, when they have special command over the weather; and it is their whim to make the weather on Friday differ from that of other days of the week. "When the rest of the week is fair, Friday is apt to be rainy or cloudy; and when the weather is foul, Friday is apt to be more fair."

In North East Scotland, it was said that when it rained it was a sign that the local faeries were baking. Perhaps the smoke from the ovens hung about the knolls like mist or low cloud.[151]

The Welsh faeries are only seen when the weather is a little misty. They prefer days when visibility on the mountains is poor, when a fine drizzly rain called *gwithlaw* covers the land. It's not clear to what extent the tylwyth teg are responsible for these conditions, but it is known that such murky days are the best times to encounter them. A shepherd living beside Llyn y Gader became infatuated with a beautiful faery woman whom he'd first met on just such a misty day, and a maid living at Cwm Glas near Llanberis used to leave a jugful of fresh milk and a clean towel for the tylwyth teg on dark and misty mornings, receiving money in return. Children were warned that it was on such days that people were abducted and carried through the air by the faeries, so doubtless the respective parents must have been very alarmed when some children in Denbighshire in the 1880s reported watching a crowd of diminutive people dressed in blue, who ran in and out of the clouds wreathing the top of a local hill.[152]

The tylwyth teg may have been taking advantage of murky days, or they may have engineered them. Certainly, in Cornwall the small people create the weather; the spriggans in particular are felt to have control over the elements. When a man went digging for buried gold on Trencrom Hill, he first saw the sky darken, heard the wind begin to roar and, on looking up at the flashing lightning of the looming storm, realised that hundreds of spriggans had emerged to chase him away from his excavations, growing larger in size as they got nearer. Prudently, he fled. On the Cornish moors and on Dartmoor, the pixies are said to conjure fog purely to lead travellers astray.[153]

---

151. Sikes, *British Goblins*, 268; Gregor, *Notes on the Folklore*, 65.

152. Rhys, *Celtic Folklore*, 33, 36, 91, 223 & 228; Owen, "Rambles over the Denbighshire Hills," *Archaeologia Cambrensis*, vol. iii, 5th series, no. 9 (1886), 72; Owen, *Welsh Folklore*, 100.

153. Hunt, *Popular Romances*, vol. 2, 245; & vol. 1, 48.

Section 3
FAERY LIFE

Chapter 7

FAERY SOCIETY

The Good Folk have their own society, material culture, and conventions of behaviour. These are distinct from those of human beings and, to interact successfully with them, it helps us to understand how their world works.

Faery Government

It may seem a shocking challenge to very well-established conventions, as respected writers such as Shakespeare and Spenser have made faery royalty such a fundamental part of our conceptions of faery society, but I wonder whether we really mean the words we use when we so casually discuss the "faery kingdom," the "faery realm," the seelie and unseelie "courts," and the king and queen of Faery. We all accept what the great poets tell us, we all take the existence of a fairy queen for granted—but is she really more of a literary creation than a folklore reality?

In her recent book *Faeries,* Morgan Daimler observed that "the social structure does seem to operate as a hierarchy ruled ultimately by Kings and Queens." Daimler was describing Celtic Faes, but examples from across Britain seem to back her up. There are, for example, said to be royal courts amongst the Dartmoor pixies, with all the pleasure and luxury that you might anticipate. This hierarchy of monarchs and subjects is allegedly reinforced by pixy law courts in which those who have offended faery morality will be punished by having to make ropes of sand—with which they're then bound. In Wales it's believed that the tylwyth teg live in communities under the rule of King Gwyn ap Nudd. There may be variation from region to region: the Highland Scottish Faes have an aristocracy and chiefs but no queen (rather like the local clans) whilst witnesses from the Scottish Lowlands and the North East coast mention meeting "the Queen of Elfame."[154]

All the same, the idea of faery royalty may be very much a projection of medieval structures by medieval writers. The idea is seen in the knightly romances of Chaucer and others and, two centuries later, Spenser, Shakespeare, and Herrick cemented the institution in our culture. Many of these writers wrote for an aristocratic audience and showed them the world they knew. Nevertheless, when we think of faeries now, we still unconsciously and automatically conjure images of Arthurian knights and ladies and all the structures of precedence and privilege that go with them. This is convention, but is it any more than that?

Our inclination to see our Good Neighbours as being organised in some parallel political structure is deep-rooted. Habitually, we speak of "kingdoms," "reigns," and "realms," but outside the literature, what's the actual evidence?[155]

Faery Reign

We are very used to thinking of Queen Mab and of Oberon and Titania, but what need do the Faes really have of rulers? In the Middle Ages, monarchs were required to perform several purposes within their simpler states. Their primary function, initially at least, was to lead the people in armed conflict and, as I will discuss shortly, although war amongst the faeries may jar with our conventional views of them, the possibility of it is mentioned in quite a few sources and might therefore justify some sort of war chief.

Monarchs also served to dispense justice. We humans are aware of no codified laws as such in Faery, although there are clearly codes of behaviour that they impose (upon humans at least), the infringement of which (by

---

154. Daimler, *Fairies*, 61; Gwyndaf in Narvaez, *Good People*, 159; Crofton Croker, *Fairy Legends*, 87.

155. Thomas Hobbes, *Leviathan*, Part One c. 12 & Part Three c. 29; Scot Book II c. 1, s. 13.

humans) is subject to sanction. Parallel with this distinct morality, there is a prevailing atmosphere of unrestrained impulsiveness in Faery.

Kings and queens served to organise medieval states, but it's hard to tell what, if any, structure there is within faery society. If we regard them as nature spirits, then they are all at the level of worker bees, it would appear. A few writers have proposed hierarchies, but these normally seem to involve different *forms* of supernatural beings rather than different *ranks*.[156]

Lastly, monarchs had a role as some sort of religious leader or high priest(ess). I'll explore later the puzzling matter of faery religion but, whilst it's an area of considerable uncertainty, there's scant evidence for holy faery queens. None of the recognised regal functions seem especially essential to Faery as we generally conceive it. The title of "queen" in truth seems redundant—or at best merely a convenient honorary title.

Secret Commonwealth

Recalling what was just said about the absence of monarchs amongst the *sith* of the Scottish Highlands, let's consider the views of the Reverend Robert Kirk, who (despite being a church minister) was deeply versed in local faery belief and is said, ultimately, to have been taken by them.

Writing in the late 1680s, Kirk titled his justly famous book *The Secret Commonwealth of Elves, Fauns and Faeries*. A "commonwealth" can merely denote a nation state, but it can also more narrowly have the meaning of "republic." Given that he cannot but have been aware of the English Parliamentary "Commonwealth" that succeeded the execution of Charles I in 1649, it's inescapable that this was the connotation intended by Kirk when he chose to describe his subject matter. That conclusion seems undeniable when we read at the head of chapter 7 of the book that "They are said to have aristocraticall Rulers and Laws, but no discernible Religion, Love or Devotion toward God ... they disappear whenever they hear his Name invoked ..."

For present purposes, we'll merely note Kirk's belief in the Faes' aversion to church and religion, and focus instead on his conviction that they inhabit some

---

156. See for example two interviews with "Irish seers" conducted by Evans-Wentz—one with George William Russell (AE) and a second with an unnamed Mrs. X. of County Dublin— *The Fairy Faith*, 60–66 and 242–3; see also C. Leadbetter, *The Hidden Side of Things*, 1913, 147.

sort of democracy regulated by rules of conduct of some description. Kirk was very familiar with (and shared) the beliefs of his parishioners, so it is telling that he chose to ascribe some sort of republican structure to their society.

Rank or Honour?

Perhaps those termed king and queen in Faery are simply those of the most distinguished character or the greatest magical power. Certainly, as far as we can judge from the experience of actual human encounters with faeries, there is little indication of any rigid hierarchy or organisation within their society. Individual faeries seem to operate quite independently of their community, doing what they please without any reference to higher authority. There may be some differentiation in status, because we do have stories of humble labouring faeries in the fields as well as meetings with "fine gentlemen" (although some of this finery may be nothing more than a projection of glamour), but there's no real sign of a true monarchy.

Some of those accused of witchcraft in Scotland in the 1500s and 1600s claimed to have had contact with a faery king or queen (some even claimed sexual relations with the royalty). For reasons I'll explain in detail later, I hesitate to rely too much on these stories, but even so there's a curious lack of ceremony and aloofness on the part of these monarchs. Several quite ordinary humans are admitted into the royal presence and are given gifts, one getting a supply of a healing white powder, it is true, but another received a plain domestic quern for grinding salt. Andro Man of Aberdeen first met the faery queen as a boy when she attended his mother as a midwife; Bessie Dunlop was also visited in person by the faery queen, whom she described as a stout woman in simple clothes who walked in, sat down on a bench, and asked for a drink of beer. These are royals who earn their own keep, run their own errands and are not averse to intimacy with perfectly ordinary humans. At the very least, we have to say that what counts as royalty in Faery is very different in status to the same position in human society. As in everything connected with our relationship to the Good Folk, then, we should be cautious to apply our conventions and assumptions too readily to their ways of doing things.

In summary, the main influence shaping our conceptions of Faery as a stratified and monarchical society, with a royal family, a court, nobility and attendants, seems to be our own way of organising things, specifically European society during the medieval period, channelled through the literature of that time. The vast body of folklore accounts of faery encounters instead suggests a much more equal and free society where each member is at liberty to behave as he or she wishes.

Faery Crafts and Industry

It's been said of the faeries that they are "very ingenious people … very clever, with very skilled artisans." They are gifted in many crafts and, despite some stories to the contrary, highly resourceful and self-reliant.[157]

Faery Workmen

The first observation that must be made is upon the contrast between these craft skills and the usual impression we get that faeries' only interest is having a good time. Sightings of faeries (other than the domestic hobs and brownies) engaged in manual labour are certainly rare in the older records. An isolated example comes from West Yorkshire in about 1850. A man called Henry Roundell of Washburn Dale near Harrogate got up early to hoe his turnips. When he reached the field, he was astonished to discover every row was being hoed by a host of tiny men in green, all of them singing in shrill cracked voices "like a lot of field crickets." As soon as he tried to climb over the stile into the field, they fled like flocks of partridges.[158]

In more recent sightings from the last seventy-five years or so, instances of working faeries have become far more common. Experiences reported in *Seeing Fairies* and in the *Fairy Census* indicate that faeries are likely to be seen involved in three main activities. Most often they will be gardening or cultivating, as in the Washburn example, and they've also been sighted digging, with a rake, tidying up leaves and twigs, or with a wheelbarrow. In addition, the faeries may from time to time be seen seemingly involved in some sort of construction work (for example, carrying a ladder) or simply in transporting burdens, whether in a handcart, in a sack, or in buckets suspended from a yoke.

---

157. Grant Stewart, *Popular Superstitions*, 73–74.
158. Roberts, *Folklore of Yorkshire*, 60.

Faery Architecture

It may seem to run counter to our intuition to think of faeries building physical structures. Most descriptions of faery dwellings imply that they were natural features like caves and hills. This is perfectly correct, but our predecessors readily assumed and accepted that a great deal more could be achieved by their supernatural neighbours. They were known to live in natural features, but they could—if they wished—construct stone towers with their doors, windows, and chimneys skilfully concealed. Indeed, faerykind seem to excel at constructing grand accommodation for themselves—they've been called "unrivalled architects" whose buildings stand forever.[159]

This appreciation of faery skills dates back a long way. In the poem "Thomas of Erceldoune," Thomas enters faeryland and sees a "faire castell" next to a town and tower; "In erthe es none lyke it." In the twelfth-century story of King Herla the faery king occupies a "splendid mansion." These tales convey some general impression of what the faeries could build, but the poem "Sir Orfeo" provides much more detail of a faery castle circled with crystal walls, buttressed with gold, and with chambers and halls of jewels and gems.

These beliefs in a parallel subterranean world of splendid palaces and fortifications persisted into the nineteenth century. Thomas Keightley recalled a conversation with a young woman in Norfolk who told him that the faeries were a people dressed in white who lived underground where they built houses, bridges, and other edifices.

These faeries were building for themselves in their own realms, but they would interact with humans in construction projects too. There seem to be three different situations in which faeries have got involved in building structures in the human world. First, this has occurred under duress. There are several instances where faeries have been compelled, against their will, to carry out tasks for a human. This might happen as the terms of a ransom for a fellow faery or because a human has gained some magical control over the Faes. For example, in Scotland a faery queen banished some troublesome elves from Cnoc-n'an-Bocan (Bogle-knowe, or Hobgoblin-hill, near to Menteith) into a spell book, *The Red Book of Menteith*. The condition was that they would only be released when the laird of Menteith opened the volume.

---

159. See too chapter 4 of my *British Fairies*; Grant Stewart, *Popular Superstitions*, 77.

Eventually, this happened by mistake and instantly, faeries appeared before him demanding work. Not knowing what work to set them to, his lordship hit upon the plan of making a road onto the island where his castle stood. They began the task energetically, but the Earl quickly realised that, if they continued, his hitherto impregnable retreat would be made vulnerable, so instead he asked them to make for him a rope of sand. They began this latter task without finishing the former, and finding their new work too much for them, they resolved to abandon it and departed, to the relief of the Earl.

Secondly, a large number of Scottish sites are said to have been built voluntarily by faeries. One, the *Drochtna Vougha* (faery bridge) in Sutherland, was for their own convenience to shorten the journey time around Dornoch Firth; however, it benefited human traffic too and, when one traveller blessed the builders, the bridge sank beneath the waves. Many famous Scottish sites—castles, palaces, bridges, and towers—are alleged to have been built by faeries, sometimes in the space of a single night, and sometimes by such laborious means as passing the stones from person to person over a great distance. All this effort to create edifices only used by humans might seem puzzling, but we are told that the church of St. Mary's at Dundee was built for gold, so the Good Neighbours' motivation in these labours might actually be very familiar indeed.

Lastly, there are numerous sites where the faeries did not build, as such, but objected to the site chosen by the human builders and overnight moved the assembled masonry blocks elsewhere using supernatural means. This would be done repeatedly until the humans accepted the inevitable and started construction on the new site. These stories mainly relate to churches, but they're found right across Britain. It isn't just religious buildings that have been moved: in Herefordshire the materials for Garnstone Manor were repeatedly transported up a hill from the original site until the human builders submitted to the faeries' will.

Usually the faeries got their way—but not always. At Stowe Nine Churches in Northamptonshire a monk stayed up all night to catch the faeries interfering with the new foundations. As soon as his suspicions were confirmed, he prayed in order to drive them off forever. A similar story, with a sting in the tale, comes from Tingwall on Shetland. Stones from an ancient broch were taken to build a new church, but nightly the work was undone by the trows, presumably because they objected to the dismantling of the ancient structure. This problem was overcome by the priest consecrating the chosen site, which drove the trows away to the nearby island of Papa Stour, after which the building was successfully completed. However, the trows had the last laugh: the priest found himself struck dumb whenever he stepped into his new church.[160]

There are several comments to make on these records. First, it's notable how most are Scottish or come from the North of England. It seems that the more northerly faeries are the skilled stonemasons, though why this should be we simply can't speculate. Secondly, whilst we can understand why they should wish to build for themselves or hinder building at places to which they had some special attachment, their willingness to work for humans (even for gold) is less comprehensible, especially as that included buildings for religious purposes—something to which they normally violently objected.

What's more, much of the impressive architecture reported by humans during visits to faeryland could have been simply "glamour"—with no physical reality. We are familiar with stories of midwives taken to assist faery women in labour who believe that they are in fine houses until they accidentally touch their eyelids with ointment intended for the faery newborn and see that, in reality, they are in a ruined building or a cave. Given their magical powers, indeed, one wonders why the Good Folk would bother at all with the labour of actually piling stone on stone when it could (presumably) all be achieved by the wave of a hand (or wand).

Faery Spinning

Whilst the Good Folk are said to indulge in several manufacturing enterprises, there is one craft activity that seems to be particularly associated with them: the making of thread and the weaving of garments.

The Reverend Kirk has this to say of the *sith* folk's skill:

---

160. See Hardwick, *Traditions, Superstitions and Folklore*, 125; Marwick, *The Folklore of Orkney*, 37; Hill, *Folklore of Northamptonshire*, 105. The churches include Rochdale, Samlesbury, Winwick, Newchurch in Rossendale, and Burnley, all in Lancashire; Gadshill, Isle of Wight; Holme on the Wolds and Hinderwell in Lincolnshire; Walsall and Hanchurch in Staffordshire; Stowe near Daventry; Knowle and Warmington in Warwickshire; Churchdown, Cam, and Bisley in Gloucestershire; East Chelborough, Folke, and Holmest in Dorset; Matchy in Essex; at Ince and Stock in Cheshire; at Kirkheaton, Kirkburton, and Thornhill in West Yorkshire; and at Gletna Kirk on Shetland. See too Bowker's story of *The Spectral Cat*.

Ther Women are said to Spine very fine, to Dy, to Tossue, and Embroyder: but whither it is as manuall Operation of substantiall refined Stuffs, with apt and solid Instruments, or only curious Cob-webs, impalpable Rainbows, and a fantastic Imitation of the Actions of more terrestricall Mortalls, since it transcended all the Senses of the Seere to discerne whither, I leave to conjecture as I found it.[161]

Quite a few other sources confirm the connection. Brownies performing household tasks will often undertake stages of the cloth making process, for instance dressing hemp (though at the same time their aversion to gifts of linen garments is to be recalled), carding wool, and spinning tow (coarse hemp fibres used for ropes and the like). Cloth working is just one of the faery abilities that can be bestowed upon favoured mortals. In one Highland case, a man who entered the faery knoll at Barcaldine came away with not only great skill on the bagpipes but a magic shuttle that helped him to weave three times as much cloth as anyone else.[162]

Logically, of course, faeries have to be able to manufacture cloth and garments for themselves. Their royal courts and nobility are marked for their splendid robes, and other costumes of green are central to many accounts. It is only really the dobbies who are habitually naked or dressed in rags. The northern faeries are said to spin with mountain flax, while the pixies of Cornwall use cotton-rush. Typical activities within the faery hills of Scotland include spinning and weaving. For example, there is an account from Skye of faeries heard "waulking" (that is, fulling) some cloth and singing as they did so. At Green Hollow in Argyllshire there was reputed to be a cloth-dyeing factory operated by the faeries of Lennox. When humans tried to steal the secrets of their natural plant dyes, it's said that the cloth workers concealed all their materials and fled. Those hidden dye-stuffs continue to stain the waters of a local pool.[163]

The Loireag is a Highland faery specifically responsible for overseeing the making of cloth through all its stages, from loom to fulling. She was a

161. Kirk, *Secret Commonwealth*, c. 5.

162. MacGregor, *Peat Fire Flame*, 2.

163. Addy, *Household Tales*, 135; Hawker, *Footprints of Former Men in Far Cornwall*; J. G. Campbell, *Superstitions of the Highlands and Islands*, 15; Evans-Wentz, *Fairy Faith*, 98.

stickler for the traditional methods and standards, apparently, and offerings of milk were made by home producers to propitiate her. Another Scottish spirit, the Gyre-Carlin, had comparable links to cloth-making. It was said that, if unspun flax was not removed from the distaff at the end of the year, she would steal it all. Conversely, if asked by a woman for the endowment of skill in spinning, she would enable the recipient to do three to four times as much work as other spinners.

Thread and cloth making are not only marvellous, but according to faery tales, the process may also be perilous. On the one hand, faeries may enter your home to carry out these tasks. In Scotland it was believed to be the solitary female creatures—the *glaistig* and the Gyre-Carlin—who would most commonly enter human homes to spin, causing considerable disturbance and noise through the night. Such intrusions were not just a nuisance and a trespass—they risked too close a contact with these unpredictable beings, and measures had to be taken to prevent it. Several Manx tales warn how a failure to disengage the drive band on a spinning wheel before retiring to bed enables the faeries to come into a house overnight to use it for their own purposes. By inviting them in, albeit indirectly, you are potentially placing yourself in the power of the "Li'l fellas." In the Scottish Highlands, this precaution was Christianised and it was said that the band should be disengaged on a Saturday night to prevent faery spinning early on a Sunday (Sabbath) morning.

The dangers associated with spinning can be greater still, though. A number of faery stories pair the faeries' spinning skills with a task imposed upon a human that can be both impossible *and* fatal if it's not completed. In many of the stories it's a cruel human who sets the hopeless task and a faery who assists with it. An example is the story of Habetrot, in which a girl must prove her female skill at the spinning wheel or face some unspecified punishment by her mother. A faery woman named Habetrot (who's been called the patron spirit of spinning) appears and assists the daughter, along with a team of helpers including Scantlie Mab.

Unfortunately, this faery assistance isn't always free and disinterested. In the tale of Tom-Tit-Tot, a girl has to spin a large quantity of yarn overnight or face beheading by the king. The imp Tom-Tit-Tot helps her on condition that she will belong to him—unless she can accomplish another impossible-sounding task and guess his name. Fortunately, she overhears it and is saved.

Sili-go-Dwt, Trwtyn-Tratyn, Terry-Top, Perrifool, and Whuppity-Stoorie are all similar British folktales in which an elf helps with spinning and demands a forfeit unless its name is guessed. Many readers will spot the similarity of these stories to the Brothers Grimm's comparable tale of Rumpelstiltskin.[164]

Occasionally it's a faery who imposes the impossible spinning task. In one Scottish example a girl is abducted by the *sith* folk under a hillock and is told that she will be held there until she has spun all the wool in a large sack and eaten all the meal in a huge chest. Despite her diligent efforts, neither diminish and she faces eternal confinement and labour until another captive soul tells her to rub spit on her left eyelid every morning. By so doing, she makes daily inroads into the wool and meal and finally escapes.

The heroine isn't always saved and isn't always successful, though. In the case of Welsh girl Eilian, she was obliged to become the wife of a faery man and live in Faery forever after she failed to finish the large quantity of wool that he'd demanded she spin.[165] In the Scottish ballad "The Elfin Knight," a human maid is told that the only way she has any hope of marrying the faery knight is to make a shirt without cut or hem, shaping it without shears and sewing it without needle and thread. This impossible task is combined with a comparable demand to sow and harvest a field subject to unachievable conditions. Needless to say, the shirt is never made and the girl doesn't get the boy.

The stories listed above link several significant themes. One is the power of knowing a faery being's personal name. If you possess that, you can overcome and escape the creature; if not, you face perpetual subjection. Intertwined with this is the obligation to perform an almost unattainable feat on pain of death (or, again, of faery enslavement). Most importantly, the tales stress the Good Folk's superior skills. Characters are reliant upon their abilities, which border on the magical, and without which there may be fatal consequences. The spinning stories also strongly emphasise a dependent relationship between the faeries and humans. Perhaps too there is some notion of exacting a high fee for the teaching of the faeries' remarkable craft knowledge.[166]

---

164. Addy, *Household Tales.*

165. Evans-Wentz, *The Fairy Faith*, 97; Rhys, *Celtic Folklore*, 212.

166. See too chapter 19 of my *British Fairies.*

Other Faery Crafts and Occupations

Over and above their renown as builders and spinners, the faeries are expert weavers, tailors, and shoemakers. The trows of Shetland are renowned for their skills working brass, iron, and other metals whilst the Manx faeries excel at the many crafts associated with fishing, such as boat-building, mending nets, and making barrels to keep herring in. The Fae are also known to mine coal and metal ores: best known amongst these are the "knockers" who are a specific tin mine faery of the South West of England.[167]

These sprites, also known as "nuggies," are frequently heard but very seldom seen, although from time to time they leave their tiny tools behind as physical evidence of their labours. They have been described as "withered, dried up creatures" the size of a one- or two-year-old child, with large heads and ugly old men's faces. They never worked in the mines on Saturdays or Christian holidays and, in respect for this, the miners avoided the workings on the same days.

The knockers will guide favoured miners to good seams or lodes by various means—through their tapping underground or by dancing in rings—and digging on the spot indicated will strike rich ore. Digging wherever a will-o'-the-wisp is seen is also reputed to lead you to a profitable lode and it's said to be good luck to see the pixies dancing in the adit of a mine. As well as pointing the way to mineral riches, the knockers will warn of impending disaster underground.

As with all supernatural helpers, they are averse to humans being too inquisitive. Although the sounds of their work indicate how and where to dig, if miners stop their work to listen to the knockers, they will also cease their labours. As with many faery types, those who offend them will be punished and those who betray the source of their good fortune will lose it.[168]

---

167. Crofton Croker, *Fairy Legends,* 27; Fergusson, *Rambling Sketches in the Far North and Orcadian Musings,* 120; Morrison, *Manx Fairy Tales.*

168. Jones, *Appearance,* no. 64; Hewett, *Nummits and Crummits,* 50; A. Craig Gibson, "Ancient Customs and Superstitions of Cumberland," *Transactions of the Historical Society of Lancashire and Cheshire,* vol. 10 (1858), 108; Deane & Shaw, *Folklore of Cornwall,* 69; Roberts, *Folklore of Yorkshire,* 102; Davies, *Folklore of West and Mid-Wales,* 136–137.

Faery Religion and Ethics

So far, we've discussed the material manifestations of faery culture, but we should also ask, "what do faeries believe in?" This may seem like a nonsensical question for at least two reasons: first, because some say that the faeries themselves are Pagan divinities and, secondly, because the faery code of morality is so distinctive and so deliberately selfish. Faeries are not concerned with good works; they are concerned with furthering their own interests and so seem outside the rules of religion and ethics as we understand them.[169]

Christianity

Throughout church history, for much of the last thousand years, the strict Christian view has been that faeries are devils or are, at best, a delusion sent by the devil to mislead us. The priests and monks disapproved of faery tales and preached against them consistently, but that couldn't stop people wanting to hear these stories or believing in their subjects. To deflect ecclesiastical criticism, a lot of storytellers made their faeries into just another god-fearing creation of the Christian deity. This is revealed, in passing, in many of the earlier romances: for example, the faery monarch in King Herla's tale exclaims "God be my witness"; the Green Children of Woolpit come from a place called St. Martin's Land and profess themselves to be good Christians.

The belief that faeries have a place in a divine hierarchy, perhaps a few rungs down the spiritual ladder from angels, has probably strengthened again in the last hundred years. As recently as the mid-twentieth century, for example, a pilgrim to the Scottish island of Iona encountered a troop of faeries whom she believed tried to communicate their beliefs by showing her a cross made of twigs and bark. This might be so, although it might also be suggested that it was a demonstration that they understood what had brought her to the holy island.[170]

Faery Salvation

The condemnation of faery belief probably only intensified after the Reformation. Protestants were quick to suggest (quite unfairly) that the faery faith

---

169. See chapters 2 and 18 of my *British Fairies.*

170. Bord, *Fairies,* 60.

was all part of the general ignorance promoted by the Catholic Church. Puritan preachers emphasised how much people endangered their souls by being tolerant of faery stories—it allowed Satan to get near them. For English proselytiser Thomas Jackson, there was no question of distinguishing between the good and bad faeries because "it is but one and the same malignant fiend that meddles in both." These attitudes have left their mark: one common explanation of the taking of children as changelings is that the faeries have to pay a tithe to the devil every seven years and, understandably, they prefer to do so with a human life instead of one of their own kind.[171]

Despite all this, ordinary people continued to believe—as did some church men, for that matter. Scottish minister Robert Kirk was convinced of the reality of elves and faeries and even felt that they were less sinful than men: "[they] yet are in ane imperfect State, and some of them making better Essays for heroic Actions than others; having the same Measure of Vertue and Vice as wee, and still expecting an advancement to a higher and more splendid State of Lyfe."[172]

The Reverend Kirk believed that, whilst they appeared to have no religion and would disappear at the mention of a holy name, the faeries could behave ethically and had the same prospect of judgement and salvation as any Christian man or woman. In fact, a number of related theories emerged as to the place of the faeries in the Christian universe. One name for the faeries was "the Hidden Folk," the origin of this name being explained in a story from Carmarthenshire told early last century:

> Our Lord, in the days when He walked the earth, chanced one day to approach a cottage in which lived a woman with twenty children. Feeling ashamed of the size of her family, she hid half of them from the sight of her divine visitor. On His departure she sought for the hidden children in vain; they had become faeries and had disappeared.[173]

171. Jackson, *A Treatise Concerning the Original of Unbelief*, 178.

172. Kirk, *Secret Commonwealth*, "Question 2."

173. Evans-Wentz, *The Fairy Faith*, 153.

Another widespread belief was that the faeries were fallen angels who had followed Satan in his rebellion but who had not yet reached hell when God commanded that the gates of heaven and hell be closed. They were left stranded in between and hid in holes in the earth. They will finally be released from this intermediate status on the day of judgement.[174]

Lastly, across Britain and Europe there are consistent accounts of incidents in which anxious faeries approach humans begging for reassurance that they too will be saved. Normally, the answer is no, to the faeries' great dismay. In line with these stories, in his poem "Friday," Sir Walter Scott imagined the faeries sitting at home on this day, "weeping alone for their helpless lot."[175]

Hell's Bells

Our faery lore has been left in a confused state by all this controversy and the exact creed of the Good Folk remains unsettled. Some people connect them with angels and imbue them with some sort of divine purpose; others see them as quite free of human morality and full of antipathy to the Christian faith.

In line with the latter view are the stories describing the faeries' strong aversion to bells and churches, which are common across Britain from the Shetland Isles to the south coast. For example, at Portland, Cadbury, and Withycombe in Dorset the church bells drove off the local pixies. This antipathy seems to be the main reason for faeries interfering in church building efforts. At Brinkburn Priory in Northumberland the churchyard is said to contain the graves of the local faeries, who were all killed by the ringing of the priory bells. Conversely, when the church bell fell at Hownam in Roxburghshire, the local faeries who had been driven away by its sound gathered there again to rejoice.[176]

One definite effect of Christian disapproval was to create the widespread popular belief that faeries are repelled by anything Christian. Possession of a copy of the Bible or some pages from it alone will be efficacious, as will saying grace, making the sign of the cross, and a number of other actions.

---

174. Evans-Wentz, *The Fairy Faith*, 85, 105, 109, 116, 129–30 & 205.

175. See Spence, *British Fairy Origins*, 165; Bett, *English Myths and Traditions*, 10; Grant Stewart, *Popular Superstitions* 59–62; & the story of the "Minister and the Fairy" printed in *Folk-lore and Legends: Scotland*, 1898.

176. Fergusson, *Rambling Sketches*, 110; Bowker, *Goblin Tales*, Appendix 9; *Denham Tracts*, 134.

For example, from the Scottish Highlands comes the story of a man invited to a faery wedding feast. The bridegroom sneezed and the guest instinctively said "bless you." This dismayed the faeries the first two times it happened, but on the third the behaviour had become so intolerable that the guest was expelled bodily from the celebrations. On Shetland it's said that the trows' power of invisibility is instantly dispelled by a pious word and that the presence of a preacher in the vicinity will drive them away. This is the aspect of faery nature that's widely recalled today and, as we'll see later, blessings and other sacred words are repeatedly endorsed as insurmountable protections against faery malice.[177]

Pagan Pixies

There has been much discussion over whether faeries are Catholic or Protestant and over the question of whether they are pure or are evil incarnate—demons and servants of Satan. It seems that on the question of faery religion, much as with faery rulers, we humans have imposed our own preconceptions on a society very different from our own.

In any case, there is a hint of another view, one that may appeal more to many contemporary readers. In William Bottrell's story "The House on Selena Moor," faery abductee Grace makes this remarkable statement about her pixie captors: "'For you must remember they are not of our religion,' said she, in answer to his surprised look, 'but star-worshippers.'"

If this truly represents Cornish belief of the late nineteenth century, it might be a relic of older ideas about the Fae and—perhaps—a connection that was made between them and "the Druids." This need not necessarily be a much older idea—it might have emerged in the previous century or so—yet it may be a tantalising hint of theories relating the pixies to worship at Cornwall's many ancient monuments.

Faery Violence

It has become a widespread belief nowadays that faeries are wholly benevolent and peaceable beings, to whom violence and antagonism toward

---

177. Browne, *History of the Highlands*, 110; Edmondston, *A View of the Zetland Isles*, 142; Marwick, *The Folklore of Orkney*, 37.

humankind is anathema. This view of the supernatural realm would surprise our predecessors, who had a very different and more complex view of Faery. Older folklore portrays an otherworld very similar to our own, with its own internal conflicts and with a range of responses to humankind, from friendly to hostile. It's important to appreciate this more perilous reality and to act with due care and caution.

Faery Warfare

It seemed entirely reasonable to earlier generations that the faeries could disagree profoundly and might engage in armed conflict amongst themselves. The Reverend Kirk said that "These Subterraneans have Controversies, Doubts, Disputes, Feuds and Sidings of Parties...they transgress and commit Acts of Injustice and Sin." As a result, they have "many disastrous Doings of their own, as ... Fighting, Gashes, Wounds and Burialls..."[178]

There are numerous Scottish accounts in evidence of these conflicts. In the Hebrides it was believed that the faery hosts always fought at Halloween, proof of which was a red liquid produced by lichens after frost which was believed to be the blood of the faery fallen. On the shores of the islands people find a substance called elf-blood (fuilsiochaire) which is like a dark red stone and is full of holes. These so-called bloodstones are connected to the red skies of the aurora borealis, which themselves are termed the "pool of blood" and are a sign of faery fighting above. The trows of Orkney were sometimes seen fighting together whilst from Speyside comes the legend of a pitched battle between the armies of the White and Black Faeries.[179]

Similar stories are told elsewhere in Britain too, such as a Glamorganshire tradition of a faery battle fought in the air between Aberdare and Merthyr. A Cornish woman called Emlyn Moyle was pixy-led in the fog on Goss Moor. She found herself near to the ancient hillfort, Castle an Dinas, and saw a pixie battle being fought on the ramparts. When the fog cleared, though, there was

---

178. Kirk, *Secret Commonwealth,* chapter 11.

179. MacKenzie, *Wonder Tales From Scottish Myths,* 11; Campbell, *Superstitions of the Highlands and Islands.*

no trace of any fighting there. It's also been said that the pixies only gained control of Devonshire and Dartmoor after a protracted war with the elves.[180]

Faeries might fight amongst themselves for possession of territory or as part of a struggle between "good" and "evil" forces. In this, they're depressingly like us. Whilst we may reluctantly accept this frailty, it's more troubling to discover that they may also turn their hostility against their human neighbours.

Faery Violence Toward Humans

Faeries impose a strict code of morals and conduct upon humans and they don't hesitate to enforce this by violent means. There seems to be little compunction over battering and injuring those amongst us of whom they disapprove. Offending individuals can certainly expect to be pinched mercilessly; they might also be jostled, assaulted, lamed, and (for the offence of seeing through the faery glamour) blinded.

The faery code is applied especially severely to those who are faeries' lovers and they can expect to be treated harshly for any perceived slights. Slaps and thrashings are common, often made worse by the fact that the man can never escape his faery lover. She's as relentless in punishing a faithless partner as she is in winning him in the first place. There are several such Scottish tales in which a man is compelled against his will to meet a faery woman, but is then apparently beaten for doing so. The battery appears to be either a means of ensuring his obedience by instilling fear—and a hint that the faery lover does not wholly trust her charms—or else it's a punishment for his temerity. Either way it suggests that faeries can be vindictive and contemptuous, even toward those they favour in some way.

Faery lovers can be tempestuous, but there are some spirits whose primary purpose seems to have been to scare and control. These beings haunted dangerous locations such as ponds or riverbanks, and children were warned of them and told to keep away. Jenny Greenteeth and Peg Powler weren't just names, nor would they merely give an errant child a fright: they would drag the disobedient infant beneath the water and drown them, using violence to warn other children.

---

180. Bruford in Narvaez, *Good People,* 131; Tregarthen, *Pixie Folklore & Legends,* 67–75; Bray, *Peeps on Pixies,* 12.

Wholly unprovoked violence is also possible—some supernaturals are malicious by nature and human encounters with them will almost invariably prove fatal. These beasts include the Highland water horses: the *each uisge* or *aughisky*, the kelpie, and the *shoopiltree* of Shetland, all of which would lure people into mounting them and would then career at speed into a river or lake or into the sea, where the humans would be drowned and/or devoured. There were other non-equine but equally maleficent and dangerous water spirits in Scotland, such as the *fideal*, the *fuath*, the *peallaidh*, the *muileart-each*, and the *cearb* (the killer). In Wales the *llamhigyn y dwr* (the water leaper) and the *afanc* were known. All of these made a habit of tearing their unfortunate victims to pieces beneath the waves.

Elf Shot

The weapon by which faery injuries have most commonly been inflicted is the elf shot, or bolt, or arrow. These implements look very like prehistoric flint arrowheads: they have been described as heart-shaped and saw-edged, made from a hard yellow substance similar to flint. One legend states that the faeries obtained them from the elves, who got them in turn from the mermaids. These arrows are never found with long shanks, apparently, because the faeries break them off so as to prevent us humans firing them back at them.[181]

The faeries kill both men and cattle with these weapons. Whilst injury to cows may be part of their attempt to steal them away, attacks on people are motivated by pure malice. It's said that the faeries shoot with such precision that they seldom miss and the resultant wound is always fatal. The arrows strike with such force that they pierce straight to the heart.[182]

A sure symptom of a cow's injury by elf shot was said to be the impossibility of getting its milk to churn into butter. In the days before farmers had access veterinary specialists, when cattle fell ill they sought out those endowed with special faery knowledge to diagnose whether elf shot was to blame and to recommend how best to treat it. On Shetland one traditional treatment involved rubbing the cow from head to tail and around the belly with a cat and then having it swallow three live crabs; another involved feeding

---

181. Grant Stewart, *Popular Superstitions*, 134; Henderson, *Notes on the Folklore*, 185; Blakeborough, *Wit, Character, Folklore and Customs of the North Riding of Yorkshire*, 142.

182. Crofton Croker, *Fairy Legends*, 43.

the cow soot and salt mixed and then burning gunpowder beneath the poor beast. Cattle might also be cured by tying a needle, folded inside a page from the psalm book, to their hair; by giving them water to drink in which an elf bolt had been dipped; or by simply touching them with another elf shot. These treatments were all thought both to heal the afflictions and also to protect against any future assaults. Furthermore, it's notable how the efficacy of the elf shot is so easily transferred into water or by contact; we'll see later how other faery magical powers can also be passed on in the same ways.[183]

Over and above their use in treating sick livestock, elf arrows are often kept as family heirlooms and are worn on cords round a person's neck as an ornament. They're said to bring a family general good luck. They protect the wearer from attack with bolts, they can act as love charms, and they will cure sore eyes. Giving away the bolt is unwise, however; the generous donor may subsequently find themselves abducted by the Fae.[184]

Faery Cruelty

Although the Good Folk are ready to torment and injure humans—and certain animals belonging to us—this doesn't appear to extend into a general cruelty toward living things. Cows are probably only victims because the faeries want to steal them for their milk and do it under the guise of their illness and death. Wild animals, in contrast, have much less economic value to either faeries or humans and are left alone.

There was a trend in Victorian faery painting to depict faeries as wantonly cruel to wildlife—most famously by artist John Anster Fitzgerald in his series of pictures of faeries tormenting and killing a robin (although he also painted scenes of faery communion with wildlife). There is no traditional support for these images. In contrast, for many contemporary faery writers and enthusiasts, faeries have become the archetype of eco-awareness and, as such, the concept of abuse of wild animals seems anathema. This appears indeed to be the more traditional view.

---

183. *Denham Tracts*, 110; *County Folklore* vol. 3, 37–9; Spence, *Shetland Folklore*, 144; Marwick, *The Folklore of Orkney*, 43; Knox, *Topography of the Basin of the Tay*, 111.

184. Blakeborough, *Wit, Character, Folklore and Customs of the North Riding of Yorkshire*, 142; Marwick, *The Folklore of Orkney*, 44.

As early as the popular seventeenth century song "The Pranks of Puck," faery protection of hunted beasts is a theme. In the ballad Puck hides himself in snares and traps left by men and scares off the hunters when they return to collect their catch. Very much more recently, the same kind of behaviour is ascribed to the Somerset pixies. In one story told to folklorist Jon Dathen, the pixies give shelter inside a tree to an exhausted fox pursued by the horses and hounds of the local hunt.[185]

Elsewhere in Dathen's book he is told (by two separate interviewees) that "if there's one thing the pixies despise, it's cruelty to animals." If they become aware of mistreatment or neglect of wild or domesticated beasts, the guilty person will be punished by the pixies, generally by the time-honoured means of vicious pinching. The pixies are described as being especially close to certain animals, including horses and robins. In *Seeing Fairies*, Marjorie Johnson's collection of modern accounts of faery sightings, there's a mention of the faeries taking care of wildlife in heavy snowfall on moorland.[186]

The Good Folk are not seen traditionally as gratuitously cruel. They injure those who offend them, but not defenceless beasts. Although more modern representations of faeries as harmless, winged, and tiny have undoubtedly compounded the perception, the concept of faeries as being in harmony with nature and protecting their surroundings seems to have deep roots.

Violence as a Way of Life?

Wildlife aside, a broader perspective on faery conduct confirms the impression of Faery as a fractious, rough, and sometimes vicious society. Many aspects of their culture depend upon violence to some degree or another: human children and wives might be taken by force to supplement the faery race; a significant portion of the food and drink consumed in Faery is stolen, usually by stealth but sometimes coercively; and, thirdly, it seems fairly clear that the faery idea of fun often involves tormenting people or their livestock—for example, the habit of "riding" horses at night, a practice which left them weak and distressed in the mornings.

---

185. Dathen, *Somerset Fairies and Pixies*, 22.
186. Dathen, *Somerset Fairies and Pixies*, 14, 72–74, 72–3 & 48; Johnson, *Seeing Fairies*, 135–136.

As this catalogue shows, traditional folk belief was a great deal less confident in the good nature of faerykind than some contemporary commentators. A more honest view of their behaviour has to be nuanced: the faeries may not gratuitously injure or torture animals or people, but these scruples may be subordinated unhesitatingly to the faeries' desire for amusement. The best counsel must therefore be to approach with care—or better still, to be on the safe side and to protect oneself with charms and to seek to avoid the "Good Neighbours" altogether. Faeries can be as variable, unpredictable, and potentially vicious as any imperfect human being.

I mentioned earlier the fear that some people have experienced when they meet faeries, as well as the animosity that is sometimes detected. In just a couple of cases recorded in the *Fairy Census,* this was taken further and there was actual violence reported against the witness. In one case this involved a terrifying attempt to abduct a woman; in another, the pursuit of a young girl by beings throwing sticks and rocks. Such cases are very rare, but we must acknowledge the fact of their existence.[187]

187. *Census* nos. 476 & 428.

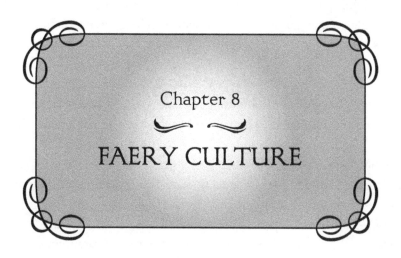

Chapter 8

FAERY CULTURE

A regular point of contact between humankind and the Good Folk is in their leisure activities, when they are dancing or feasting, for example. This chapter looks at these different aspects of faery culture and how we humans should best approach them.

Faery Leisure

Although I've just described faery crafts and building skills, our abiding image of the Good Folk is of a people living an uninterrupted life of leisure. This seems, on the whole, to be pretty accurate.

The Fae are a highly social people and many of their pastimes are participatory, whether it's playing music, dancing, or taking part in games. The Good Folk enjoy team sports such as hurling and football and, in fact, the earliest pixie sighting in Cornwall was of a hurling match held in a cornfield at Boscastle in August 1657. The supernatural identity of the players was confirmed by their disappearance over a cliff into the sea and the fact that there was no sign of damage to the crop afterward.

Given the faeries' contrary nature, they may sometimes react violently if they are intruded upon in these activities, but they equally may welcome humans joining in. We'll see this particularly with musicians, but there are comparable accounts of men being asked to make up numbers in a team for a sports match.

Faery Music

The faeries' liking for music and song is a key aspect of their pleasure-seeking nature. According to John Dunbar of Invereen in the Highlands, the faeries were "awful for music, and used to be heard often playing the bagpipes." In the Shetland Isles the trows were renowned for their love of both music and dancing (although their dancing appeared ungainly and ludicrous to humans—they crouched and hopped about the floor).[188]

As mentioned already in connection with faery rings, dancing used to be regarded as the faeries' distinctive activity—their major preoccupation. Now it's seldom witnessed, being mentioned in only around 9 per cent of modern reports. Perhaps this is because the faeries are busy doing other things—like working—or because they have retreated from their former dance sites as we humans have got more numerous, more noisy, and more intrusive. Equally likely, as we'll see soon, is the possibility that the Fae may simply have moved inside more convenient human buildings for their revels.

Whilst dances are seen less frequently, hearing faery music is still reported, nonetheless: it's a feature of 16 per cent of the most recent sightings. We can seldom dance with the faeries (not least because it's a dangerous thing to do, as it's often the way they lull people into a false sense of security before abducting them) but we may often and more safely hear their music, which is renowned for its enchantment and otherworldliness. Where may you hear faery music and what will it sound like?

Music Hills

The Fae's music is often heard coming from particular knolls, hills, or barrows, in which the faeries are taken to reside. This is a very common local report and it can be found all over Britain from the Faery Knowe on Skye to

---

188. Evans-Wentz, *The Fairy Faith*, 95; Saxby, *Shetland Traditional Lore*, 116; see chapter 11 of my *British Fairies*.

the "music barrows" of Southern England, for example at Bincombe Down and Culliford Tree in Dorset and at Wick Moor, near Stogursey in Somerset.

The otherworldly nature of the music nevertheless quite often gives witnesses problems trying to judge exactly where the tunes are coming from. Firsthand accounts not infrequently seem to find it hard to place the source. For example, music heard at Ditton Priors on the Clee Hills in Shropshire was "up in the air" and this wafting, immersive impression is common. Other witnesses have located the music "from the ground," "in the air all around," and "in the air as faint as a breath dying away and coming back again." It might even be described as sub-audible, something you are aware of without hearing it—in fact, something that ceased to be audible as soon as you tried to focus upon it.[189]

Irish mystic and friend of poet W. B. Yeats Ella Young had many experiences of hearing faery music. She described a further problem with saying exactly where it came from. To her, the orchestral sound was something that was in motion; it was a "wave or gush of wind." Fascinatingly, a witness in the Clent Hills near Birmingham during the 1960s was caught up in something similar—"a real singing whirlwind"—and another in Ireland experienced the music as sweeping around her house.[190]

Learning Faery Tunes

Faery musical skills—and even instruments—can be granted to fortunate humans. There are several sets of bagpipes in Scotland that are alleged to have been faery gifts.

The receipt of faery musical ability can be a blessing that makes a man and his heirs rich and famous. The favoured player might just be well paid: one Jeems o' da Klodi on Shetland was given a bag full of threepenny coins, for example. Another Shetland fiddler on his way to perform at a wedding was waylaid by a "little grey man." The musician said he hadn't time to play at the trows' dance, but was assured that, if he agreed to perform for them, he'd still get to his first appointment on time and that outstanding skill on the fiddle would run in his family for nine generations. On that basis the man

---

189. Burne, *Shropshire Folklore,* Part I, 58; Johnson, *Seeing Fairies,* 60, 231, 330 & 331; *Census,* nos. 384, 406 & 489.

190. Johnson, *Seeing Fairies,* 44 & 146.

agreed to go under a hill to the dance, although once there he found himself rooted to the spot and unable to stop playing until the trows freed him from their spells and delivered him to the wedding party.

Faery skills could also be a curse, too: the favoured one might die young, being taken back by the faeries to play for them, or he might lose his wits. As is always the case with faery transactions, discretion is the key. A man carried off into the air by the Shetland trows was kept by them for a whole twelve months; when he returned home, he never spoke of what he saw or heard, other than to play a tune he'd learned whilst he'd been away. Another Shetland fiddler, John Scott of Easting, so impressed the trows with his playing that he was told he would never want for money—he had simply to put his hand in his pocket and coins would be there. Eventually, he got drunk one night and spilled the beans to his drinking companions—and his endless supply of cash was gone.[191]

Musical skills might be willingly shared with some. A man called Fyfe from Reay in Perthshire spent many hours with the faeries, enjoying their music and honing his own skills on the bagpipes. Because of the time he spent with them, his music became imbued with a magical charm that made him much in demand at dances. Even better, Fyfe could rely upon the faeries always to carry him to his destinations, so that he was sure to arrive on time whatever the weather. Sometimes this conferring of musical ability seems almost incidental: A faery woman visited a Perthshire home and tuned the family's bagpipes for them. She played a few tunes and then left, but the three sons of the family were endowed with great prowess as pipers thereafter.[192]

Conversely, talented human musicians were from time to time abducted to satisfy the powerful faery need for music and dance. Almost always they met the fate of all those who tarry in Faery. They believed that they had played for just a night, but found all transformed on their return home.[193]

Despite what's been said, faery music can prove notoriously hard to remember. In his 1779 history of Aberystruth parish, the Reverend Edmund Jones reported that "everyone said [the music] was low and pleasant, but

191. Saxby, *Shetland Traditional Lore*, 65–66; Marwick, *The Folklore of Orkney*, 34.

192. Sutherland, *Folklore Gleanings*, 27; Murray, *Tales from Highland Perthshire*, no. 186.

193. Evans-Wentz, *The Fairy Faith*, 40 & 103; MacGregor, c. 2.

none could ever learn the tune." On the Isle of Man, one musician had to return three times to the same spot where he'd heard faery music to be able to commit it to memory. It's only very occasionally that humans are able to learn a faery tune and then contribute it to the mortal repertoire. One such is "Be nort da deks o' Voe" from Shetland, but there are several such so-called "ferry tüns" from the far northern isles. Two Welsh examples are "Cân y Tylwyth Teg" ("The Faery Song") and "Ffarwel Ned Pugh" ("Farewell to Ned Pugh"). There's a downside to this too. Rather like the price that may be paid for having the faery musical gift, it's said that some of those who commit faery music to memory will be otherwise addled for the rest of their lives.[194]

Faery Orchestras

There's a conceit, which may be almost entirely poetic rather than being based upon experience, that faery music is produced not from instruments but by animals. Anna Bray, for example, said that the Dartmoor pixies danced to tunes played by crickets, grasshoppers, frogs, bees, and owls. This notion is predominantly part of the literary tradition of exaggerating the perceived quaintness and tininess of faeryland, but one modern experience lends substance to the idea. A woman visiting a rainforest in New South Wales during the 2000s heard "something off by the river, almost like music—but all natural sounds." She went on: "I could tell it was the sound of crickets, the wind, the river, and frogs [but] they were all harmonized with a distinct tune."[195]

Most witnesses, however, agree that faery music is played on instruments or is sung by choirs. Irish poet and mystic George William Russell (AE) first listened to the music in the air on a hillside in County Sligo. He heard "what seemed to be the sound of bells, and was trying to understand these aerial clashings in which wind seemed to break upon wind in an ever-changing musical silvery sound." Over the summer of 1917 and into 1918, AE's friend, Ella Young, repeatedly heard the *ceol sidhe* and reported that this faery music was played by a "myriad, myriad instruments" among which she identified cymbals, bells (both silvery tinkling and deep tolling), trumpets, harps, violins, drums, pipes, organs, bagpipes, and "stricken anvils." The very recent

---

194. See Marwick, *The Folklore of Orkney*, 34; Sikes, *British Goblins*, c. 7; Evans-Wentz, *The Fairy Faith*, 118 & 131—two examples from Man; Young & Houlbrook, *Magical Folk*, 131.

195. Bray, *Description*, 173; *Census* no. 455.

Faery Census has also reported music played on bells, accompanied by pipes and drums.

Interwoven with this instrumentation might be voices singing in an unknown tongue, either solo or resembling Gregorian chant. Faery author Lewis Spence once heard "faerie singing, wordless and of wonderful harmony" whilst a Cornish witness described domestic pixies singing in the evenings "like a Christmas choir."[196]

Several times, though, Ella Young was unable to compare the sounds to anything she knew from earthly ensembles: she heard "very high notes—higher than any human instrument could produce," "something like a Jew's harp," and "a curious reedy instrument." Young isn't alone in being unable to say how the sounds were produced. On the Isle of Man in the 1720s islanders would hear "Musick, as could proceed from no earthly instruments" and a modern hearer on Iona felt that she could not ascribe anything so beautiful to an earthly source.[197]

Faery Scores

If it's hard for listeners to say what the *ceol sidhe* is being played on, it's unsurprising to discover that they've also frequently struggled to say what it sounds like. Everyone seems to be agreed that it surpasses most human compositions but saying anything more definite than that has proved difficult.

Some witnesses struggle with vague terms: "tunes not of this world, unlike anything a mortal man ever heard, being the finest, grandest and most beautiful kind." Music that ravished those listening at Holderness in East Yorkshire was described as "delectable and harmonious"; a Lake District writer recalled "aerial music, which for rich and thrilling harmony far surpassed the most exquisite warblings of the Swedish nightingale." In the 1880s some gypsies camping near Ditton Priors in Shropshire heard unearthly music that was "wonderful clear and sweetsome."[198]

---

196. Hawker, *Footprints*, "Old Trevarten."

197. Evans-Wentz, *The Fairy Faith*, 61; Young & Houlbrook, *Magical Folk*, 173; Johnson, *Seeing Fairies*, 330; Hawker, *Footprints*.

198. Evans-Wentz, *The Fairy Faith*, 124 & 24, 32, 47 & 57; Nicholson, *Folklore of East Yorkshire*, 82; Young & Houlbrook, *Magical Folk*, 81; Palmer, *Folklore of Shropshire*, 141.

Modern witnesses are scarcely more informative. We have impressionistic offerings such as "tiny—and soft and quick and light" or "plaintive yet joyful." Ella Young spoke of "orchestral [music] of amazing richness and complexity." Its melodies could be exquisite, she said, with "delicate and intricate rhythms" in a variety of tempos—sometimes like very fast reels, at others slow and wistful. On August 27, 1917, she described "a certain monotony like slow moving waves with a running melody on the crests." Ultimately, she despaired of her descriptive abilities: it was "not music I can describe... it is beyond words."

Comparison to other genres may be a little more informative and such descriptions as "weird folk," Middle Eastern, medieval, and traditional Irish have all been offered. One witness even suggested "a mixture of birdsong and Celtic."[199]

What stands out most clearly, perhaps, is the otherworldly character of faery music and the range of responses it evokes. It's not modelled on the familiar scales or time signatures nor can it conveniently be described with our conventional terms. Some people mention mysterious long chords; some hear repetitive, circular tunes; others are amazed by rich melodies. To some hearers it's melancholy, to others joyful.

The best summary of *ceol sidhe* I can offer may be to say that it is lovely, complex, and immersive. What *is* consistent in all the witnesses' descriptions is the wonder it evokes.

The Effect of Faery Music

Whatever its nature, the experience of faery music can be powerful, not least because it has an aura of mystery. It can have a magical or enchanting effect on listeners: Ella Young described the "sense of freedom and exultation" it gave her. Some people find it "intoxicating;" a recent Irish witness heard "Streams of music which was hypnotic, but made me feel sick!" Coleridge in his poem "The Eolian Harp" rightly described the "soft floating witchery of sound / As twilight Elfins make."[200]

---

199. Johnson, *Seeing Fairies*, 186; *Census,* nos. 73, 87, 172, 310, 331, 376 & 479.
200. Johnson, *Seeing Fairies*, 156, 328 & 331; *Census,* nos. 73, 87, 144, 172 & 310.

The response may not be solely emotional. Some witnesses from Ireland tell stories of how, on hearing the *ceol sidhe*, they felt compelled to dance—and then had to continue until they dropped from sheer exhaustion. On the Isle of Man, it could have an opposite effect, freezing people and animals to the spot whilst it lasted, for periods of up to forty-five minutes.[201]

The Meaning of Faery Music

The music of the Good Folk is one of the ways in which their world intersects with ours—and it is possibly the most beautiful and the most tantalising of these. Hearing the music is rare, but it is an intensely affecting experience because the medium itself is so evocative. Whilst faery encounters are always astonishing, we feel better able to judge the reality of what we *see* and to trust the evidence of our eyes. We believe we can assess the subject of a vision to determine whether it's potentially tangible and to estimate its height, distance, weight, and colour. What's *heard* is far harder to assess and to locate with certainty. It makes us much more likely to doubt our senses. As Ella Young herself fretted—was it all in her head? Was she going mad? Readers may be reassured to read that hearing faery music is an experience that occurs often enough to be taken seriously and that part of its nature is its elusive and tantalising quality.

For all its ethereal beauty, though, our last word should be a note of caution. Faery music is notorious as one of the ways in which people are lured into faery abduction. For example, a story from St. Allen in Cornwall tells of a boy who wandered off, enticed by the sound of music in some woods, and was absent for several days in Faery. Just like faery beauty, *ceol sidhe* can be alluring, but we need to keep our wits about us.

Faery Food

There is considerable difference of opinion over what faeries eat, whether we would recognise their food as edible, and even whether they need to eat at all. As I've argued already, there's plenty of evidence to demonstrate that the

---

201. Evans-Wentz, *The Fairy Faith*, 69; Waldron, *A Description of the Isle of Man*, 37 and footnote 53.

Fae are as solid and fleshly as we are and, that being the case, I feel sure that they need (and enjoy) food and drink just as much as we do.

Some sources suggest that faery food is not all it seems, though. One Perthshire woman who was abducted to Faery said that the food she was offered looked very tempting, but that when she saw through the faeries' glamour, it was "only the refuse of the earth." Another Scottish abductee said grace over a meal and then realised that it was nothing but horse dung. These ideas doubtless explain why faery food has a reputation for being unsatisfying and why inedible fungi are often popularly called "faery butter" and the like.[202]

To set against these accounts is other evidence that the faery diet is much like our own. The Fae are widely known to bake (as we'll see) and from both the north of Scotland and (especially) from the Isle of Man come accounts of faery fishing fleets. There are also numerous stories of faeries entering human homes asking to borrow flour or oatmeal. Not only are these loans returned, but they are often repaid several-fold. This has to indicate that the faeries have their own supplies of grain and flour and (of course) that they must be storing it because they eat it.

All of these accounts show, pretty convincingly, that the faery diet is understood to be very similar indeed to the human one. That being so, how do we fit in the experiences where witnesses are served such non-food items as tree leaves to eat (as in the story of St. Collen and the Faery King)? Probably what we're seeing here is grand displays of faery "glamour" intended to delude and entrap humans and the feasts laid out don't represent the true nature of faery cuisine.

Vegetarian Fae

There are two very old sources that suggest that faeries avoid meat. In the early twelfth-century reports of the Green Children of Woolpit, when the faery brother and sister are first found, they are pale, their skin is tinged green, and for some time after their discovery they will only eat raw green beans, refusing offers of bread and other human food. Secondly, the writer Gerald of Wales told the story of Elidyr, who had visited faeryland in his

---

202. Graham, *Sketches Descriptive*, 111; Campbell, *Superstitions*.

youth. He claimed that the little people he met there "never ate flesh or fish" and instead lived upon various milk dishes, made up into junkets with saffron (a junket is a mixture of curds and cream, sweetened and flavoured). The faery preference for dairy products was often mentioned in Elizabethan folklore. There is some good evidence, then, that faeries prefer a vegetarian diet, though not a vegan one.

Overall, however, there are contradictions and inconsistencies in the sources. Elidyr also told Gerald that the tiny beings he visited kept horses and greyhounds. The latter are hunting dogs and the elves were plainly equipped for the chase. In the poem "Sir Orfeo" the hero meets the king of Faery when he is out hunting wild beasts with his hounds; the king is also said to hunt wild fowl, such as mallards, herons, and cormorants, with his falcons. The Gabriel Hounds of Lancashire are faery dogs; they are also called Gabriel Ratchets, a ratchet being a hound that hunted by scent rather than by sight. The Manx faeries too are particularly known for their love of hunting across the island.

The pursuit of all this game was presumably for some purpose other than mere sport. We have to assume that the deer, boars, and birds that were caught were all eaten and that these particular faeries were very far from veggie. The *bucca* living on the beach at Newlyn in West Cornwall were given a share of the catch by local fishermen and they were doubtless expected to eat those fish. The Highland water horses, the *cabaillushtey* and the *each uisge,* both carry off and consume cattle and children, as does the Welsh *afanc.*

What are we to conclude? The folklore evidence is not unanimous, but then it seldom is. There are different sorts of faery and each will naturally have its own tastes and preferences. Nonetheless, there is clearly a very old strand of belief that some faeries eat a limited diet excluding flesh, perhaps as an indicator of their otherness or of their sympathetic links to the natural world.

Faery Bread

The faeries are known for baking bread and cakes. According to one account, they were inexplicably noisy when doing so. So familiar is the link that certain echinoderm fossils are known as faery loaves and, if you find one, it's said that you will never want for bread.[203]

Tantalisingly, one Scottish writer tells us that faery bread tastes like a wheaten loaf mixed with honey and wine and that it will last for a week at least without going stale. Cornish woman Anne Jefferies, who was imprisoned for suspected witchcraft, was fed by the faeries during her captivity and a person who tasted the bread they gave her described it as "the most delicious… I ever did eat, either before or afterward."

Intriguing as these loaves sound, the same Scottish writer also recorded that the faeries would subsist upon silverweed roots, called *brisgein*. This was known as "seventh bread" but may well sound a good deal less appetising than the conventional loaf. In fact, the plant has been cultivated since prehistoric times and, in the Highlands, the crop was grown up until the potato was introduced (and was still used subsequently in lean years). The roots could be boiled, baked, or ground into flour and tasted a little like parsnips. The leaves are antiseptic and were used to treat a range of conditions. We should also bear in mind that faery food will be proportionate with its makers: from the Scottish island of Muck comes a report of a meeting between two boys and a faery family in a boat. The boys were offered some bread; the faeries were tiny and so too were their loaves, being the size of walnuts, although they tasted very good.[204]

The folklore confirms that the Good Folk have their own bread ovens: we've heard of the noise they make and that, in the north of Scotland, rain was a sign that the faeries were baking. Just as they might prefer human spinning wheels to their own, they may enter our homes at night to do their own baking. In one story from the Isle of Man, because the maid hasn't put out any water for them, they take a drop of blood from her toe to mix their dough. They eat most of the cakes they make but conceal bits of some under the cottage thatch before they leave. The next day the girl falls ill, but a visitor who had overheard the faeries at their baking is able to cure her with some of the hidden cake crumbs.[205]

---

203. Bourne, *Antiquitates Vulgares*, 1725, c. X; Wright, *Rustic Speech*, 208.

204. Aitken, *Forgotten Heritage* 5; Cunningham, *Remains*, 242; Bord, *Fairies*, 63.

205. Evans-Wentz, *Fairy Faith*, 127–128.

They have their own delectable loaves, but how do the Fae feel about human bread? On the Isle of Man, the faeries are said to object to baking after sunset, but otherwise they will help with the process so long as a piece of the dough is stuck to the kitchen wall as an offering. If such an offering isn't made, the baker will face problems. It's believed that one of the regular pranks of the tylwyth teg is to enter kitchens and to "robin" bread dough— that is, to make it too sticky and stringy to rise. If this happens, the solution is to sacrifice an old slipper (later we'll see shoes being burned in Scotland too to scare off faeries). A prank of the Cornish pixy is to spoil bread in the oven, making it come out full of "pixy-spits."[206]

Evidently, the faeries have a taste for the results of human baking: this is confirmed by several stories in which Welsh lake maidens are lured to tryst with a mortal man by the offer of bread. They are very fussy about the bake of their loaves though: first the bread will be too hard, then too soft, until finally a happy medium is found and true love blossoms. In another of these Welsh stories, concerning the maiden of Llyn y Fan Fach, the man baits a fishing hook with bread in order to catch himself a faery wife. Once again, he tries first with a hunk from a well-baked loaf—and fails—and then tries with half-baked bread and lands his bride. In addition, it's not just the quality of the bake that seems to matter: the faeries don't like salt in their loaves. As a general rule, it's a substance they can't abide.[207]

The Welsh stories just outlined are interesting not just because of the importance of bread in them: as many readers will know, it's dangerous to eat the food offered when in faeryland because then you will never escape; here that concept is reversed and a faery is lured into the mortal world by consuming our food.

There is something mysterious and semi-magical about bread, certainly. It can provide charmed protection for people or bestow supernatural powers, although the sort of meal used and the manner of preparation seem to vary widely. In one Scottish story a man who has stolen from the faeries is pursued by them and they cry out, "You wouldn't be so fast if it wasn't for the hardness of your bread." In a similar tale, a Perthshire man was troubled

---

206. Moore, *Folklore of the Isle of Man*, c. III; Lewes, *Queer Side*, 130 & 114; Davies, *Folklore of West and Mid-Wales*, 135; Harris, *Cornish Saints and Sinners*, c. 19.

207. Rhys, *Celtic Folklore*, 3–6 & 27–30; Roeder, *Manx Folk Tales*, 14.

by faery cattle eating his crops. He could never catch them until one day, as he futilely chased a dun cow around his land, a faery woman appeared to him and advised that he'd do better if he ate barley bannocks turned on the griddle and milk from black goats. He followed her advice, caught the faery cow and thereafter had the best milk herd in the district. The bread magic works both ways: an incident from the Hebrides involves a mermaid escaping into the sea; she's nearly caught by a man and she tells him his failure can be ascribed to the dryness of his bread—whereas if he'd eaten porridge and milk, he'd have overtaken her.[208]

Bread somehow works to protect people from faery ill will. It was widely believed throughout Britain that carrying a crust was a sure way of protecting yourself from malign influences. Witness Stuart poet Robert Herrick's rhyme:

If ye feare to be affrighted,
When ye are (by chance) benighted,
In your pocket for a trust
Carrie nothing but a Crust:
For that holy piece of Bread,
Charmes the danger, and the dread.

The verse seems to imply that, originally, people carried a piece of consecrated host, but eventually any sort of bread was thought to be just as good. Right across in Scotland oatcakes were thought to have protective powers: a bannock hung over a cottage threshold would protect a mother and her newborn child inside and burning an oatcake would drive off the faeries.

As we'll see later, new babies are thought to be especially vulnerable to faery interference and bread products are a particularly effective way of safeguarding them. From Cornwall in South West England comes a belief that a child can be protected from faery abduction by baked goods: a mother must take a cake with her to her baby's baptism and then give it to the first person she meets in the road. This guarantees her child's safety from the pixies. There's an identical practice in Sutherland in Scotland, involving oatcake and

---

208. MacPhail, *Hebrides II,* 384; Stewart, *Ben Nevis,* 261; Murray, *Tales from Highland Perth-shire,* no. 167.

cheese, whilst on the Isle of Man the practice was to provide "blithe meat" (bread and cheese) for people who came to visit a mother and her newborn child. A portion of this would be scattered around for the unseen visitors, too—partly perhaps to win their favour as "godmothers" and partly to guard against the risk of abduction.[209]

The Faery in the Dairy

The faery preference for dairy products has already been mentioned and the theme was often employed by Shakespeare and his contemporaries. Queen Mab loved junkets, according to Milton, and Ben Jonson has her consuming cream, too. In the Scottish story of a goblin called Gilpin Horner, he's found lost and wandering and is taken in by a farmer. When he's eventually called home by his parents it's quite a relief for the smallholder, because the boy consumed so much cream during his stay.

It seems that it's not just cows' milk that our Good Neighbours like. They also drink the milk of goats and deer, which explains why the banshee of Glen Nevis is often to be seen driving as well as milking herds of deer. So strong has been the link between faeries and the dairy (its work, as well as its products) that in Sussex the name of the local brownie, Dobbs, was invoked as part of a charm which was repeated three times to help butter to come in the churn. Milk might even have magical properties for the Fae: in the ballad of Young Tamlane part of the spell to free Tam from faery thrall is to dip him in milk.[210]

The Good Folk will be found haunting dairies, both as helpers and as filchers. They insist upon cleanliness and neatness, but then shamelessly skim the cream from the milk. In these circumstances, a major part of the interaction between farmers and faeries has comprised efforts to protect dairy products from theft.

A range of defensive measures were recorded, some very simple indeed. They were employed at different stages of the dairying process: you might take steps either to defend your livestock or their products. Cows can easily be protected by tying a coin to their tails; a more complex charm involves

---

209. Deane & Shaw, *Folklore of Cornwall*, 93; Sutherland, *Folklore Gleanings*, 26.

210. See Appendix Two of my *British Fairies*.

passing a hot coal over their backs and bellies. Another version of this spell involves a cat drawn around the cow. One common faery pastime was to ride both cows as well as horses at night. A witch-stone or hag-stone (a naturally holed stone) hung just above the animals in their stalls would prevent this. On Shetland it was said that if a farmer suspected that the trows were stealing milk from his cows, he should try to hear them doing it in the byre. This would bring good luck, but to actually try to spy on them as they milked would lead to ill fortune.

Once the animals had been milked, the dairy products could be protected, either directly or indirectly. In Leicestershire hanging a witch-stone over the dairy doorway once again stopped the faeries getting in and tainting the milk; usefully, it also gave more general protection against illness and warts. Twigs of rowan, bramble, or ivy placed under a milk pail could be sufficient to safeguard its contents; sprays of rowan, elm, and witch hazel were tied to churns in Herefordshire to deter the Fae and facilitate the butter making. In Worcestershire, to keep faeries away, the practice was for everyone entering the dairy to stir the cream. Finally, salt thrown in a churn will avoid any interference with the butter making process.[211]

Despite this list of remedies, we ought to mention that denying the faeries their dairy treats might not be wise. We'll discuss their reaction to meanness later, but here's a dairy based example. A Cumbrian farmer had left a churn of milk outside his cottage overnight to keep it cool. Next morning a little of the milk was missing and he guessed the faeries had filched some. Annoyed, he fetched some of the salt he kept in his cottage to ward off evil spirits and threw it into the churn. When the faeries sampled the milk the next night they were outraged by his response and retaliated by spitting it out all over his smallholding. Wherever they sprayed the salty milk, the grass died and would not regrow.[212]

It might be suggested that we only have ourselves to blame for these problems, as we have encouraged the Fae's taste for our produce. Milk products were traditionally the recompense given to brownies and Pucks for their

---

211. *Printed Extracts 3*, Leicestershire, 16; Edmondston, *A View of the Zetland Isles*, 217; Leather, *Folklore of Herefordshire*, 18; Wright, *Rustic Speech*, 210; Cumming, *Guide to the Isle of Man*, 22.

212. Thomas, *Cumbrian Folk Tales*, 82.

household work. For example, in the North of England brownies would expect to receive "oatcakes warm from the mill and spread with honey or cream..." In the Scottish Highlands the same arrangements were in place with local beings such as *gruagachs*, *glaistigs*, *urisks*, and Loireags. If a nightly share of the milking were not left out an angry response was bound to follow: the cattle and goats would be enchanted in the field and their milk taken, or the calves would be put amongst the cows overnight so that there was no milk left for the household in the morning. If the milk offering was forgotten for a second night, worse would follow: the cattle might be let loose in the cornfield or a cow might fall over a cliff. The *gruagach* at Balieveolan cared for the family and the neighbours' cattle and was satisfied with a simple bowl of whey every night; however, when one evening a careless servant put out boiling hot whey, she drove the *gruagach* away forever.[213]

This situation was further aggravated and complicated by the fact that offerings of milk would be made to the faeries as a whole, seeking their favour and protection, blurring the distinction between rewards and gifts and perhaps creating a sense of entitlement to the produce amongst the Good Folk.

In many parts of Scotland, the practice was to pour milk, or the wort of beer that was being brewed, into a depression on a so-called "brownie stone" to ensure favour and protection from the household spirit. Most districts had such a stone. On the island of Colonsay milk was poured into the rock basins annually. Additionally, on the first occasion each year that the cattle were left out overnight in the summer pastures, a single cow's whole milking was sacrificed. Similar offerings might be made when bringing the cattle in again at the end of summer, whenever a cow calved or simply when passing one of the stones with a full pail of milk. On Shetland the practice was to sprinkle every corner of a house with milk when butter was to be churned. Neglecting these offerings would ensure loss and bad luck. At least as recently as

213. Henderson, *Notes on the Folklore*, 248 (see too *The Cobler of Canterburie*, 1608); MacGregor, *Peat Fire Flame*, cc. 4 & 5; Carmichael, *Carmina Gadelica*, 306 & 320; D. MacKenzie, *Scottish Folklore & Folk Life*, 218; MacDougall, *Folk Tales*, 217.

the 1950s milk was still put out overnight for the pixies on one Dartmoor farm.[214]

In fairness, we should round off this survey by observing that the faeries didn't just like to consume other people's produce—they made their own and would assist human households with their dairy production too. In the Lake District the faeries were particularly known for churning their own butter and it was said to be lucky to eat faery butter (although there may be some confusion here with the fungi called faery butter discussed earlier). Many of the domestic sprites—brownies, dobbies, and the like—are known for their particular aptitude for caring for milk cattle and undertaking dairy tasks. Also in the Lake District, tradition tells of a farm in Little Langdale where the local faeries visited and churned the household's butter at night. Doubtless their help was welcome, but they were untidy workers, apparently scattering bits of butter in the nearby woods as they left in the morning.[215]

In conclusion, a good way to show respect for and encourage contact from the Good Folk is going to be offerings of milk, cream, and such. They are almost certain to be better disposed toward you and to start to frequent your home.

Extracting the Goodness

Part of the reason it has sometimes been said that faeries don't need solid food like humans is the way they steal provisions from us. Frequently, rather than taking a whole cheese or a pail of milk, the faeries will instead extract its nutritional substance—what's called the *foison* in England or the *toradh* in Scottish Gaelic. The advantage of this is that it looks as though nothing has been stolen, although in fact the nourishment in the food stuff is wholly gone. The Reverend Kirk described this effect with cheese, saying that what was left floated like a cork on water.

---

214. Browne, *History of the Highlands,* vol. 1, 106 & 113; Martin, *A Description of the Western Isles of Scotland,* 391; Grieve, *Colonsay and Oronsay,* 177; Dalyell, *The Darker Superstitions of Scotland,* 530; MacGregor, *Peat Fire Flame,* c.4; *County Folklore* vol. 3, 47; Marwick, *The Folklore of Orkney,* 40; Addy, *Household Tales,* 141; Brand, *A Description of Zetland,* 169; R. St. Leger Gordon, *The Witchcraft and Folklore of Dartmoor,* 21.

215. Briggs, *Remains,* 223; H. Cowper, *Hawkshead,* 308; Hodgson, "On some surviving fairies," *Transactions of the Cumberland and Westmorland Antiquarian and Archaeological Society,* vol. 1, 116.

Something similar happens to food left out overnight specifically for the faeries and the advice has always been to throw it away the next day. Faery contact with food very often taints it for humans in one way or another: eating faery food in faeryland may trap you there and that malign influence can carry over to our world. In a case from Dunadd in Argyll, the Fae one night washed a stolen child in milk left out for them by a farmhouse fire. This milk was wisely thrown away by the farmer the next morning, but his sheepdog lapped it up—and instantly died.[216]

Conversely, it's worth remarking here that it seems to be completely safe to eat food provided by faeries outside faeryland. As we'll see later, they will sometimes feed those they favour or who have helped them. In such cases the gifts of faery meat and drink, consumed in the mortal world, can be accepted confidently.

Faery Sexuality

If we're concerned with the relationship between humankind and the Good Folk, we must inevitably discuss one of its most difficult aspects—that of personal relationships between humans and faeries. Just as they share our bodily appetites for food and drink, they can be quite as keen on sex as humans. Faery lore expert Katharine Briggs described the Good Folk as "dangerously amorous"—and that's certainly a good starting point for this discussion.[217]

We've spoken already about faeries' physical charms and, inevitably, some men and women will want to get better acquainted with the Good Folk. This interest has been heightened by the ways we've chosen to present faery culture and morals in our art and literature. Faery has long been imagined as a place of uninhibited pleasure and of sexual freedom.

Many of the most famous paintings of faeryland are full of naked, writhing flesh and the Victorian painters certainly didn't invent these ideas. Generally, the traditional view of faeries is that they are wanton and libidinous. In the medieval romance of "Sir Launfal," the knight encounters the faery woman Tryamour reclining upon a couch in a pavilion. It's a hot summer's day and she's loosened some of her clothes. Presented with this alluring pros-

---

216. Pegg, *Argyll Folk Tales*, 35.
217. Briggs, "English fairies," *Folklore*, vol. 68 (1957), 274.

pect, Sir Launfal responds predictably and "for play, lytylle they sclepte that nygt." The powerful effect of the faery female (at least in the minds of medieval poets) is also attested in the story of "Thomas of Erceldoune," which is dated to around 1425. Thomas meets the faery queen, a "lady shining bright," and is so overcome with desire for her that "seven times he lay by her." Eventually she has to literally push him off, protesting, "Man, you like your play…let me be!"

It is not just that faery females are said to be far more attractive than human women. These physical attributes are combined with an active interest in physical contact with humans, so that there's a long history of sexual relations between mortals and faeries. This has been known since the Middle Ages at least and several of those accused during the Scottish witchcraft trials claimed to have had faery partners, including the Queen of Elfame herself in at least one case.[218] These liaisons were known still to occur in Highland Scotland into Victorian times. For example, describing Perthshire in 1810, one writer complained how "in our Highlands there be many fair ladies of this aerial order, which do often tryst with amorous youths, in the quality of succubi, or lightsome paramours or strumpets, called lean-nan-sith."

His words echo those of Reverend Kirk, who, around 150 years earlier, had condemned the "abominable" goings on between faeries and humans. It wasn't just elves and faeries either; men often took mermaids as their brides, whilst in the Northern Isles it was believed that all a woman had to do to attract a selkie lover was to shed seven tears into the sea at high tide.[219]

Visits by both male and female faery lovers were once thought to have been common but by the early nineteenth century they had grown rare, although there was a shoemaker from Tomintoul, in Moray in the Highlands, who claimed a *Leanan sidhe* partner. On the Isle of Man, the faery lover, the *lhiannanshee*, was a very strong tradition. They were believed to attach themselves to men and to haunt them constantly, whilst remaining invisible to everyone else. They would become an intolerable burden to their chosen partners and the men were frequently desperate to escape them, even emigrating to the other side of the world in an attempt to shake them off.

---

218. Browne, *History of the Highlands*, vol. 1, 108; *Metrical Chronicle*, 196.

219. Graham, *Sketches Descriptive of Picturesque Scenery*, 275; Kirk, *Secret Commonwealth*, c. 11.

In one case, the faery women were said to have lured all the males of the island into the sea.[220]

The reason for these contacts, over and above simple passion, seems to have been to widen the Fae gene pool.[221] Sex with flesh and blood has practical purposes for the Fae over and above any pleasure, but although they may benefit in turn from the faery gifts of knowledge, prophecy, and good advice, it can be a risky interaction for the human partner. Fae can be possessive and even violent lovers sometimes. The relationship can be passionate to the extent of being emotionally obsessive for the human, too, and at the worst a disease called "Night Hag" was said to be the result. Relations between faery men and human women have been said to be solicitous and passionate, but mortal men might be placed under spells and put in danger of their lives by their female faery lovers. These males have been said to suffer from a frenzy and a "wandering madness," causing them to roam restlessly during the day and to leave their homes at night to rendezvous with their Fae lovers.[222]

The consensus on faery beauty, coupled with consciousness of their liberated sexuality (or, at any rate, our fantasies to that effect) can impel individuals to make assumptions about the desires and behaviour of the Good Folk and to rashly seek close acquaintance with the Fae. Even today, questions of faery sexuality are a very popular search subject online, as there is a lively interest in the possibility of sexual relations with faeries. As I'll discuss next, we should hesitate and proceed with care in such relationships, because the Good Folk's charms are tempered by a jealous and demanding nature. As with several issues that I'll cover later, we must be alert to the fact that what we think we know about the faeries can often be what we've chosen to believe about them—and, as such, possibly says more about humans than about them. They remain independent individuals, acting in accordance with their own principles and aims, and we should never forget that, especially in the case of such intimate relationships.

---

220. Hobbes, *Leviathan*, 436; Grant Stewart, *Popular Superstitions*, 103–105; I. H. Leney, *Shadowland in Ellan Vannin*.

221. Dalyell, *The Darker Superstitions of Scotland*, 534.

222. See Robert Amin, *The Valiant Welshman*, 1615, Act II, scene 5; Reginald Scot, *A Discourse Concerning the Nature and Substance of Devils and Spirits*, 1665, Book II, c. 4, 14; J. G. Campbell, c. 1.

Section 4
CONTACT WITH
THE FAE

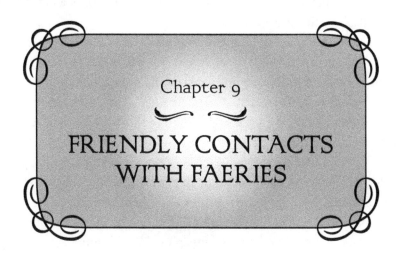

Chapter 9

FRIENDLY CONTACTS WITH FAERIES

As stated at the very start of this book, we can only experience Faery through our interaction with its inhabitants. That relationship between mortals and supernaturals has, in fact, always had its stresses and difficulties. Nonetheless, it is inescapable: we are tied together in a strange kind of barter economy with the denizens of faeryland; there is an interdependence that, whilst it may not always be mutually beneficial, has shaped both communities for centuries.

Faeries in the House

We should start by admitting that, at some times and in some places at least, contact with the Fae may be unavoidable. They can display an overwhelming curiosity about humankind which makes them hard to exclude from our houses.

The faeries are said to be able to enter all homes and to be impossible to keep out. They can get in through any tiny aperture, such as a chimney or a keyhole, and once inside will behave however they wish. Worse still, some faeries are already inside, living under the house and having access through the hearth. One Scottish story tells how the trows stole freshly baked oatcakes simply by slyly raising a floor slab and snatching them away as they cooled, although they may have felt an element of entitlement in this situation: on the

Isle of Man the practice certainly was to leave the last cake of a batch behind the "turf-flag" for the little people.[223]

As we already know, faeries are at large on Fridays and this is when they will invade homes in broad daylight, brazenly peering into cooking pots, getting into closets and cupboards and generally meddling with things. In South Wales it was also believed that stormy weather drove them in for shelter, although often stories from the region simply show the tylwyth teg taking advantage of any available space in houses and barns for dancing and other get-togethers. Besides sheer nosiness, the faeries seem prepared, happily and unapologetically, to commandeer human homes and other places whenever they need them. There are numerous stories of them entering cottages, mills, inns, barns, and the like at night and using them for their own purposes— spinning, baking, feasting, bathing, gossiping. "What's mine is yours" operates both as a charm to release abducted people from their clutches and as a summary of their attitude to human premises and property.[224]

Some houses are more vulnerable to intrusion because they are built on faery places. In such locations the faeries will make a terrible nuisance of themselves, teasing and disturbing the inhabitants. They will appear each evening, making noise and interfering with things. If a room is left empty a racket will start and if you go back in, quick as lightning the faeries will fly up the chimney or out of the doors and windows.[225] It seems that there's only one remedy to such a problem, and that's to move. In one Scottish story a housewife was troubled by faery women suddenly appearing at her cottage asking to borrow items or, unbidden, undertaking household tasks for her. On advice from a local wise man, the decision was made to demolish the house and rebuild it elsewhere. The thatch and rafters were, however, left behind and were burned after sprinkling nine dishes of seawater upon them. Later some men quarrying near the spot found bones buried, confirming for them that the place was frequented by ancestral spirits.[226]

---

223. MacGregor, *Peat Fire Flame*, 3.

224. Simpson, *Folklore in Lowland Scotland*, 101; Jones, *Appearance*, no. 46, 65, 87, 117 & 57; Crossing, *Dartmoor Pixies*, c. VIII—"The Pixies' Revels."

225. Gregor, *Notes on the Folklore*, 59–60.

226. J. Campbell, *Waifs & Strays of Celtic Tradition*, vol. IV, 83–86.

Most of us aren't in a position to knock down our homes and relocate, so if we're pestered by pixies we will have to find other remedies, which are discussed fully later. One example remedy comes from Dorset, but it is not for the faint hearted. To prevent access down the chimney a bullock's heart is hung up there. The efficacy of this charm is improved if the heart is studded with pins, nails, or what are called "maiden thorns," those that have grown in the same year they are picked.[227]

The other option—and one that many readers may prefer to consider—is to accommodate the supernatural visitors and to make them welcome. For many this may be the natural inclination in any case, but given the possibility of reprisals from faeries who feel neglected or unwelcome, there are good practical reasons for making the effort. The Good Folk appreciate a tidy, clean house so it makes excellent sense to leave your home in good order overnight and to make your visitors as welcome as you can, banking up the fire, hiding any knives and iron implements that might offend them, and putting out fresh water for them to bathe in (although in Wales it's said that the tylwyth teg prefer to wash their children in the water in which human infants have already been bathed). If you don't make these preparations, be warned that they may wash in any liquid available (even if this is meant for cooking or drinking) and they can sometimes be nastier still. A Scottish fisherman who had been dozing by his fire awoke to find a trow using his feet as a clothes horse for drying her child's clothes. When he moved and the washing fell in the ashes, she slapped his leg in irritation. As a consequence, for generations afterward, there was always someone in that family who limped.

People have long understood that they will have to share their homes and accepted that the best thing to do is to accommodate our Good Neighbours as best they can. This will range from making the house welcoming, or perhaps leaving the door open at night, to much more major adaptations. For example, in East Cornwall the practice once was to leave holes in the walls of newly built houses so that the pixy routes weren't blocked; in 1852 a man living at Polyphant near Launceston was asked why he'd allowed his cottage wall to remain in disrepair for years. He said that this was so the pixies could continue to come and go as they always had. Putting up with such apparent

---

227. Udal, *Dorsetshire Folklore*, 276.

discomfort must either be a sign of great respect or of the considerable anxiety that thoughts of faery displeasure could instil.[228]

Faery Flits

Common enough amongst humans, moving house is, surprisingly, something for which faerykind is also known, contradicting preconceptions of their timeless presence in particular localities, under certain distinctive faery hills, in groves, or near standing stones. You may well meet the Good Folk just as they are leaving, or arriving in, your area. For certain, this constant motion from house to house may explain some of the faeries' notorious elusiveness.

Our best and most picturesque account comes from the Reverend Robert Kirk in *The Secret Commonwealth of Elves, Fauns and Fairies.* In chapter 2 he describes how

> They remove to other Lodgings at the Beginning of each Quarter of the Year, so traversing till Doomsday, being imputent and [impotent of?] staying in one Place, and finding some Ease by so purning [journeying] and changing Habitations. Their chamælion-lyke Bodies swim in the Air near the Earth with Bag and Bagadge; and at such revolution of Time, Seers, or Men of the second sight, (Fæmales being seldome so qualified) have very terrifying Encounters with them, even on High Ways; who therefoir uswally shune to travell abroad at these four Seasons of the Year...

Aside from the wandering tendency of the *sith* folk, what is noticeable too is that they seem tied to the points in the human calendar when leases tended to expire. That this habit still applies has been confirmed by a twentieth-century witness, who saw the Somerset pixies during one of their quarterly relocations.[229]

Secondly, there is Kirk's quaintly appealing image of the faeries floating along with their luggage. Given their magical powers, you might suppose there were easier ways to move house, but apparently not. One sighting from

228. Leather, *Folklore of Herefordshire*, 43; Courtney, *Cornish Feasts*, 125; *Notes & Queries* 1st series, vol. 5, 173.

229. Dathen, *Somerset Fairies and Pixies*, 17.

Sutherland during the late 1860s portrayed the flit as even more prosaic: the witness saw three carts laden with furniture and other household possessions being dragged over the moorland where there was no road and in a direction in which no human habitation lay. On the Isle of Man, when the flour mill was built at Colby, the local faeries abandoned their former haunts. Early one morning they were seen climbing up into the mists and solitude of the mountain glens, with all their household goods on their backs.[230]

Over and above a natural preference for novelty and change, there are a few other reasons why faeries might switch their residences. As we've just seen from the Isle of Man, some are driven from their homes: the supernaturals may find themselves obliged to move either because they no longer feel welcome in their abode or because physical conditions there have become intolerable. The first situation tends to arise with brownies: well-meaning householders will try to give them clothes as a reward for their hard work or in pity at their nakedness, but this always causes offence and can lead to loss of the being's voluntary labour. The second impulse for a faery departure is very frequently the noise of church bells, which the creatures can find unbearable. Such stories come from Inkberrow in Worcestershire and from Exmoor. The pixies residing on a farm at Withypool had to retreat to the other side of Winsford Hill, a distance of around four to five miles, to escape the sound of the "ding-dongs." For this they begged use of the farmer's cart and horses, another instance of the very physical inconvenience caused to them by moving (just as is the case with us).

Thirdly, domestic faeries may flit because their human families are doing so—or, should we say, are trying to do so. Sometimes humans can find their supernatural housemates (typically boggarts) so vexing that they resolve to move away and leave them behind. This always proves impossible; at some point during the removal it will be discovered that the *entire* household including the sprite has packed up and is on the move; a voice from within the cart piled high with belongings will confirm "aye, we're flitting," in reply to a question from a neighbour come to see the family off. Very frequently the response to this is simply to turn around and head back to the old, familiar home. Interestingly, in one case where trying to escape from the faeries had failed, the householder persuaded them to move on anyway by tricking them into believing

---

230. Sutherland, *Folklore Gleanings*, 22; Herbert, *The Isle of Man*, 1909, 177.

that the household had fallen on hard times and barely had enough to live on. The unwelcome housemates abandoned the humans forthwith.[231]

These accounts make faeries seem much like us: their tenancies expire, their neighbours get on their nerves and, rather than sorting out the problem where they are, they move on. It humanises and domesticates them for us as well as stressing their inextricable links with humankind.

Perhaps the other aspect of these reports is to instil in us an expectation and acceptance that faeries may remove themselves from our locale. For many hundreds of years, it has been said that "faeries used to be seen round here—but no longer." Herein lies the reason: they haven't ceased to exist, they have simply moved elsewhere. The explanation may help us sustain our belief; we don't see them anymore, but someone else does now and—perhaps —some others might move into our neighbourhood soon if we're lucky. This conjecture gains confirmation from an encounter that took place on the Scottish island of Muck in about 1910. Two lads playing on the beach met two tiny boys in green who had disembarked from a small boat off shore. The faery youths told them "We will not be coming back here anymore, but others of our race will be coming."[232]

Faery Childcare

The standard account of the faeries' dealings with human children is a sombre one: they steal infants and leave changelings in their place, bringing grief to mortal families. We will examine this in a later chapter and we've already alluded to the Fae's potential for violence and cruelty. Reassuringly, this is not the whole story. Our Good Neighbours have been known to help children in need, much against their accepted character.

From Norfolk come the little known hyter (or *hikey*) sprites. They are small and elusive faeries, but they are said to be favourable to humans and will return home lost children they come across (and stray donkeys too). Oddly, nevertheless, the threat of the sprites was actually more frequently deployed by parents as a sort of nursery bogie to get children to behave.

A similar report is made of the Scottish Highland spirit called the *gille dubh* (the gilly doo or black boy). His hair is black and he dresses in moss

---

231. Jenkyn Thomas, *Welsh Fairy Book,* "Getting rid of the fairies."
232. Bord, *Fairies,* 63.

and leaves, haunting the woods at the southern end of Loch a Druing near Gairloch. He was known and often seen in the latter half of the eighteenth century and once found a girl called Jessie MacRae wandering at night in the woods. He looked after her kindly, filling her arms with flowers before he took her home in the morning. Jessie was, in fact, the only person to whom the *gille* was ever known to have spoken.

More generally, the Scottish faeries were reputed to take care of children whom they found forgotten.[233] In one story a cowherd fell asleep on a faery hillock and his young son who was with him wandered off. When the man awoke, he presumed that the faeries had abducted the boy until a voice told him that the child had been safely returned home. The *glaistig, connall,* and (less predictably) the Headless Body of Morar all had reputations for looking after lost infants. It was also said of the *glaistigs* that they had particular affinity with those with mental disabilities.[234]

The faeries didn't just care for stray infants: they might participate in the daily childcare of a household. Domestic brownies' duties certainly included rocking the family baby in its cradle. Particular mention should be made of one of the Lowland Scottish brownies called Red Gauntlet who was so trusted by his human household that he would be left to look after the children or to guard the gold when the family and servants were absent from home.[235]

Many faeries also displayed a more general concern for the welfare and good treatment of children. In one story a brother who had agreed to look after one of his sister's children neglects to do so and is punished by the Fae as a result. Faeries might protect, help, and teach children and, from time to time, they have to educate the parents or guardians too, giving them lessons in proper childcare. A woman who neglected her grandchild after its mother's death was reminded of her proper duties by the Fae: whilst she was out the faeries dressed the infant in its mother's clothes and left it lying on the hearth, which was sufficient to reform the woman when she returned. Very similar is the story of Bettie Stogs from Cornwall. She was a drinker and was neglecting herself and her home as well as her baby. The pixies removed the

233. J. G. Campbell, *Superstitions of the Highlands and Islands of Scotland*, c. 1, 40.

234. J. Campbell, *More West Highland tales*, vol. 1, 481, fn. 3; MacGregor, *Peat Fire Flame*, c. 5; MacKenzie, *Scottish Folklore*, 178–9.

235. Dalyell, *The Darker Superstitions of Scotland*, 530; Aitken, *Forgotten Heritage*, 27.

infant, washed its clothes, and left it near the cottage, covered in flowers, by way of a salutary lesson to her.[236]

Setting aside the suffering caused by the faeries' traditional wish to acquire human infants, it was widely accepted that those stolen children would be well cared for when they were in faeryland. There was also reciprocity. A family in Shetland found a lost trow girl, fed her, and put her to bed with their own children. The next morning the trow mother was heard calling and the girl disappeared, but the human children whose bed she'd shared always prospered after that night. Sometimes, too, faery children would be fostered long-term upon humans. If they were well cared for, the Fae parents would show their appreciation with generous gifts (although human neighbours weren't always so understanding: Janet Drever of Shetland was scourged and banished when she admitted she had fostered a trow child in the hill of Westray).[237]

Despite painting this benevolent picture of some faeries, we should confess that, like any parents, their patience might be strained from time to time. From Orkney comes the story of one unfortunate little girl who so pestered the local trows with repeated visits to their underground homes that, in their irritation, they breathed on her and paralysed her for life.[238] This may seem something of an overreaction, but it is reflective of faery tendency to go from one extreme to another.

Faery Gifts

The Good Folk can be generous, spontaneously and unexpectedly, as well as in response to friendly acts toward them. They may choose to endow some people with wealth and good fortune inexplicably, simply because they seem to have taken a liking to them. In other cases, their munificence is less unprovoked largess than a part of the semi-commercial interaction between us that has persisted for centuries.

To those who are prepared to help them, or who happily join in with their games, the faeries can be generous in return—sometimes disproportionately so. A faery in need will always request, and insist upon, a limited amount of flour or meal but the reward can be of far higher value. A Strathspey farmer

---

236. Addy, *Household Tales,* 31 & 42; Davies, *Folklore of West and Mid-Wales,* 102.

237. MacKenzie, *Wonder Tales,* c. IX; Fergusson, *Rambling Sketches,* 14; Owen, *Welsh Folklore,* 60.

238. *County Folklore,* vol. 3, 22.

was asked by a faery woman for a gift of some corn and a song to go with it; he readily complied and in turn received a sack containing a supply of grain that never ran out. On the Isle of Pabbay a faery woman who was either pregnant or nursing and needed food asked for help at a house; she was fed and spent the night there. The next morning, before leaving, she pronounced a spell that no woman of the household would ever again die in childbirth. Other payments have included articles that can heal diseases, the ability to cure or to lessen pain, skill as a midwife that was inherited by subsequent generations, and lifelong success and prosperity.[239]

A regular feature of all such faery gifts is the duty of discretion concerning their source. It is never acceptable to boast about your good fortune nor to show ingratitude, for "if you once throw away faery gifts, you never, never get them back again." The faeries insist upon respect for their privacy and it seems that this extends to their good works, so circumspection is essential. Some people, often for no apparent reason, are lucky enough to be favoured with gifts of faery money. These will appear regularly and sometimes increase exponentially each time. They'll be continued indefinitely so long as discretion is maintained, but as soon as anyone is told, the favour will cease. In some cases, the recipient's lapse in discretion can be far more harshly punished by illness and death.[240]

Related to gifts of money is faery aid in finding hidden treasure. It's not a gift much mentioned now, but certainly until the seventeenth century it was regularly claimed as a faery favour. For example, in June 1499 Marion Clerk of Great Ashfield in Suffolk was prosecuted before a church court for claiming that the faeries helped her locate buried treasure; they had given her a rod of holly for this purpose. Much more recently, in Cornwall, it was believed that catching a faery or spriggan could lead you to gold secreted around the ancient cromlechs, quoits, and barrows. Other soothsayers and healers have claimed to be able to discover lost or stolen goods with the Good Folk's aid.[241]

239. McPherson, *Primitive Beliefs*, 99; or Grant Stewart, *Superstitions*, 125–7; MacGregor, *Peat Fire Flame*, 11; Grant Stewart, *Popular Superstitions*, 105.

240. Roberts, *Folklore of Yorkshire*, 60; Davies, *Folklore of West and Mid-Wales*, 134; Rose Fyleman, "Jan and the Magic Pencil," in *The Rainbow Cat*, 1922; Owen, "Rambles over the Denbighshire Hills," *Archaeologia Cambrensis*, vol. iii, 5th series, no. 9 (1886), 72; *Y Cymmrodor*, vol. 9, 1886, 384.

241. Bottrell, *Traditions and Hearthside Stories*, vol. 1, 72.

Lastly, trying to abuse faery favour will ensure that it's withdrawn completely. There are several examples of this. A farmer who mended a faery tool was rewarded with a supply of food and drink—until he tried to steal a silver spoon that came with his meal. At Cusop near Hay-on-Wye the faeries used to provide dinner to the haymakers in the fields. When one of the men stole one of the faeries' knives, they gave up their helpful ways, even after the man tried to make amends and return the implement. We'll return to this issue in the next chapter.[242]

Offerings

One way of keeping on the right side of the Good Folk is to make gifts to them. This shows respect and, hopefully, encourages their favour. Colliers in North Derbyshire used to leave coal in the mine each week as an offering, doubtless hoping that faery favour would sustain rich seams and prevent pit collapses. The Dartmoor pixies always appreciate a gift of pins or ribbon left at the Pixies' Cave on Sheepstor and will reward the donor.[243]

There seems to be a very fine line, though, between gifts made out of respect and something less voluntary. Sometimes we seem to be dealing with a sacrifice to an angry deity. One Dartmoor sheep farmer's flock was plagued by disease; he concluded that the only remedy was to go to the top of a tor and slaughter a sheep to the pixies—a move which promptly alleviated the problem. A contemporary example comes from a schoolchild in Highland Scotland: he'd knocked down some toadstools and, as these might have been a faery's "wee house," he placed some money under his pillow for the Tooth Faery to take, in order to say he was sorry. There's a good deal of confusion here between old and new ideas: the Tooth Faery seems to have been chosen as a familiar and friendly representative of faerykind generally and as one who's in the habit of entering into deals with children. In this case, however, she's being given coins instead of leaving them in exchange for milk teeth, a reversal of her conventionally recognised role. Although this child's understanding of the function of the Tooth Faery was unusual, he had nonetheless fully grasped the fundamental dynamic of the human relationship with supernaturals—they

---

242. Palmer, *Radnorshire*, 98; Leather, *Folklore of Herefordshire*, 44; Simpson, *Welsh Border*, 72.
243. Addy, *Household Tales*, 141; Coxhead, *Devon Traditions*, 50.

are a dangerous people who should be propitiated, so something is offered to them in the hope of forgiveness and future goodwill.[244]

On other occasions people's "gifts" to the Good Folk bear a closer resemblance to a protection racket. Faery lore expert Katharine Briggs noted that the Good Folk can be "arrant thieves" and that making offerings to them is a way of deflecting their mischief and displeasure. She described it as a form of blackmail and there definitely seems to be some truth in this.[245]

There is one special class of offerings that deserves particular attention. This is the practice of making donations, or gifts, of clothing to the Fae. We find these being made usually to brownies, but boggarts, hobs, and even banshees have also been offered clothes. It's a problematic area because of the varied and unpredictable reaction of the faery to the items presented. One thing is for sure: the faeries can be very touchy on the subject. At Upleatham near Redcar the hob attached to the Oughtred family was outraged by the mere sight of a workman's jacket mistakenly left hanging overnight on a winnowing machine in the barn.

Some faeries accept clothes with delight; some are deeply offended by the idea of wearing human garments. In either instance the outcome seems to be the same: whether the faeries put on the clothes or reject them, they will depart from the service of the family or house for whom they had previously toiled so devotedly. An example of this comes from the Scottish Highlands. One family had a spirit called a Caointeach (keener) attached to it; she would wail and moan before any death. One wet, cold, and windy night she was heard outside a house in which a family member lay ill. One of the company present put a plaid outside and called to the Caointeach to put on the tartan and move herself to the side of the house sheltered from the gale. She was never heard to mourn again.[246]

There seems to be a variety of reasons why clothing can alienate faeries. One story about the Manx brownie, the fenodyree, reveals that the offence can arise from the fact that wearing our clothes will make him ill, causing aches in head and feet.

---

244. V. C. Clinton-Baddeley, *Dartmoor*, 1925, 97; Bennett in Narvaez, *Good People*, 111–112.

245. Briggs, "English Fairies," 274.

246. Roberts, *Folklore of Yorkshire*, 97; Taylor & Troon, *Midlothian Folk Tales*, 112; L. Spence, *The Fairy Tradition in Britain*, 36–37; MacDougall, *Folk Tales*, 215.

Some faeries appear to want clothes (and even ask directly for clothing in recompense for their labours) but they may still be upset by the quality of what they're given—in most cases finding garments of coarse hemp or linen unacceptable (because presumably they wanted cotton or wool). Once again, the perceived insult will lead to their prompt departure.[247]

Sometimes humans get it wrong and give the wrong sort of clothes. In other cases, a gift is wanted—but it isn't garments. This is set out for us in a ballad, "The Life of Robin Goodfellow," published in 1628. In response to being presented with a linen waistcoat, Robin exclaims,

> Because thou lay'st me himpen, hampen,
> I will neither bolt nor stampen.
> 'Tis not your garments new or old,
> That Robin loves; I feele no cold.
> Had you left me milke or creame,
> You should have had a pleasing dreame;
> Because you left no drop nor crum,
> Robin never more will come.

The faeries in all these cases have undertaken voluntarily to attach themselves to a household and to work there without acknowledgement or substantial reward (other than the classic bowl of milk or cream—and this sharing of food might be seen as accepting the brownie as part of the household and not as a mere worker). Providing payment in kind seems to violate this unspoken arrangement and to seek to formalise it on quasi-contractual grounds. Food left out at night doesn't seem to create the same bond or obligation as arises from providing clothes made specially. There may be a connotation of livery or uniform here, too—of the brownie's subjugation to control and organisation of the human household. Perhaps, as these faeries tend to choose to go about naked or dressed in tatters, the offer of human clothes may also be offensive because it represents another aspect of subjection to human society and behaviour.[248]

---

247. Spence, *The Fairy Tradition in Britain*, 36–37; Barton, *North Yorkshire Folk Tales*, 3; Roberts, *Folklore of Yorkshire*, 96–98.

248. Bailey, *Lancashire Folk Tales*, 91.

There is one anomalous account from Dartmoor of coins being left out for the pixies at night. Nevertheless, paying for the work to be done by the Fae is not how this relationship functions and to attempt to commercialise it will virtually always prove to be a bad idea.[249]

Politeness and Respect

A cheerful helper or participant is what the faeries prefer. A man from Northamptonshire joined in with a faery game of football, perhaps a little over-enthusiastically: he kicked the ball too hard and it burst. The faeries vanished instantly and he fell down in a faint but, when he awoke, he found their punctured ball had been left behind and that it was full of gold coins.[250]

Anyone who genuinely and honestly deals with the faeries on their terms may expect good treatment. A man who went to a faery market and bought a pewter cider mug—which he paid for in gold and for which he received his change in dry leaves—did not grumble or question the bargain. He accepted it cheerfully and so, the next morning, found that his mug was silver and his change was lumps of gold. In a related incident, a man came across a pixie fair between Pitminster and Blagdon on the Blackdown Hills in Somerset. He too bought a mug—and was presented with pebbles as his change. He made no protest at this and was not surprised to find, when he got home, that the mug had changed into a giant puffball mushroom. When he awoke the next morning, however, he discovered that the pebbles had become gold.[251]

All the same, there seems to be a fine line here. A good principle to follow is to never say thank you. This isn't just a matter of avoiding verbal gratitude: gifts to faeries that acknowledge some obligation on their part—or that might even suggest some reciprocity may exist between our two worlds—are as likely to offend.

Kindness and Sharing

Another way of retaining the Good Folk's goodwill is to be prepared to share with them. A Scottish miller who let the Fae use his mill to grind their corn

---

249. Crossing, *Tales of Dartmoor Pixies*, c. 3.

250. Sternberg, *Dialect and Folklore*, 137.

251. Mathews, *Tales of the Blackdown Borderland*, 57.

at night was favourably treated. When his son succeeded him and tried to prevent their nightly takeovers by shutting off the mill leat at the end of the day, misfortunes and accidents were visited upon him. Loans of tools, mending broken implements, and help finding lost items are all appreciated and rewarded, especially if the person who helps is themselves deprived or inconvenienced in some way. A faery woman visited a Highland home and asked for a cup of flour. Even though supplies were low, as it was nearly time for the new harvest, the housewife gave her visitor what she asked for—and in return was granted a never-ending supply of meal.[252]

The Fae will always reward good deeds by humans, such as caring for faery infants or providing food or other goods when they are in need of them. Housewives and servants who remember to leave out fresh water for the faeries at night regularly are rewarded with a gift of money. Where exactly all these coins that are given to favourites come from is an interesting question. The Good Folk have little need for currency and from the information we have, it seems that their economy works solely on the basis of barter. We have to conclude that the money they leave is actually stolen, or perhaps comes from a hidden hoard they have discovered—which may explain the ancient or unknown coins that are sometimes received.[253]

It's comforting to know that a good turn won't be forgotten, either. Although, as we'll mention in the next chapter, faery grudges can be long-standing, a person who's behaved well toward them may get their reward many years later. A story often told concerns a person whose drains were flowing into a faery house underneath his front door. The faeries complained and he took prompt steps to remedy the fault. Years later, facing execution for some offence, a faery suddenly appeared on the scaffold to rescue him.[254]

The Good Folk can also show favour to those who are poor and needy. For example, in the story of Gowan Dell, a sheep farmer whose stock were dying in a severe drought was helped with a gift of faery gold. He bought two new cows and the faeries then revealed to him a rich pasture hidden in the nearby

---

252. Aitken, *Forgotten Heritage*, 7; Allies, *On the Ancient British, Roman and Saxon Antiquities of Worcestershire*, 418–9; Anon, *Folklore and legends: Scotland*, 98.

253. Aitken, *Forgotten Heritage*, 14 & 15; Anon, *Folklore & legends*, 1; see Bottrell, *Traditions and hearthside stories*, vol. 2, 162—faeries bartering at a market.

254. Bett, *English Myths and Traditions*, 14.

dell. The cows produced plentiful milk and the grass was never exhausted. At Morewood's Farm, Holmesfield, in Derbyshire, the faeries tidied a woman's home whilst she was absent at her daughter's funeral and in Northumberland an overworked housewife and mother was assisted in her many chores by a hobthrush—until she drove him away with a gift of clothes.[255]

It's clear again from the last case that the faeries ask nothing for their gratuitous labours except perhaps a gift of food or drink. Material reward is not looked for in return for their kindnesses, but a properly expressed sense of gratitude still seems to be. Some Sussex faeries helped a sick workman by undertaking his thrashing whilst he slept, but when he awoke and laughed aloud in surprise at what he saw, their goodwill was withdrawn.[256]

The faeries may also help those in peril. Doonie, a type of Scottish Lowland brownie who lived in the wilderness, once caught a man who had fallen over a cliff whilst out hunting. Even so, he was warned not to seek prey there again—or else Doonie might not be there to save him. In this story, the brownie has a role as guardian of the natural environment, it seems, but she is probably also acting to preserve her privacy from intruders.[257]

In Wales the tylwyth teg are thought to help those lost in mist on the mountains—sometimes by accompanying them home, sometimes by conjuring inns or other accommodation which provide warm beds and food but which disappear the next morning. The faeries might even prevent men and women from committing crimes: the Fae would set up ropes at night to keep people away from places where they would get themselves into trouble. An attempt to get over the ropes would leave the potential miscreant entangled until morning. This wish to keep mortals on the straight and narrow is surprising given the faeries' own thieving proclivities, but it is nonetheless a recurring element of Welsh folk belief.[258]

Lastly, there are examples of people in need or in danger invoking faery aid. A farm labourer in Aberdeenshire called on the "red cappies" to come and help him thrash the corn and with their supernatural aid he got through

---

255. Aitken, *Forgotten Heritage*, 21; Addy, *Household Tales*, 135; Grice, *Folk Tales*, c. 7.

256. J. Simpson, *Folklore of Sussex*, 52; see also Gwyndaf in Narvaez, *Good People*, 176.

257. Aitken, *Forgotten Heritage*, 37.

258. Palmer, *Gloucestershire*, 145; Gwyndaf in Narvaez, *Good People*, 177.

the work in record time. A boy from Rhayader in Powys was lost at night and asked the faeries to guide him; they sent lights to lead him home. Lastly, an inhabitant of the Scottish island of Barra found himself stuck whilst climbing the cliffs at Mingulay. Unable to go either up or down, he cried out to anyone who would help him. The *sluagh,* the faery host, answered his call and carried him up to the clifftop. However, in this case, the charitable rescue came at a price, because from that time forward he was at the mercy of the *sluagh* and was liable to be carried away by them at any moment.[259]

Summary

Successful relationships with faeries are tricky to manage. The Good Folk can prove touchy and finicky and dealings with them have to be cautious and sensitive. The best guidelines may be a reserved respect and willing reciprocity; there's always a fine balance to be struck between openness toward them and anything that might be taken as prying. By way of example: in one Shetland folktale a traveller came across two trows fighting each other. He stayed to watch at a respectful distance but was eventually noticed by the trows when they had stopped fighting through sheer exhaustion. We might anticipate that they would have been offended that he had spied upon their private disagreement, but instead they felt kindly toward him—partly because he was footsore and tired and partly because he had not tried to intervene in the fight nor shown any partiality to either side. For this, they used their magic to carry him swiftly over the remaining distance to his home.[260]

Much of traditional faery lore shows that people's attitude toward the Good Folk has been one of nervous appeasement. Nevertheless, we should never seek blatantly to solicit their favour and it's useless to be supplicants. Their friendship can only be bestowed and there's no certain way of earning it. If they do look kindly upon us, though, they are good friends to have: they can be generous, scrupulously fair, and committed allies.

---

259. McPherson, *Primitive Beliefs,* 98; Palmer, *Radnorshire,* 99; J. MacPherson, *Tales from Barra,* 178.

260. Nicolson, *Folktales and Legends.*

Chapter 10

DANGEROUS CONTACTS—HARM DONE BY FAERIES

The problem with the Good Folk is that they have a natural tendency to mischief and, where they are offended or simply maliciously inclined, this can shade into outright vindictiveness. It has been said of Scottish faeries that they are "as active as squirrels and as numerous as rabbits," taking an "embarrassing interest in human affairs" and, as a result, often proving "terribly troublesome." One Herefordshire man defined the Fae simply as "little people that come into folk's houses to steal things." These comments may seem harsh but, as I suggested earlier when discussing faery religion, the Good Folk do not seem to be guided by a code of moral principles so much as by caprice, self-regard, and self-interest.[261]

The Good Folk are unpredictable, as capable of being vengeful as grateful, as likely to show spite as kindness. They will borrow from humans—and return the compliment, often several-fold—but they might prefer just to steal. Although the so-called trooping faeries were said to steal cattle only when they were involved in one of their periodic relocations, the "Good

---

261. Aitken, *Forgotten Heritage*, 1; Leather, *Folklore of Herefordshire*, 43.

Neighbours" who live in close proximity to humans all the time have come to have a more proprietorial attitude to human possessions. They are thought to be engaged in daily thefts.

Given the attention paid to humans by their Good Neighbours and given their temperament, it's obviously advisable, wherever possible, to avoid conduct that's likely either to attract their attention or to antagonise them. They are a people who are "easily offended and who are implacable in their resentments." They've been described as "good friends to those men and women who pleased them [but] relentless enemies to others."[262]

Mischief

Writer Mary Lewes described the Welsh faeries as "mischievous if thwarted, but kind and good-natured otherwise." Pixies seem to have an especially bad reputation: they may sometimes be good and kind, but they are more frequently mischievous and harm those they spite. Mischief is in their nature, so much so that it's even been said that their king deliberately sends his subjects on errands to torment and trick us humans.[263]

Sometimes the Good Folk are mischievous for the pure fun of it; sometimes they may be punishing a human misdemeanour. Pixies especially seem to love to annoy us by plaiting the manes and tails of horses at night, but even so on Dartmoor it was believed to be bad luck to try to comb the hair smooth again. The only remedy was to cut the plait out, but despite this, it was said that the horses were spoiled after the experience.[264]

As noted in the last chapter, the Good Folk will enter houses at night, purely to mock or scare the inhabitants, to play and to make noise. A particular delight seems to be disturbing the occupants' slumbers, whether that's by clattering about in the kitchen or, more directly, by bouncing on the sleep-

---

262. Jones, *Aberystruth*, 74; Lewes, *Queer Side*, 119.

263. Lewes, *Stranger than Fiction*, 160; Bray, *Description of the Part of Devonshire Bordering on the Tamar and Tavy*, 173–4; Wright, *Picturesque South Devonshire*, 16.

264. See too Mercutio's famous speech about Queen Mab in Shakespeare's *Romeo & Juliet* (Act I, scene 4, line 91): elf-locks, "once untangled, much misfortune bodes."

ers, pulling off their bedclothes or dragging them by their heels from their beds and down the stairs.[265]

Worse, the faeries have a range of tricks designed purely to hinder and irritate people in their domestic routines. They may change coins for imitation "faery gold," eat the children's porridge, ride horses, blow out candles, kiss people unexpectedly, and steal butter. A favourite prank, even today, is to hide keys. The charm used to deal with this in Herefordshire is to place a piece of cake on the hearth and then get the entire household to sit in a circle, silent and with their eyes closed. The Fae will have to return the hidden keys, flinging them against the wall behind the sitters.

Amongst the household spirits like hobs and brownies, mischief might manifest itself in *undoing* work that's already been done: Robin Round Cap of Spaldington Hall near Selby in Yorkshire delighted in mixing chaff into the winnowed wheat, putting out the fire, or upsetting the milk pail. Other nuisances that would interfere with farm work include setting the livestock loose or turning them into the clover, hiding tools, tripping up people carrying full buckets, stopping butter churning, making yeast go stale, and souring the milk and cream.[266]

Brownies and hobs who have been permanently alienated by the household in which they have been living may desert it or, probably worse, they may stay but only in order to cause a nuisance. It's sometimes said that a brownie scorned becomes a boggart. In West Yorkshire some homes were so notorious for the trouble caused by the vexed household sprite that they came to be known as "boggart houses"—and quite a few of these can still be found. In fact, even helpful hobs might spend their leisure time elsewhere, scaring innocent travellers. There was a tradition that boggarts would disguise themselves as stones on moorland tracks, deliberately to trip up passersby. Animals, especially horses, can see them better than people can and often when they rear up unexpectedly it's because they have "taken the boggart"—they've spotted one, even if it doesn't look like a boggart.[267]

---

265. Sir Walter Scott, *Owlspiegle and Cockledemoy*; Dixon, *Gairloch in North West Ross-shire*, 159; Harland, *Lancashire Legends & Traditions*, 56.

266. Lewes, *Queer Side*, 119; Harland, *Lancashire Folklore*, 53; Roberts, *Folklore of Yorkshire*, 98.

267. Roberts, *Folklore of Yorkshire*, 99–102; Billingsley, *West Yorkshire Folk Tales*, 37–41.

One last, and very curious, example: It appears that faery dancing might also be used as an opportunity for mischief. In 1884 a postman on the Isle of Man found his horse and cart surrounded one night by a group of faeries. They encircled him, dancing around in a ring, and proceeded to throw the mail sacks out of the cart into the road. As fast as he replaced them, the Fae threw them out again. This went on for nearly four hours until sunrise. It is perhaps an example of the faeries combining business with pleasure …[268]

Pixy-Leading

The Good Folk's greatest form of mischief is the sport of pixy-leading people at night—steering them astray from their path, even in places they know very well indeed. On Dartmoor there are so-called "pixy lanes" where you will always lose your way and a popular saying is "he got out of the muxy (mire) and fell into the pucksy (a bog)"; the bog-cotton that grows in those marshy spots is known as "pixy-grass." Many people are pixy-led just for the fun of it, but the faeries will also mislead those who have trespassed on their ground, insulted them, taken their property and, more generally, whose conduct they disapprove of. A man from Bishop's Lydeard in the Quantock Hills came across a faery grindstone and decided to keep it as a curiosity; a mist promptly came down and he was led through brambles all night as a result. Another Somerset farmer, who cheated customers at market; who was lazy, thieving, and drunken; and who mistreated his wife and children, was punished in the same way.[269]

Although the commonly used phrase is "pixy-led," we shouldn't suppose that it is just the pixies of South West England who like to cause mischief for travellers. Two girls from Llandysul in Wales were returning home one evening from Lampeter Fair. They got as far as the field next to their home, but then spent several hours trying to find their way out, even though it was a moonlit night and they knew the field intimately. In another Welsh case something similar happened in a man's own bedroom. He awoke to see a group of faeries feasting and dancing on the floor. He was unable to rouse his wife to witness the revels and lay there for about four hours watching with

268. Bord, *Fairies*, 42–43.

269. Coxhead, *Devon Traditions,* 50; Tongue, *Somerset Folklore,* 114 & 115.

a mixture of fear and amazement. Eventually the faeries departed and the man got up to see if they'd moved elsewhere in the house. He was unable to find the bedroom door—or to get back to the bed—and it was only when his panicked cries awoke the rest of the family that the spell was finally broken. Very often those who've been led in circles for hours by the Good Folk are only able to escape by attracting a third party who intervenes to save them.[270]

Very similar to the Dartmoor pixy-lanes, on Shetland there are grass "gaits" (paths) along which it's known that the trows process in the evenings when they emerge from their hills and at dawn when they return. It's unlucky to cross these at twilight and those who do so will find themselves separated from their companions and led astray.[271]

Generally, the impact of being pixy-led is frustration, confusion, and perhaps mild panic. Occasionally the consequences can be far more serious. In a case described by the Reverend Edmund Jones, a John Jacob of Bedw in Monmouthshire was travelling at night when he lost his way. The faeries misled him, appearing as shapes ahead of him and then vanishing as he drew close. Eventually he stumbled across a neighbour's house and was taken in, but his ordeal was not over. He fell mute and heavy, soon sickened, and then died. A similar story comes from Dartmoor: A man walking home drunk at night was led in circles until he was giddy and fainted. When he awoke, he was able to get home, but he straightaway took to his bed and was dead within a few days.[272]

I mentioned the protective powers of bread earlier and one of the surefire ways of avoiding being pixy-led is to carry a piece of bread with you at night (the Scottish Highland equivalent is to have oatmeal in your pocket or sprinkled over your clothes). Another simple remedy, if you do find yourself lost and going in circles yards from your own front door, is to turn your pockets or your coat inside out or to reverse your hat—this too is guaranteed to dispel the enchantment. Turning your gloves inside out and throwing them at the pesky pixies also seems to work. Given the simplicity of this remedy, prudent travellers at night have been known to reverse an item of

---

270. Davies, *Folklore of West and Mid-Wales*, 192 & 123; Mathews, *Blackdown Borderland*, 58 & 62.

271. Firth, *Reminiscences of an Orkney Parish*, 75.

272. Jones, *Apparition*, no. 82; *Transactions of Devonshire Association*, vol. 8 (1876), 722.

clothing before they even set out, so as to ensure protection throughout their journey. In extreme cases, stripping off your clothes and sitting on them for five to thirty minutes—as long as is necessary for the mental (or real) fog to dissipate—is recommended.

A final mention should be made of the so-called will-o'-the-wisp. This supernatural being exists solely to lead travellers out of their way and into ponds and marshes. As recently as 1965 people confessed that they were afraid to venture onto the moors near Warleggan in Cornwall because of the dancing red, white, and blue lights that would lead them into peril.[273]

Faery mischief in all its forms casts an interesting light on our relationship with our near neighbours. In many respects, the Fae seem to regard people as their playthings. One commentator called them "veritable little demons" because of their "endless" pranks, but this satanic allusion is misplaced. The Good Folk are agents of neither hell nor heaven. Their ethics are their own. Whilst moral lessons may sometimes be enforced by their tricks, as a rule they seem merely to take delight in taunting and annoying us.[274]

Eavesdropping

I mentioned the faery habit of listening in to human conversations when I described the medieval Welsh account of the *Coraniaid* (see chapter 2). They were regarded as a plague by the population because nothing could be kept secret from them. This ability to overhear has since been inherited by the modern Welsh tylwyth teg, but the problem is by no means limited to Wales.

An example of the faeries' alarmingly acute hearing and their constant proximity is found in the ballad of Lady Isabel and the Elf Knight. Sitting in her bower, Isabel hears the knight's horn sound and wishes to herself that he might be there with her, sleeping in her bosom. Instantly, he is at her window. His designs upon her are murderous rather than amorous, so there's also a suggestion in this tale of the idea of letting in a vampire.

The faeries don't like to be spoken of and, as they can always be present yet invisible, the best advice is to speak of them with respect, especially on those days when their power is at its greatest. They will always exact ven-

---

273. Deane & Shaw, *Folklore of Cornwall*, 90; see too Charlotte Dacre's poem, *Will O' Wisp*.
274. Page, *Dartmoor*, 37.

geance on those who've spoken ill of them, but also anyone who has spoken unwisely. This will include those who invoke or make promises to the faeries, those who make rash wishes, and those either who don't appreciate faery favour—or their own good luck.

Faery Punishments

If they're displeased with you, the Good Folk have various ways of demonstrating their ill will. They may take away your good fortune, they may deprive you of (second) sight, and, most commonly, they may cripple you. We've already noticed several cases where people have been lamed or otherwise disabled for some slight (perceived or otherwise).

These injuries are normally inflicted by means of a direct blow to the limb in question. They may be temporary and curable (such as a girl's dislocated leg) but they are in most cases lifelong afflictions. Disablement is a punishment deliberately applied in the vast majority of cases, but in one source there's also a hint, at least, that it may be a consequence of simply spending too much time with the Good Folk. In 1499 a Suffolk woman, Agnes Clerk, told a church court how, as a young woman, she had spent a lot of time talking with "les Elvys." The effect had been for her head and neck to become twisted backward, a condition which was finally cured with a blessing—a good indication of its supernatural nature, as we'll see soon.

Strains, sprains, and stiffness in joints and limbs were so much identified with the faeries that one medieval writer, Hereford friar John of Bromyard, even noted down a charm for healing the sprains termed "the bite of elves." The lameness caused by a faery blow has no visible wound and comes on suddenly; it marks out the afflicted persons within their community as ones who have offended the Fae, making them a constant reminder to themselves and to the others of the cost of showing insufficient respect and consideration toward our Good Neighbours.

Faery Filching

The faeries will take anything that has been lost, destroyed, discarded, or rejected by humans; they've been described as "thieves by inclination"— habitual criminals, if you will … For example, liquids that are spilled and crumbs of food dropped during cooking or eating go to the faeries, as do goods that are destroyed by fire, and cattle that have died. It was thought in the Highlands that when a cow fell off a cliff, the only way to stop the Fae taking the carcase was to act quickly and put a nail in it.[275]

As well as asserting a right to wasted items, the faeries seem to claim some sort of tax or tithe on the rest of our goods. A woman who gleaned too thoroughly in the fields after harvest was roughly handled by the faeries because she had deprived them of what they regarded as their customary share of the grain (the same consideration may well lie behind the practice of leaving some apples in an orchard at harvest time, as mentioned before). Undoubtedly related to this is the Cornish idea that to ensure a good harvest the reapers should always throw a piece of bread over their shoulder and spill a few drops of their beer at meal break. We will see how the tin miner called Tom Trevorrow, who never left a crumb of his lunch for the knockers in the mine, lost all his luck because of his meanness. These ideas seem to be somewhere between an offering and an indication of the faeries' sense that they're entitled to a share of all the goods and food that we produce.[276]

This attitude of entitlement easily shades into out-and-out theft by the Good Folk. There appears to be little compunction about this and the nocturnal household invasions described earlier will often be for more than just playing pranks. I've already mentioned the faeries' notorious habit of stealing milk and cream. Other goods and foodstuffs are equally vulnerable. Northamptonshire poet John Clare recorded the popular sentiment on this: mice were not reckoned greater thieves, he wrote, and the faeries were compared to wasps in a grocer's shop, streaming in through the keyholes, "pop, pop, pop."[277]

Food is the most commonly stolen item across Britain, but the faeries have even been known to take cooking implements. In the Highlands it used to be the case that hand mills were particularly vulnerable to theft. The way to protect them was always to turn the grindstones sunwise during use. The trows of Shetland will even steal fire from a human hearth if their own goes out.

---

275. Lewes, *Stranger than Fiction,* 160; Grant Stewart, *Popular Superstitions,* 122–124; MacGregor, *Peat Fire Flame,* 3.

276. Murray, *Tales from Highland Perthshire,* no. 103.

277. John Clare, *January.*

The faeries will steal from anywhere, too. Cattle in fields are vulnerable, homes will be entered, and they are confident enough to enter shops and markets and steal openly there. For example, from the English Lake District we have an account of faeries mingling with the crowds at Ambleside market. When they found an item they wanted, they blew in the eyes of the stall-holders, rendering themselves invisible, and then made off with the goods.[278]

Curiously, whilst the faeries show no qualms over taking human property, it is forbidden for them to steal off each other. The story is told on Shetland of a trow boy who was often seen wandering alone and miserable. Apparently, he had stolen a silver spoon from another trow and his punishment was to be banished from beneath the hills. It seems that faeries can be strict about how they should treat each other, as well as how humans should behave toward them, yet they can be blissfully amoral in their treatment of us.[279]

Another irony is that, whilst the faeries don't hesitate to steal, they don't like to be unjustly accused of theft. A man called Rob o' t' Deans who lived at Walsden in West Yorkshire was very prone to thieving off his neighbours, but he would always seem very concerned over their losses, helped to search for the missing items—and would loudly blame the faeries. The Fae took note of his calumnies and, eventually, they got their revenge. He was crossing the moor one night, carrying home some stolen cloth, when he came upon a faery dance. He sneaked up and watched it for hours, eventually falling asleep where he was hidden. The faeries knew all about his presence, of course, and Rob stayed fast asleep until the next morning when early risers discovered him, still holding the stolen bolts of worsted.[280]

Vampire Faeries

There's a couple of references suggestive of an even more sinister aspect to the character of some faeries, involving the theft of humans' life forces, their breath, or their blood. This "vampire behaviour" is something rarely mentioned but it is not wholly out of character with more widely reported examples of malign faery conduct. We've mentioned already the abduction

---

278. Cowper, *Hawkshead*, 307.

279. Saxby, *Shetland Traditional Lore*, 140.

280. Billingsley, *West Yorkshire Folk Tales*, 156.

or "taking" of people. This can involve the abstraction of their vital essence, leaving an inanimate stock behind: their soul is in Faery and a lifeless shell remains. Related perhaps to this is the Shetland belief that trows can only appear in human form if they can find someone who's not been protected by "saining" or blessing with holy words. This form of faery "possession" can be deadly.

Breath

Let's begin with a few lines from Shakespeare's *Comedy of Errors*. The character Dromio of Syracuse exclaims,

> This is the faeryland. O! The spite of spites,
> We talk with goblins, owls and elvish sprites:
> If we obey them not, this will ensue,
> They'll suck our breath, or pinch us black and blue.[281]

Many of you will be familiar with the idea of pinching as a regular faery punishment; it's a fairly harmless sanction for the relatively minor transgression of poor housekeeping. But, "suck our breath"? We must assume that Shakespeare was aware of a genuine tradition when he wrote these lines: he seemed to draw on authentic folklore for much of his faery material, so this presumably reflects something he'd encountered.

Relevant to this brief allusion may be a fragment from Rudyard Kipling. He wrote a story called "Fairy-Kist" that describes the mental state of a man who'd been wounded and gassed whilst serving in the Great War. He was left in a poor mental state, "practically off his head," a condition which his family labelled "fairy-kist." This appears to be a West Country phrase meaning kissed by the faeries. In both these brief mentions, we have the suggestion of oral assault, a possibility of an authentic folklore source, and a description of the impact upon the victim's mental health.

The idea of faery breath being perilous is certainly widespread, from Ireland and Britain to the Scandinavian countries. It's known variously as elf-wind, gust, or blast and can cause blisters. It's a frequent feature of British

---

281. William Shakespeare, *A Comedy of Errors*, 1594, Act 2, scene 2.

faery stories that human midwives who have abused the faeries' ointment and rubbed it on their own eyes will be found out and blinded by a puff of breath in the face. In fact, "elf-wind" is still a term used today in Nordic lands for medical conditions, just as in English "stroke" (from "elf-struck") is still employed. In Norway it's said that a person will be afflicted if they stand on a spot where an elf spat on the ground. Doubtless derived from Norse belief, on Shetland it was thought that elf-winds often blew on a person and caused a skin disease. The cure was to open a Bible and brush the affected part a few times. Also in the Northern Isles there lived a creature called Nuckelavee, part horse and part man, whose breath was believed to be extremely venomous, blighting whole neighbourhoods with pestilence.[282]

Blood

Next, we have a chilling tale of faery vampirism from the Highlands of Scotland. Four hunters on the Braes of Lochaber stayed overnight in a bothy. Shortly after each had lamented the absence of their girlfriends, the women themselves entered the hut. Whilst the others were in their lovers' arms, one man was suspicious and held off his alleged sweetheart with his knife and by playing a (metal) Jew's harp. The women disappeared at cockcrow and it became clear that they had not been the girls at all but *glaistigs*. The three trusting companions lay dead, their throats cut and their bodies drained of blood.

It was said in both Scotland and the Isle of Man that water was left out for the faeries overnight not so much as a courtesy, but to give them something to quench their thirsts so that they would not take the sleepers' blood. Consumption was thought in Scotland and Ireland to be the progressive result of such faery bleeding. In Cromarty it was believed that the "lady in green" carried her child from cottage to cottage at night, bathing it in the blood of the youngest inhabitant. There are similar Highland tales of birdlike green women who crack bones and drink blood; there is, finally, a tale from Skye

---

282. Marwick, *The Folklore of Orkney*, 23 & 45; Crofton Croker, *Fairy Legends,* 117; conditions such as dermatitis, urticaria, shingles, herpes, and hives are all denoted.

similar to that of the four men of Lochaber: eight girls tending cattle were attacked by an "old woman" who sucked the blood of all but one.[283]

There are faery beasts that exist solely to catch and consume hapless humans. The vampire-like faery maidens I've described here are somewhat different, and they are using their physical allure for novel ends; nevertheless, seduction by faeries with a view to abduction to Faery is a familiar enough theme, although this is a gruesomely different version.

Summary

Living with the Good Folk as our neighbours involves accommodations. We have to accept that their attitudes to privacy and personal property are different to our own and that the best view we should take of our relationship is that they will expect to exploit and play tricks upon us. If we approach them on this basis, and adapt and prepare accordingly, we should be relatively safe and will sometimes be pleasantly surprised. If we respond badly to their interventions, they may make us suffer; if we antagonise them purposefully, the response may be even worse—as we are about to see.

---

283. Spence, *The Fairy Tradition in Britain* chapter XIV, 268–269; Miller, *Scenes and Legends of the North of Scotland*, 15.

Chapter 11

DANGEROUS CONTACTS—HARM DONE TO FAERIES

Throughout this book I've stressed the need to approach the faeries warily, because of the risk of harm from them—whether provoked or not. In this chapter I'll examine those situations where humans harm faeries—deliberately or not—and the consequences of doing so. The harm inflicted may be nominal—an insult to faery dignity, perhaps—and the response may be disproportionate to the offence caused or injury inflicted. Usually, then, we still come off worst, but this needn't always be the case, as you may be surprised to see.

Doubt and Insults

It may hardly need to be said that loud proclamations of disbelief in Faery, a frivolous or contemptuous attitude toward the faery folk, or a declared intention to injure them or steal from them are all bound to be heard and answered. One Cornish tin miner called Trevorrow mocked the knockers' purported powers and refused to share his lunchtime *fuggan* (cake) with them. He was first hit by a fall of stones underground and, when he did not take the hint, a rock fall completely buried the lode he was working as well as all his tools. He had to abandon mining completely and become a farm labourer. Another miner called Barker announced that he was going to spy on the knockers and to try to steal their tools. They were, of course, very well aware of his plan and lamed him for his presumption.[284]

Disbelief in the face of tangible proof of the faeries' existence and capabilities is especially hated. Not infrequently, in the stories of humans who win faery favour by mending broken tools, there will also be a companion who doubts and mocks any such assistance. In a Sussex version of the story of the broken peel mended by a ploughman his mate scorns the whole idea—and dies a year to the day later. The least violent of these types of tale may be the Dartmoor story of Nanny Norrish, whose scepticism is answered one night when she meets the pixies piled up before her in a pyramid and all chattering loudly. Nanny appears to have got off lightly, as another writer averred that the pixies' "malevolence will know no end" toward one who's spoken ill of them.[285]

Just as much as lack of faith, the Good Folk don't like to be contradicted or to feel that their wishes have been thwarted or ignored. A Shetland man who stumbled across a trow dance one night unwisely got into an argument with them. One of the dancers struck him on his heel with a heather stalk, leaving him crippled for the rest of his life. A woman of Trevethin parish in South Wales, when she was still a child, discovered the Fair Folk dancing under a crab apple tree. For several years she would meet them twice daily, on her way to or from school, and would dance with them. When she ceased her visits and no longer joined in their revelry, they dislocated her leg as a sign of their displeasure.[286]

Deliberately abusing or offending the Fae is also to be avoided. In the last chapter we examined the touchy nature of brownies and how they can abandon their homes if they feel insulted by a gift of clothes. Mocking or criticising when the faeries are assisting you can be a terrible misjudgement. One Cornish brownie went on strike when he felt slighted. An old mill in mid-Cornwall benefitted from the presence of this domestic pisky,

---

284. Deane & Shaw, *Folklore of Cornwall,* 69–70.

285. Simpson, *Sussex,* 53; Crossing, *Tales of Dartmoor Pixies,* c. 7; Page, *Dartmoor,* 37; see too Saxby, *Shetland Traditional Lore,* 157, & Billingsley, *West Yorkshire Folk Tales,* 41.

286. Jones, *Appearance of Evil,* para. 117.

who worked hard at the grinding and was scrupulously honest. One day a dispute arose over a failed delivery of grain. At first the miller blamed his wife; then he accused the pisky of causing the mix up. The pisky heard this, of course, and swore an oath not to do another stroke of work for the next two generations. It's hard to say whether the response in the following story from Scotland was better or worse. A new servant of a family in Glenfeochan made a disparaging remark about the *gruagach* that served the household; in response, she received a slap that twisted her neck. The only way this could be righted was by asking for the *gruagach*'s forgiveness—and a compensating slap in the opposite direction.[287]

Others who've cursed or maligned the faeries have faced far more serious consequences. Disparaging their work can even prove fatal. A Sussex farmer discovered the faeries threshing his grain in his barn at night. He laughed at the tiny beings' exertions and was struck with a flail, a blow from which he never recovered. A Highlander called Hugh Ross met three women playing in a tree; unwisely, he decided to interfere and told them they ought to be at home doing their wifely chores. Although they were all dressed in green and behaving oddly, he had not realised they were faeries—but this foolishness did not spare him. One of the women climbed down and struck him in the face with a twig. He immediately fell to the ground but recovered enough to get home, where he took to his bed and soon died.[288]

You may well feel that in at least some of these cases the humans did not deserve their treatment, but—as in everything—the Fae can be unpredictable and disproportionate. Caution, gratitude, politeness, and a preparedness to do what *they* want are generally the best ways of keeping on the right side of the Good Folk.

Meanness and Ingratitude

The faeries like those who show them generosity. The flipside of this is that any perceived meanness in their treatment will be treated severely. At Farnsdale, in North Yorkshire, a son and his new wife inherited a farm from his father. With it came the resident hob who did many of the chores around the

---

287. Harris, *Cornish Saints and Sinners*, c. 19.

288. MacKenzie, *Scottish Folklore*, 212; Simpson, *Sussex*, 53; MacDougall, *Folk Tales*, 223; see too Hunt, *Popular Romances*, 97.

holding. The wife, being unused to faery helpers, begrudged him his nightly jug of cream and left out just thin, watery whey instead. The indignant hob duly departed, taking the farm's prosperity with him. A similar case on a farm near Whitby in 1824 provoked the hob into making noise, pulling off bed covers at night, and killing the poultry. There is a sense of entitlement to their offerings and the Fae will punish those who neglect them and breach this unspoken contract.

The faeries particularly dislike people who try to take back their gifts. In Herefordshire a faery woman disguised as a beggar visited a baker's shop and begged for a piece of dough. She was given a small piece which she then asked to be allowed to bake in the oven. As it cooked, it swelled magically in size, as a result of which the baker's daughter confiscated the loaf to sell in the shop instead. This was repeated two more times until the faery woman lost her temper and turned the greedy and selfish daughter into an owl.

As we've also already seen, generosity to the faeries when you're in need yourself will be appreciated, but pretending to be unable to help when in fact you're well able to do so will inevitably be punished. If they come begging to borrow flour and you say you have little when you have plenty, it's a sure-fire way of ensuring that you do end up with very little.

Promises made to the Fae should always be kept. In Cornwall a tin miner called Trenowth had promised the mine faeries, the knockers, a share of the profits of a rich lode if they let him exploit it, but he then decided not to keep his side of the bargain. The knockers noted his actions but didn't act immediately. However, when his son too kept all the proceeds for himself, they took their revenge: the lode failed and the young man drank away the remaining money his father had left. This story underlines another important aspect of faery vengeance: it may be postponed for generations, but the grudge won't be forgotten.[289]

Reprisals can be taken for as little as not appreciating their gifts. This can range from as minor an affront as showing caution about eating their food to failing to appreciate much larger advantages. A Scottish miller who allowed the faeries to use his mill at night was given some of their ground flour to try.

---

289. Barton, *North Yorkshire Folk Tales,* 85; Roberts, *Folklore of Yorkshire,* 99; Halliwell, *Popular Rhymes,* 167; Deane & Shaw, *Folklore of Cornwall,* 69; Rhys, *Celtic Folklore,* c. VII.

He did this appreciatively, but his dog refused to taste it—and had the mill door slammed on its head in vengeance. In the same way, faeries were known to enter country houses and have fun at night fooling with the servants and labourers. In the mornings, butter, cheese, and bread would be left behind for the staff to eat; any who refused to do so could expect misfortune. As we saw earlier, this suspicion of the faeries' food is understandable, but misplaced: faery food is perilous in Faery but is safe in the mortal world so that here *not* eating the food—whether it's intended for faery consumption or is explicitly meant for humans to eat—becomes the risky course of action.[290]

With the Good Folk, it seems that you should never look a gift horse in the mouth—and this certainly extends beyond any generosity with a single meal. In Devon a story is told of a family living in the town of Topsham on the Exe estuary who had the good fortune to be given a never-ending barrel of beer by the Fae. No matter how much they drank, it never ran dry. This wonder lasted until a curious maid pulled out the bung to look inside. All she saw was cobwebs—and no ale ever ran again. Identical stories come from Scotland, concerning an inexhaustible supply of meal—until someone takes a peek in the meal chest.

Human farmers have been known to benefit from faery livestock in their herds, and once again prudent and respectful handling of those beasts is the only way of ensuring that the good luck lasts. A Scottish couple had moved onto the deserted island of Pabbay and had found there an abandoned cow. From this they had bred their entire herd. Eventually, because the cow was old, they decided to slaughter it. The beast overheard their plans, gave a bellow, and led all her daughters into the sea after her. It transpired that the animal was one of the *crodhmara,* the faery sea cows, and the couple's careless and ungrateful attitude had cost them their entire livelihood. Very similar is the story of the white faery cow at Mitchell's Fold stone circle in Shropshire. It fed the local people during a famine, on the unspoken understanding that people would only ever fill one vessel at a time and never try to milk it dry. If this was respected, the cow's milk would never cease. Inevitably, one greedy

---

290. Aitken, *Forgotten Heritage,* 7; Reginald Scot, *A Discourse Concerning the Nature and Substance of Devils,* 1665, Book II, c. 4, s. 8.

woman tried to exploit this and the cow left forever. The offender, moreover, was turned into one of the standing stones that make up the Fold.[291]

Cheating the Faeries

Deliberately setting out to cheat and exploit the Good Folk is definitely a bad idea. A man living at St. Briavels in the Forest of Dean decided to sell some cider to help pay his rent. Although he did not immediately realise it, the purchaser was a faery man, who asked for the cider to be poured out on a grassy area near the town. The vendor thought this a foolish waste and instead poured out a barrel full of water. The faeries were not to be cheated though; they laid a curse on the family that many of its members would bleed to death over the generations.[292]

Abusing faery generosity is another breach for which vengeance will be exacted. A Scottish woman who visited faeryland, and was shown the sights there, stole a box of magical dew that dispelled faery glamour. Her violation of faery hospitality was found out and she was deprived of the second sight she had acquired by such underhand means. In a second case, a man was visited at night by three faeries, whom he treated with great hospitality. For his warm welcome they offered him the gift of whatever he chose. He asked for a harp and received a magical instrument that he was able to play beautifully and whose music none could resist. People would start to dance as soon as he picked it up and could only rest when he chose to stop playing. Realising his newly acquired power, the man abused the gift, playing the harp to his neighbours and never letting them pause for breath, despite their cries for mercy. For this maliciousness, the faeries took back their gift.[293]

Intrusions

The Good Folk are a secretive folk and bitterly resent intrusions upon their privacy, whether these are perceived or real, committed on purpose or unwitting. They may flee human trespassers—or they may blight them in revenge. It's been said of the tylwyth teg in Wales that "many were hurt by

---

291. McPherson, *Barra,* 188; Simpson, *Welsh Border,* 79; see too Lewes, *Queer Side,* 134.

292. Palmer, *Gloucestershire,* 145.

293. Aitken, *Forgotten Heritage,* 14; Lewes, *Queer Side,* 139; see too Jenkyn Thomas, *Welsh Fairy Book,* "The fairy password."

going inadvertently where the faeries were, when they had little or no occasion to go that way … everyone that had done so had received great damage by it." Often, the Fae will inflict wounds that are very hard to cure; nonetheless, sometimes they will let an incursion pass. The faery response can be hard to predict, but a clear distinction certainly seems to be made between deliberate and accidental intrusions.[294]

Sometimes the faeries are disturbed unintentionally. For example, in Victorian times near Crowle in Lincolnshire there used to be an unfinished road which had been abandoned by the faery workmen as soon as a man came across them at work upon it. It was believed locally that, following this disturbance (albeit unwitting), the work would never be completed by them.

The faeries will always react more seriously to intrusions that they perceive to be deliberate, although the response will tend to reflect the degree of disturbance and offence that's been caused. In a mid-twentieth-century incident, a woman sitting on a log in woods near Berry Pomeroy Castle in Devon received an unprovoked slap in the face from an angry pixie—presumably because he resented her perceived encroachment upon his solitude. She might have been forgiven for not realising her fault, but on other occasions the faeries plainly reckon that you ought to know better. One Scottish man was beaten simply for sitting down on a faery hill; a Manx boy who played on one was crippled for life: he never grew any taller and his mouth became twisted.[295]

It would seem that just getting in a faery's way when he's in a hurry can constitute grounds for retaliation. In an apparently unprovoked attack on Islay, a faery ran past two children walking along the road and touched one, a boy, as he passed. The child was left paralysed for the remainder of his life. His sister was spared, it was believed, because she was dressed in green, although usually it is thought that wearing the faery colour is what antagonises them, as it is treated as an affront and a usurpation of their rights.[296]

Those who spy on the faeries' gatherings—dances and summer markets—can fully expect to suffer in consequence. You might stumble unwittingly

---

294. Jones, *Appearance of Evil*, para. 63.

295. Addy, *Household Tales*, 135; Young & Houlbrook, *Magical Folk*, 51; and MacDougall, *Folk Tales*, 191; *Yn Lioar Manninagh*, vol. III.

296. Briggs, "Some Late Accounts of the Fairies," *Folklore*, vol. 72 (1961), 516.

upon them, of course, but if this happens, you shouldn't linger. At Bodfari near Denbigh in March 1772 four children spied some dwarf-like beings, who were dancing in a field. They watched curiously for a while but were spotted, at which point one of the small men came racing across the field toward them, with a "grim countenance and a wild and somewhat fierce look." He nearly caught one of the children as they struggled desperately to escape over a stile and the whole experience left them feeling very scared, but otherwise unharmed. Contrast the case of a man walking home across the Yorkshire Wolds to Whitby who came upon some faeries dancing in a secluded dell. He watched for a while and was so taken by their habit of crying "Whip! Whip!" and cracking their hunting whips that he joined in. Outraged, they broke off their dance and whipped him most of the rest of the way to Whitby. Finally, a Northumberland faery tale records how a little girl gathering primroses by the River Wear came upon some faeries bathing. For this invasion of their ablutions, she was abducted by them that same night and her father had to follow a complex ritual to recover her (see next chapter).[297]

Deliberate spying upon the Fair Folk is definitely unadvisable. They will always punish or blight those who intentionally seek them out and watch them. For instance, Broonie, king of the trows on Orkney, did not like to be overlooked at his work around the islanders' farms and would scatter the hayricks if he felt he was being observed. Far more seriously, a Northamptonshire man who tried to catch a glimpse of faeries in a barn at night by peeking through a knothole in a door went blind in the eye he'd used; in a Welsh variant of this, dust was thrown in the man's eyes so that he lost his second sight.[298]

If the intrusion causes long-term or permanent disturbance to the Fae, or if they are actually injured by it, their revenge can be severe. Fortunately, they will sometimes choose to warn the intruder off first. Three Perthshire men set out to strip turf from the top of a faery hill. When they got there, they all felt suddenly exhausted and lay down for a nap. On awaking later, each had been carried off some distance, one finding himself a quarter of a mile away

---

297. Addy, *Household Tales,* 135; Bovet, *Pandaemonium,* 1684, 207; Jones, *Appearance of Evil,* para. 34; *Notes & Queries,* 4th series, vol. 4 (1868), 132; Grice, *Folk Tales,* c. 15.

298. *County Folklore,* vol. 2, 21; Sternberg, *Dialect and Folklore,* 133—compare Roberts, *Folklore of Yorkshire,* 63; Owen, *Welsh Folklore,* 90.

in a pool. If the human won't take the hint, he must accept the consequences. An Orkney farmer who dug into a faery mound was confronted by a little grey man who angrily told him that, if he dared to take another spadeful, six of his cows would die and, if he still persisted, there would be six funerals in the family. The man went on—with predictable results.[299]

Serious violations of faery privacy and dignity will meet with serious reactions. The miller of Rothley's son discovered that the faeries were using the mill's kiln to cook their porridge at night. The youth objected to the faeries feasting in his father's premises and he thought it would be amusing to drop a large stone into their cooking pot. Of course, this splashed boiling porridge everywhere, burning and scalding those crowded around and, just as inevitably, the faeries immediately chased him to exact their revenge. He received a blow which left him lame for the rest of his life; had he not made good his escape, things could have been much worse. When the building of Fernworthy Hall on Dartmoor disturbed the local pixies, they abducted the family's child in revenge, and in a case from Cornwall in 1952 the son of a family who'd unwittingly picnicked in a faery ring soon afterward was injured and died.[300]

The most significant and coordinated example of an adverse faery response to disturbance comes from the fens of East Anglia. As noted in chapter 2, for many centuries the local people had co-existed with a marshland sprite called the "Tiddy Mun." If the floodwaters rose too high, invoking his name would be guaranteed to lower them. From the seventeenth century onward, however, concerted commercial efforts were made to drain the fens—and the Tiddy Mun responded badly. Some of the drainage engineers were found dead whilst blight settled upon the population and their stock and crops. The only way to abate the faery's anger was to propitiate him by pouring out offerings of water into the dykes, symbolically replacing what had been drained away.

---

299. Murray, *Tales from Highland Perthshire*, no. 85; Marwick, *The Folklore of Orkney*, 41. In the similar story of "The Fairies of Merlin's Craig," the offending turf cutter was abducted and forced to swear never to take turves again before he was freed—*Folklore & Legends—Scotland*, 106.

300. Grice, *Folk Tales*, c. 10; Coxhead, *Devon Traditions*, 75; Deane & Shaw, *Folklore of Cornwall*, 92; contrast E. Tregarthen, *North Cornwall Fairies and Legends*, 115, where the punishment for trespass is merely eating some biscuits.

Some individual members of the Good Folk are more tolerant than others, naturally, so that what enrages one may not vex another. Nonetheless, their capacity for being seriously offended is clear and it only makes sense to adopt a cautious and respectful approach. If a warning is given, it should be accepted for what it is and heeded. It will doubtless help, too, to be sensitive and alert to clues that the faeries are displeased.

An example of the right sort of response dates from the early twentieth century. A girl used to go fishing on Loch Awe in Argyllshire accompanied by an old ghillie (an attendant on fishing and hunting expeditions); when lunchtime came she would find a place on the shore to tie up the boat and picnic in his company. One day she took a fancy to eating by a little burn running into the loch. The ghillie tried to dissuade her and, when she would not change her mind, he set her down alone and ate nearby. She found a little pool shaded by a rowan, an oak, and a hawthorn and sat down to eat her lunch of three sandwiches and an orange. She had eaten half the first sandwich when the orange slipped off her lap and fell in the pool. She scrambled down to get it, but it was not there, nor anywhere else in the stream, so she said aloud, "Well, whoever it is, is welcome to my orange." She went back for the rest of the picnic but only her cushion was there, not the sandwiches. "You're welcome to them," she announced and lifted the cushion, under which she found her sandwiches. "Thank you," she said and sat down and ate them. When she'd finished her lunch, she spoke up again: "You're welcome to my orange, but could you give me some fruit in exchange?" Looking down as she spoke, she saw a bush of ripe blaeberries, even though it was only June. She ate them with thanks and returned to the boat. Later the girl looked up the name of the little stream on the map and found that it was Alltna Sith, the Faeries' Burn (although, we may suspect that the faery trees growing by the pool should have been another warning to her). This explains the ghillie's wariness and the faeries' reaction to the girl's intrusion. Luckily, she responded with patience, politeness, and good humour.

Catching Faeries

We are very familiar with the idea of faery folk stealing humans, whether that is infants swapped for changelings or older men and women taken as lovers, wet nurses, and midwives. Surprisingly, there is also some evidence of the reverse process—for faeries being captured by humans.

There are three principal reasons for deliberately attempting this dangerous and difficult task. The first, obviously and understandably, is pure curiosity. The second may be a desire for revenge against a nuisance faery—and the third is the equally human motivation of greed. It's said that catching a leprechaun brings good luck and that catching a faery may cause him to reveal the whereabouts of hidden treasure.[301] A warning though—never trust an elf; in one poem a man who frees a goblin from a hunter's net is rewarded with gold, only to find later that all he'd been given was dead cowslips. What's worse, the faery who's been forced to act against her will might also curse the scheming captor.[302]

Needless to say, faeries are very hard to catch, first because they are well aware that we may want to do this and are alert to the risk. They're thieves and nuisances to us and they deliberately stay out of our clutches: Thomas Hobbes described in *Leviathan* how "the faeries are not to be seized on or brought to answer for the hurt they do." Secondly, the Fae are hard to capture because they have magical powers: they can disappear at will, they have some knowledge of the future, and they may be able to shapeshift. That said, in one instance it was the change of form that was the problem for the Fae. A Lake District farmer caught a fine hare that he intended to have for his supper. To his surprise it began to call to its faery father outside the farmhouse and then asked to be set free; in the circumstances, the farmer felt that he had to comply, even though he was losing his evening meal. In most cases, all the same, the Good Folk are highly elusive. It's said in North Yorkshire that the reason faeries' underground houses are never found when people are digging wells, mines, or foundations is because, as the workmen dig down, the faeries will just make their homes sink deeper out of reach; comparably, in Dyfed in South Wales it's said that you can never reach the place where the faeries are dancing: you'll see them from

---

301. Graham Tomson, *The Luprachaun*; "And will you come away?" in F. Olcott, *A Book of Elves and Fairies*, 1918, 62.

302. Graham R. Tomson, *Ballade of Fairy Gold*; Spence, *Fairy Tradition*, 52–3.

one mountain peak on another, but if you make your way to the second they'll have moved on again.[303]

As might be expected, therefore, faeries are captured extremely rarely and when it happens it seems to be a combination of extremely good luck, cunning, and agility. In two of his poems, "Europe" and "The Fairy," William Blake describes catching faeries in his hat. In the former verse, he does this "as boys knock down a butterfly." Speed and surprise are predictably essential to catching a magical creature—in one story from Dartmoor it's only an incredibly lucky jab with a fork that pins a pixie to a stool and prevents his escape from a house. Nevertheless, most of the cases suggest that agility and numbers will never be enough on their own. In one case from Wales two parishes had organised a football match at the village of Pencarreg Caio. When the two teams assembled, they saw faeries dancing nearby and decided to capture them. Despite the number and fitness of the young men, they were unable to surround or reach the Fae—they were always somewhere else.[304]

Forward planning is the other ingredient fundamental to successfully catching a faery. A man was able to capture a *glaistig* at Lochaber because he had taken a charmed belt with him for just that purpose; Highland water horses *(each-uisge)* have been secured by procuring a magic bridle.[305]

Faeries are not always caught intentionally. From across Britain come variants of a story involving faeries trapped accidentally by thieves. In the Lancashire version, two poachers were out ferreting and, instead of rabbits, flushed two faeries from a burrow into their sacks. They were so alarmed by the voices crying out from inside the sacks that they dropped them and ran home. The next day the sacks were retrieved, empty and neatly folded, and the men were said to be reformed from their criminal habits by the shock of their unexpected catch.[306]

---

303. Hobbes, *Leviathan*, 1651, Part 4, 436; Hodgson, "On Some Surviving Fairies," 117; Blakeborough, *Wit, Character, Folklore and Customs of the North Riding of Yorkshire*, 143; Davies, *Folklore of West and Mid-Wales*, 128.

304. Crossing, *Dartmoor Pixies*, c. VIII—"The Pixies' Revels"; Davies, *Folklore of West and Mid-Wales*, 130.

305. Spence, *Fairy Tradition*, 53; Mackinlay, *Folklore of Scottish Lochs*, c. XI.

306. Rhys, *Celtic Folklore*, 139—Welsh otter hunters; Simpson, *Folklore of Sussex*, 60—pig thieves.

The faeries in these last folktales apparently bear no ill will over the incident (indeed, in the Sussex version the faery's own curiosity gets it into trouble, as it climbs into a sack with a stolen pig). Likewise, in the story of Skillywidden, a pixie captured at Treridge near Zennor, the faery does not seem too put out by his ordeal. A farmer was cutting furze when he spotted a young pixie asleep. He scooped it up and took it home where it was named Bobby Griglans by his family and would play contentedly by the hearth with the children. The pixie child promised to reveal to the farmer where gold was buried on a nearby hill as soon as the nights were moonlit. However, one day when the youngsters all slipped outside to play, the pixie's parents appeared searching for him and he readily went home with them. Readers may like to note that there is a farm called Skillywadden to the south of Trendrine Hill where this incident took place; this may therefore be prime faery-catching country.

Deaths in Captivity

The recorded incidents of faeries taken captive break down into three types, depending upon their outcomes. In some stories, the imprisoned faery dies; keeping faeries as playthings in the human world is cruel and dooms them, attractive as the idea may initially sound. In the Suffolk story "Brother Mike" a faery is caught by a farmer in the act of stealing corn from his barn. He puts the creature in his hat and takes it back to the farmhouse for the amusement of his children. The captive is tethered to the kitchen window and there he sickens and dies, refusing all food. This sad incident compares to the story of the Green Children, also from Suffolk: after they had strayed from Faery into the human world, the boy of the pair steadily pined away and died of grief. In these first two examples the decline takes place over a period of days, but it can be merely minutes. From Cheshire and Shropshire come tales of the water faery called the asrai. This mysterious being, in the form of a young, naked woman, is from time to time dredged in fishing nets from lakes and meres. When exposed to the air they never last long, simply melting away in the bottom of the fishing boat before it reaches the shore. Related to this, perhaps, is the case of a faery baby found once during haymaking in North

Yorkshire. Although cared for by the finders, before the day was over the child had dwindled away until it was gone.[307]

Ransomed Faeries

In some stories the captive faeries are forced to act against their will by their human captors, whether that involves marrying a human, carrying out near impossible building works, making promises of good behaviour or, as we have already mentioned, disclosing hidden treasure. For example, at Rockingham in Northamptonshire a local elf called the "redman" was pestering three brothers for food. The two older siblings were simply irritated by his presence and drove the elf away; the youngest saw an opportunity. He seized the creature and held it until it revealed where its crock of gold was hidden, thereby making himself a very rich man. Sometimes the captive faeries will buy their freedom by offering some benefit in return for their release: a captured *glaistig* granted prosperity and the second sight to be set free, for instance. Mermaids will make similar bargains when caught in fishermen's nets or stranded on the beach.[308]

Elvish Escapees

In many accounts the captive faery sooner or later escapes. This may be due to human carelessness, as in the case of a Dartmoor farmer who caught a pixy in his barn and trapped him in his lantern, but then left the door of the lamp open, allowing the pixy to get away. Sometimes the captive faery simply uses its magic powers to vanish. This was the experience of a Dartmoor woman returning from market who was able to snatch up a pixy and shut him in her basket. After some initial complaining the pixy fell silent and on opening the lid to check, she found that he'd disappeared. In a similar incident from North Yorkshire, a drunken man making his way home one night came across a faery dance. In his inebriated state he tried to join in but the faeries objected, pinching and kicking him mercilessly. He fled, but not before he'd snatched up one of the Fae, thinking it would make a fine living doll for his daughter. When he got home, though, his pocket was empty. This

---

307. Atkinson, *Forty Years in a Moorland Parish*, 54; and see the poem *The Opal Dream Cave* by Katherine Mansfield.

308. Hill, *Folklore of Northamptonshire*, 152; Spence, *Fairy Tradition*, 51.

man was fortunate that his presumption was chastised only with some rough treatment. In a comparable Manx story, a man caught a faery that hopped out of tree and took it home as a doll, but as a result he became very ill. He was only able to cure himself by returning to the spot and setting the captive free. As well as demonstrating the skills of faeries as escapologists, these two stories highlight the perpetual risk of close contact with a supernatural being—it is not always healthy for a human.[309]

Freed Faeries

Sometimes, of course, the faery's released voluntarily by its captor. From North Yorkshire comes a story of a faery girl found lost and alone near Tower Hill, Middleton-in-Teesdale. A woman took the child home, sat her by the fire and gave her bread and cheese to eat but the girl cried so bitterly that the woman took pity and returned her to the place by the river where she'd been found and where it was believed that the faeries came to bathe, in the hope that her parents would return for her—and several of these stories indicate that they will do just that.[310]

It's notable from many of the examples cited how often it's the case that a juvenile faery is caught. Presumably the reason for this is quite simply that, like the juveniles of many species, they are less cautious and less alert to danger than their parents. Secondly, whilst contact with faeries is generally something to be discouraged, in most of these cases there are no ill consequences for the captors; in fact, in several cases the human children play with the faery child on terms of amity and equality. In some of the other cases, it appears that the faeries may have accepted that it was their own want of care or simple bad luck that led to their capture and, as a result, no vengeance is exacted. This isn't always the case though—and knowing faery character it would be odd if this was so. A North Yorkshire man, who declared that he'd catch a faery and trap it in a bottle if he ever saw one, was overheard by them, as he was bound to be, and was then pixy-led for two hours in punishment for his boldness.[311]

---

309. Crossing, *Tales of Dartmoor Pixies*, c. 5; Roberts, *Folklore of Yorkshire*, 63; *Choice Notes & Queries*, 1859, 26.

310. Bord, *Fairies*, Appendix; R. H. Horne, *The Elf of the Woodlands*.

311. Blakeborough, *Wit, Character, Folklore and Customs of the North Riding of Yorkshire*, 143.

Sometimes the faery is simply lost and is invited in by humans, but even helping stray faeries can have its disadvantages. In the Scottish story of Gilpin Horner some men found a lost goblin and allowed it to move into their house. He was happy to take their offer of shelter and stayed with them a while before being called home to his family. During his stay though, he consumed vast quantities of cream from the dairy, so that the departure of their unusual pet was little regretted.[312]

Killing Faeries

It's a widespread belief that the Fae are immortal. In fact (and surprisingly) the folklore evidence—scattered as it is—clearly contradicts this. Faeries are mortal and, it follows, they can be killed. Dramatic confirmation of this comes from Dartmoor in Devon, where there's long-standing animosity between the local foxes and pixies, which has led to an ever-increasing effort by the latter to protect themselves. The foxes hunt the pixies, digging them out of their underground homes and devouring them. The pixies have responded by making iron shelters.[313]

Faeries aren't immortal, but their life spans are considerably longer than ours, which probably explains the common misconception. Nonetheless they do die eventually, something the Reverend Robert Kirk expressed with his usual style: "They are not subject to sore Sicknesses, but dwindle and decay at a certain Period, all about ane Age."[314]

English writer Reginald Scot affirmed that they were "subject to a beginning and an end, and to a degree of continuance." Another Scottish account of faery life spans states that they live through nine ages, with nine times nine periods in each:

---

312. Aitken, *Forgotten Heritage*, 17.

313. R. King, "Folklore of Devonshire," *Fraser's Magazine*, vol. 8, 1873, 781.

314. *Secret Commonwealth*, chapter 7.

Nine nines sucking the breast,
Nine nines unsteady, weak,
Nine nines footful, swift,
Nine nines able and strong,
Nine nines strapping, brown,
Nine nines victorious, subduing,
Nine nines bonneted, drab,
Nine nines beardy, grey,
Nine nines on the breast-beating death.[315]

That the Fae will eventually sicken and pass away is confirmed by several pieces of evidence. First, faery funerals have been witnessed. William Blake most famously described one, but his account is more poetic than authentic. Witnesses have, however, from time to time stumbled upon faery funeral processions (for example, that of the Faery Queen at Lelant in Cornwall) and the Reverend Edmund Jones, living in Monmouthshire in the late eighteenth century, told of several such funerals seen which also foretold deaths in the mortal world, quite often that of the witness.

Secondly, we find a few allusions to faery cemeteries. One was believed to be at Brinkburn Priory in Northumberland; generally, in the North of England it used to be said that any green shady spot was a faery burial ground.

Next, it was believed that, amongst the trows of Orkney, a father would always die when his son reached adulthood. It is also said that there are no trows left in the Orkneys because of a disaster that killed them all. Long ago they decided to leave the mainland and live only on the island of Hoy. To do this they assembled one night on the shores of the bay of Stromness and threw a straw rope across the water. Just at the point that all the trows were in the process of passing over the waves, one end of the rope slipped loose, plunging them into the sea. They were all drowned.

Age, sickness, and misadventure will ultimately overtake even the faeries. This is sad, but not necessarily shocking. More disturbing is the evidence that faeries can be killed prematurely. I discussed faery warfare earlier; it's almost unavoidable that blood will be spilt in such conflict, but we might

---

315. Scot, Book II, c. 1, s. 12; A. Carmichael, *Carmina Gadelica,* vol. 2, 334.

still not think it so remarkable that one magical being can slay another. The truth is, though, that humans can murder supernaturals as well.

Nymphocide (I've just invented this word, by the way) may occur accidentally. One version of the story from Brinkburn Priory is that it was the ringing of the bells of the church that killed them.[316] I've mentioned before faeries' aversion to church bells; this particular story takes it to extremes.

Other faery murders are just that—deliberate and premeditated killings. One case from Shropshire concerns some nuisance boggarts in a farmhouse. The story follows the pattern of the "we're flitting too" type of tale, in which the family try to escape their unwelcome companions by moving house, only to find that the boggart comes with them. In most versions the humans reconcile themselves to their unwanted housemates and often give up the move altogether (see Faery Flits earlier). In the Shropshire version, the household takes matters to their logical conclusion. Unable to give the boggarts the slip, the humans trick them into sitting in front of a blazing fire in the hearth and then topple them into the flames, where they're held in place with forks and brooms until they're consumed. In a Manx version the troublesome Fae are bundled into a barrel and chucked in the sea whilst a Scottish water kelpie that was terrorising a home and family was killed with two red-hot spits by a blacksmith. In this last version, the use of iron is sure to be part of the reason for the killer's success; we know iron is a good defence against faeries, so it seems only reasonable that it should be fatal for them too.[317]

Some other nymphocides seem to be crimes of passion or are committed in the heat of the moment or in self-defence. On the Hebridean island of Benbecula a mermaid was accidentally slain by a stone thrown at her head during an attempt by some fishermen to capture her. In one Highland story a man fights off and kills a *gruagach* with a sword. The Reverend Robert Kirk also mentions a man with second sight who, during a visit to Faery, "cut the Bodie of one of those People in two with his Iron Weapon." These examples

---

316. *Denham Tracts*, 134.

317. Roeder, *Manx Folk Tales*, 23; Gregor, *Notes on the Folklore*, 66.

again illustrate the efficacy of cold steel. Water bulls were said to be invulnerable, except to silver bullets.[318]

Whilst it may be possible to deal with a nuisance faery by killing it, it probably hardly needs to be said that this may not be a wise way of proceeding. Faery vengeance will often follow. From Shetland comes a story of a mermaid who was caught up in a fishing boat's lines; to get rid of her one of the crew stabbed her. She sank out of sight and the hook was freed, but the man never prospered after that time.[319]

Summary

The overall impression gained from this chapter must be that the faeries can be violent and unprincipled and must be approached accordingly. In fact, force and compulsion often appear to lie at the heart of human-faery relations. Incontestably, this is part of the reality of our interactions with them. To assume that offence might be taken, and that retribution will follow—albeit within timescales much longer than our own—is possibly one of the most prudent preparations you can make before meeting the Good Folk.

Always remember that faeries do not think or act like humans and that they want to keep us at a controlled distance. Observe this rule and you will—by and large—be safe. Some faeries are actively friendly and helpful, as we've seen, but the initiative and the approach should always come from them.

---

318. J. Campbell, *Popular Tales of the West Highlands*, vol. 1, 7; Dalyell, *The Darker Superstitions of Scotland*, 542; see the Scottish ballad, *Lady Isabel and the Elf-knight*, in which the heroine either stabs or drowns the wicked knight.

319. Brand, *Description of Zetland*, 172.

Chapter 12

FAERY ABDUCTIONS

There is a very particular form of perilous contact with the Good Folk that must be examined separately, which is the taking of adults, children, and babies from the human world. The risk of abduction has been a source of deep anxiety for people for many centuries, but the real interest of this subject is what it has to tell us about the Fae: about their motivations, their methods, and the ways in which they may be overcome and the abductee rescued. The tenor of these accounts is of a society besieged: humans face constant alert hostility and must perpetually be on their guard. I've stressed before the constant proximity of the Good Folk and their eavesdropping proclivities. This perception of them as always watchful, always waiting to pounce, adds a sinister aspect to our relationship.

Taking Adults and Children

The faeries are known for their propensity to steal people away. This occurs far more often than the very occasional capture of a faery by a human. It is without doubt the most fraught part of our interaction with the Fae and, as such, the most revealing.

The fate of the abductee varies. Some stay in Faery forever; some are held for a term of years, and are then released, and some provide a service (for example musicians and midwives) but are then allowed to go home. Even then, the returnees may not find that the world they return to has changed—or that they have changed.

Who's Taken and Why?

Adults may be taken for their skills—especially if they are talented fiddlers or pipers. Women are frequently taken as nursemaids: it seems human milk is very beneficial to supernatural infants and that faery women produce little of their own. In consequence, mothers recently delivered of their babies who have not yet been "churched" have always been considered especially vulnerable. By way of contrast, it's interesting to note that human midwives and nurses will almost always be dealt with on a temporary and commercial basis: they will be taken to the faery hill when their help is required but will be returned home once the baby is safely delivered (and will suffer no ill effects from any differential passage of time).

Children seem to be abducted more frequently than adults, most especially boys. This is said to be because of a faery belief that such a mortal infant, if brought up and indoctrinated in the faery ways, may become the faeries' champion on reaching adulthood and then lead the Fae hosts to victory against humans.[320] Some children are simply wanted as playmates for faery offspring. As I've already mentioned, and as will be clear from these stories, these stolen children will be well looked after in Faery. Nonetheless, mortal families would still dread the theft of their offspring and go to considerable lengths to protect them, such as dressing boys as girls as a way of disguising them from the watchful Fae. In one interesting Scottish story, a girl used to regularly play with the faeries under the Hill of Tulach at Monzie. One day the faeries cut a lock of her hair and told her that next time she visited she would stay with them forever. The girl informed her mother what had happened and the woman immediately took various (unspecified) magical precautions and never let her daughter out to play again.[321]

---

320. Aitken, *Forgotten Heritage*, 5.

321. Murray, *Tales from Highland Perthshire*, no. 33.

Some abductions are only temporary and appear much more like what we'd now term a "possession." In one Shetland story two children appear at the Yule revels; they dance with unnatural skill yet have staring eyes and fixed grins. When their unsuspecting mother sees them there, she utters a blessing which causes them to vanish. After a search, they're found dead in the snowdrifts the next day. The mother had forgotten to bless the boys before going out for the night and, thus unprotected, they were left vulnerable when the trows came looking for a human form to use so that they could join in with the dancing. This seems a very harsh and utilitarian exploitation of the infants, using their bodies up and then casting them off, but it typifies the faery attitude in many such circumstances.[322]

Nonetheless, abductions don't always seem forceful or against the human's will. It is not uncommon for a person to be lured into the faeries' abode under the pretence of being invited in as a guest. The visitor will be treated well and offered food and drink; accepting this hospitality is the dangerous thing. Once you've partaken of faery fare, you're trapped with them for seven years at least. If you're on your guard and refuse what's offered, you may well be lucky and find yourself released. Enticing men and women to join the faeries' dancing is the other very well-known means of entrapment. Other traps have been tried: in one reported case the Fae attempted to lure a farmer's sons away from their work thrashing grain with invitations to play with them, and a poem describes how the faeries tried to persuade a farmer to accept the honour of milking the faery queen's cow. The man was suspicious of their offer and refused to go with them, which was undoubtedly wise: the faeries want humans not primarily for their company but because they can provide some sort of service. Women, for example, often end up seemingly enslaved and responsible for cooking and cleaning for the whole faery community. In fact, the faeries' general preference in the older stories for females and children probably reflects the fact that they were known to be the ones who had to do most of the household chores in the human world. I guess that the Fae attitude was that these groups could therefore fairly easily be compelled to suffer the drudgery in Faery too, freeing their captors for

---

322. Jones, *Appearance*, no. 67; Edmonston, *The Home of a Naturalist*, 141.

more pleasurable activities, such as feasting, dancing, and playing pranks on humans.[323]

Faery Host

There's a particular form of abduction that is especially prevalent in the Scottish Highlands, which is for a person to be snatched up and carried along with the *sluaghsith* (slooashee), the faery host. This flock of spirits is believed to fly about the night sky "like starlings," fighting battles between themselves and injuring men, women, and beasts on the ground.

The host rides over the countryside and even over the sea into foreign lands. Sometimes humans are invited to journey with them; sometimes they overhear the magic words that launch the faeries into the air and travel with them that way; sometimes they are abducted. This is a temporary form of taking, although it may happen repeatedly to the same individual. For example, I mentioned earlier a man trapped on cliffs on the island of Barra who wished to be saved and who was lifted to safety by the faeries; the price he paid for his rescue was to be snatched up at any time of day or night to travel with them.[324]

The *sluagh* may travel high above the clouds or they may move at ground level as a whirlwind of dust. The trips may be for pure pleasure, to visit inns or to raid wine cellars, or they may have a more malign purpose, quite often to shoot elf bolts at people and their livestock. It's said that the host themselves can't discharge these arrows, which is why they capture humans to take along with them.[325]

One way of rescuing a person carried off like this is to throw a piece of iron or handful of earth into the whirlwind; instantly, the victim is set free. In an interesting Cornish variant upon this phenomenon, a whirlwind was

---

323. Wilson, *Folklore and Genealogies of Uppermost Nithsdale*, 76; Gregor, *Notes on the Folklore*, 62; Jones, *Appearance*, no. 46; Leather, *Folklore of Herefordshire*, 43; Graham R. Tomson, *The Ferlie*.

324. MacPherson, *Barra*, 178.

325. Jones, *Appearance of Evil*, paras 67 & 68; Sutherland, *Folklore Gleanings*, 28; Murray, *Tales from Highland Perthshire*, nos. 88, 157, 191 & 204.

used to blind a mother to the taking of her baby and its substitution with a wizened old changeling.[326]

The actual experience of travel with the *sluagh* can be unpleasant. Not only are you suddenly snatched away, you may fly at terrifying height or so low to the ground that you're buffeted by bushes and trees. The Reverend Jones in South Wales told of a man who was carried off one night and spent his time being dragged through thorns and briars. Part of the time he was insensible and he came back looking sick with exhaustion and scared.[327]

Protecting Adults against Abduction

Over the centuries, people have developed a range of tried and tested methods to repel the faeries and to prevent abductions. All of these are more or less magical and there is considerable crossover between this section and some of the matters discussed in the next chapter.

Amongst the simple and effective protections are

- blessing yourself or someone else with a Christian invocation scattering holy water around a property;

- carrying a Bible—or even a single page from one debating with the faery who's threatening you and outwitting its magic with your superior wits. In one Scottish faery song the faery thief tries to persuade a young mother that her child is sickly and would be better off living on the moors tending the faeries' sheep and cattle; she counters every argument with its opposite and thereby saves the boy;[328]

- wearing or carrying lucky charms. These have included a bone taken from a sheep's head and worn as an amulet, an iron knife or a piece of torch fir. Dressing children in the morning whilst holding them upside down (easier said than done), tying a red thread around their necks, or giving them a rowan cross to wear are all effective means of protecting them exploiting the power of the herb called *mothan*

---

326. Bord, *Fairies,* 209; J. Harte *Explore Fairy Traditions,*146; Tregarthen, *North Cornwall Fairies,* 185.

327. *Appearance of Evil,* para. 68.

328. Campbell, *Waifs & Strays of Celtic Tradition,* vol. 5, 140–148.

(pearlwort). In the Scottish Highlands, if a cow grazed on this plant, its magical properties would infuse the milk. If that milk was then made into cheese, anyone who ate the cheese would gain protection from the faeries, as would all their property;[329] and

- protecting yourself with burnt items. This was especially effective. At New Year the Highland practice was to burn a special strip of skin cut from the chest of a sheep slaughtered over the Christmas period. It had to be oval in shape and could not be removed with a knife. The head of each household would set it alight and then pass it around the family members sunwise, getting each to smell the fumes in turn. If it went out, it was bad luck for whomever happened to be holding it. Burnt hide from the neck of a cow was equally protective and beating a cow hide on New Year's Eve also helped drive the faeries away from the farmstead. Lastly, if you're out and about and meet with a faery whom you fear has designs against you, drawing a circle around yourself and declaring "God be about me" or lying down and sticking a knife in the ground at your head.[330]

On Shetland, if a child began to "dwine," to sicken, and appeared to be in imminent danger of being "trow-taken," there was a special procedure to protect it. This was a meal composed of "nine women's meat," which involved the mother visiting nine neighbours whose firstborn children were sons and begging from each of them three items as ingredients for the dish. If the child didn't recover after being fed this mixture, nothing more could be done; it was said that "the grey men's web was about the bairn," meaning that the infant would inevitably be taken. A comparable treatment from the east coast of Scotland involved families cutting oak and ivy branches in March. These faery plants were woven into garlands and preserved until the autumn. If anyone in the family started to look lean or like they were pining away, they would be passed three times through the garland.[331]

---

329. Gregor, *Notes on the Folklore*, 136.

330. Grant Stewart, *Popular Superstitions*, 114; Marwick, *The Folklore of Orkney*, 36.

331. Spence, *Shetland Folklore*, 147; & Edmondston, *A View of the Zetland Isles*, 217; Saxby, *Shetland Traditional Lore*, 130; Crofton Croker, *Fairy Legends*, 41.

These precautions may be effective, but bear in mind that the Good Folk won't necessarily react well to their plans being thwarted. Taeder, a Shetland man, had just escorted the midwife home and was returning to his wife and newborn child when he saw the trows approaching his cottage. He managed to get ahead of them and placed a razor blade before his door, preventing the abduction of his family. This success notwithstanding, the next day he found the blade broken on the path and his best cow gone. Another Shetland man who managed to save his brother's wife and child from abduction later lost one of his own sons instead.[332]

Rescuing Abductees

If the preventative measures don't work, all is not lost. In fact, releasing a captive from faery thrall can be often achieved by the same means as would protect someone in advance. For instance, blessing a taken person will instantly break the spell placed over them. Usually, however, rather more effort is needed.

Persons lured into faery dances can only be freed again a year and a day later and that by means of reaching into the circle, where they will still be found dancing. The dancer may then be dragged out or may simply be touched with a long stick made of that efficacious wood, rowan (*prencriafol* in Welsh). It's further believed in Wales that, even after the rescue has been successful, the recovered person still needs to be watched. Cold iron should not be allowed to touch their skin, otherwise they may become invisible and may be taken again. As an illustration, a Welsh farm girl taken for a year and a day by the faeries was rescued from their dance and for a while seemed to be her old self once more. One day, however, she was helping to saddle a horse when the metal bit touched her hand; she instantly disappeared and was never seen again. A belief related to this was that those who have willingly partaken of faery food are able to return to their earthly homes after seven years but, nonetheless, they will be reclaimed by the faeries and disappear forever after another seven years.[333]

---

332. Edmondston, *A View of the Zetland Isles*, 214.

333. Lewes, *Queer Side*, 120; & Grant Stewart, *Popular Superstitions*, 91; Davies, *Folklore of West and Mid-Wales*, 109; Crofton Croker, *Fairy Legends*, 16.

Sometimes quite complex rituals are needed to free a person who's been taken. A very good illustration of this is a story from Stanhope in Northumberland. A little girl had been picking primroses by the side of the River Wear. This was a known faery haunt and the flowers, being yellow, were known faery blooms, so her father rightly feared that she might very soon be taken. He sought the advice of a local wise woman who counselled him to defend his home by making sure everything was completely silent. He locked up all his livestock and stopped all the clocks but he overlooked a little dog that slept on the bed with his daughter. It barked when the faeries arrived and, as a result, the girl was abducted. To recover her, the father had to go to the faeries' caves holding a sprig of rowan and bearing three gifts for them: a light that shone without burning (he took a glow worm), an animal that had no bones (he took an unhatched egg), and a limb shed without the loss of a drop of blood (he took a tail shed by a lizard). The faeries had no option then but to free the girl. A similar rescue in Scotland required a man to put three knots in his wife's bridal shawl before going to the faery knoll to recover her and their child.[334]

Apparently, some captives are able to negotiate their way out of Faery. In one Scottish story a nursing mother had been taken but she was able to escape by agreeing to give the faeries the family's best milking mare. It was eventually returned to the owners when the faeries had no further use for it, but it came back looking very lean.[335]

Lastly, there are a few Scottish stories of abducted wives that are interesting for the fact that the husband *doesn't* recover the woman. Curiously, abductees often seem to be able to come back to ask their family for help and to give instructions on how they may be saved. Frequently this rescue will involve throwing an item into the faery rade as it passes and claiming the victim (faeries are unable to refuse this demand for an exchange, regardless of what's being swapped, so a cap will often save a captive). However, in the case of failed rescues, fear generally seems to inhibit the husband. In one case the elders of his church advised the man against recovering his wife as she had been in the land of the dead and would never be accepted again by the community. You can

---

334. Grice, *Folk Tales*, c. 15; MacGregor, *Peat Fire Flame*, 5.

335. Gregor, *Notes on the Folklore*, 62.

see the wisdom of this advice, but you also can't help wondering if sometimes the man wasn't secretly glad to be rid of his spouse. In a few of the stories an added complication is that the husband has remarried in the interim. Often, he genuinely believed that his spouse was dead, because he has buried a "stock" in the form of his wife's corpse. In a few cases, you suspect he may not regret his restored bachelor status. For sure, in the last case described, after the husband has failed three times to rescue her, the aggrieved wife reappears and curses him so that his luck fails, all his cattle die, and he has to surrender his farm.[336]

Taking Cattle

We know already how partial faeries are to milk products. They will persistently steal from the dairy and they may also take the milk cattle themselves. How this might be done is illustrated by an incident from Shetland. A man out early one day saw two "grey men" approaching a cow lying down in a field. They walked up to it and then ran away from it backward; the cow immediately stood up and followed them to the limit of its tether. It died later that day, a clear sign that the trows had abducted it.

On the assumption that faeries are averse to Christian religion, making a habit of regularly blessing your livestock has been recommended as a sure way of protecting them.[337] Many have felt safer employing more elaborate preventative measures, though, and the treatments mentioned include

- wrapping a page from the Bible around a cow's horn;
- giving the cattle water in which an elf shot (a flint arrow head), a crystal gem, or an "adder stone"—that is, a stone with a natural hole through it—has been dipped;
- using iron tethers for the cattle in the byre;
- mixing "dirk grass" into their bedding (contact with this plant defeats the Fae);
- feeding the cattle "*mothan*" (pearlwort)—as seen earlier, eating this herb protects the cow as well as anyone consuming its milk; and

---

336. Murray, *Tales from Highland Perthshire*, nos. 15, 27 & 201.

337. Miller, *Scenes and Legends*, 16.

- drawing a cat or a hot coal the length of the back and around the belly of a calved cow.[338]

Other chattels might also be pilfered by the Good Folk. It was believed that "adder stones" were also a cure for whooping cough and were valued accordingly; one recorded example was kept in an iron box to protect it from the faeries, though whether this was to stop them taking it or from damaging its healing properties (or even both) is not entirely clear.[339]

Stocks and Substitutes

The Fae often like to cover their tracks when making off with living people and livestock. The question of living changelings exchanged for human babies will be discussed in the next section; here we're concerned with inanimate decoys.

In place of an adult a so-called wooden "stock" might be left, made from a piece of timber such as alder or moss oak; the trows of Shetland and Orkney were renowned for their particular skills in this malign craft. In one account from New Deer in North East Scotland a man overheard the faeries discussing the stock they were making in the likeness of the local blacksmith's wife. He immediately ran to the couple's house and blessed the woman. A thump was heard outside and, when they looked, a piece of bog fir in her rough likeness was discovered. A cabbage stalk or ragwort stem might be left in place of a child.[340]

A story from Craignish in the Western Highlands encapsulates many of our themes. A shepherd's wife who had gone out to tend his flock was found dead on the moor, her body unmarked. A week after the funeral the man came home to his children to be told that their mother had been with them during the day and had told them to let him know that she was alive and well, having been taken by the faeries, and that only a stock had been buried. If he could have her coffin disinterred, only a dry leaf would be found inside it. The husband sought the advice of his local minister, who told the

---

338. Pennant, *A Tour in Scotland*, 99; *County Folklore*, vol. 2, 37 & vol. 7, 32.

339. Dalyell, *The Darker Superstitions of Scotland*, 141.

340. Gregor, *Notes on the Folklore*, 62; and see the tale of *Sandy Harry*; Aitken, *Forgotten Heritage*, 16; Browne, *History of the Highlands*, 111; Anon, *Folklore & Legends*, 52.

shepherd to pay no attention to such nonsense. A few days later, both the priest and his pony were found dead out on the moor. This may have been the revenge of the frustrated wife or of the faeries, whose existence and powers had been doubted.

Not just whole people might be taken. In Shetland it's thought that if a person is paralysed or loses the use of a limb, this is because the faeries have taken the good member and have left a log behind. The lack of feeling in the limb is demonstration of its substitution. By way of example, a tailor sleeping in a cottage one night was awoken from his slumbers by a faery dance taking place in the main room of the house. He could not restrain himself from saying a blessing—at which point the revel vanished, but not before one faery woman had touched his toe, leaving it numbed for the rest of his days.[341]

Occasionally it is not an animated log that is left behind, but a faery impersonator. A couple lived at Braemore in the far north of Scotland. One day the wife went out visiting and, on her return, didn't seem quite the same as she had been. She did however become more efficient and productive in her domestic chores, an improved state of affairs which continued for a year until she suddenly fell sick and died. After another six years the original wife returned, believing herself to have merely been absent for the space of one dance under a faery hill. It was clear that, to conceal the abduction for a while, a faery woman had taken her place, although it seems that the faeries can only live in human form for a year at the most. This substitute was a kind of changeling for an adult, but a lot more agreeable than the usual infant kind (see next section).[342]

In the case of cattle, the faeries will always leave something resembling it in its place. This is often a slaughtered cow's hide stuffed to look something like the stolen live beast. Sometimes, rather like a changeling, the hide contains an old faery. To the farmer, the animal will appear to have taken ill. It will lie immobile and won't fatten or produce milk but it will still display a ravenous appetite. Somewhat akin to these incidents are the stories in which the faeries are seen to slaughter and eat a prize cow. They save the hide and

---

341. Edmondston, *A View of the Zetland Isles*, 77; S. Hibbert, *A Description of the Shetland Isles*, 194.

342. Sutherland, *Folklore Gleanings*, 24.

the bones, though, and at the end of the feast bundle them all up together and bring the cow back to life, as healthy and whole as it was.[343]

Changelings

This section considers the theft of very young children and babies and their substitution with a faery—termed "the changeling." The changeling phenomenon is a particularly strong feature of faery belief: "among the wicked propensities of the faeries is their inclination to steal children, in which they display particular sagacity," as one authority put it.[344] Whilst a healthy human infant is removed, an old or infirm faery seems always to be left in its place. This contrasts with the situation just described, where an adult woman was replaced by a faery who undertook, and even performed better at, her chores—and this with the ostensible aim of concealing the substitution. In changeling cases, no effort is made to disguise what's been done.

In the case of children, it appears that the Fae anticipate reciprocity from humans and so will leave one of their own behind in exchange for the stolen child. The process is therefore a mutual, if involuntary, exchange of care.

Although nowadays we have developed a generally beneficent and indulgent view of pixies, it's fascinating to learn that in the past they were regarded as being amongst the worst culprits when it came to stealing children. "Devonshire is, above all other lands, the land of changeling boys and girls" one writer declared—and a contemporary of his felt that in Victorian times there was a changeling to be found in every Dartmoor village.[345]

Who's Taken and How?

A widespread belief is that pretty, fair-haired, and blue-eyed babies are the most vulnerable to being snatched away. Along the border between England and Wales it was said that "fine and solid" country babies were preferred. From the Cornish story of Selena Moor we gather two key facts: first, that faery babies are born rarely, which explains the need for human recruits; and,

---

343. *County Folklore*, vol. 3, 26; Edmondston, *A View of the Zetland Isles*, 211; Macgregor, *Peat Fire Flame*, 9.

344. Crofton Croker, *Fairy Legends*, 39.

345. Bowring, "Devonshire Pixies," *Once a Week*, vol. 16 (1867), 205; Richard King, "The Folklore of Devonshire," in *Fraser's Magazine*, vol. 8, 1873, 781.

secondly, that in late Victorian times there was some concern over a decline in the human stock, which was said by the pixies not to be as strong as before "for want of more beef and good malt liquor."[346]

Contemporary of Shakespeare George Puttenham encapsulated many aspects of the belief in these words:

> alluding to the opinion of Nurses, who are wont to say that the Fayries use to steale the fairest of children out of their cradles and put other ill-favoured in their places, which they called changelings or Elfs.[347]

Babies, whether in bed with their mothers or alone in their cots, were consistent targets. In the circumstances, it often fell upon those caring for the new mother to ensure that the proper steps were taken to protect both her and her offspring. The mother would be too exhausted and distracted to take precautions, so midwives, friends, and families had to be alert instead. It was common practice indeed, in the Highlands, for as many as a half-dozen women to stay with the new mother for three or even eight days around the birth. They would stay awake and watch over the cradle. In Shropshire the safeguards extended even further: it was thought to be risky to speak of an expected baby, as this would only serve to alert the faeries to its impending arrival. In Wales it was said that Midsummer, around St. John's Eve, was the time of year when children were particularly vulnerable to being exchanged, presumably because it was a magical season of the year when the tylwyth teg were frequently out and about.[348]

One source from the sixteenth century includes an oath taken by midwives "not to suffer any other bodies child to be set, brought or laid before any woman delivered of her child in the place of her natural child." Amongst the means used by midwives and neighbours to protect mothers in labour were

---

346. Simpson, *Welsh Border*, 73; Bottrell, *Traditions & Hearthside Stories*, vol. 2, 94.

347. Puttenham, *The Arte of English Poesie*, 1589, Book III, chapter XV; see too Richard Willis, *Mount Tabor*, 1639, 92–3.

348. Firth, *Reminiscences*, 74; Palmer, *Shropshire*, 150; Davies, *Folklore of West and Mid-Wales*, 133.

- sprinkling salt around the house;

- hanging fern or oatcakes over the threshold;

- blowing across a Bible into the mother's face, or copying out powerful holy words on slips of paper and hanging them about the bed; and

- weighing down the mother in labour with nine blankets—a lucky number.[349]

Once the child was delivered, a further range of protective measures was available. These included

- the use of the preservative powers of iron. At night parents would pin the baby's clothes to its cot and fasten its curtains with pins in a cross shape. During the daytime a baby might be pinned closely to its mother's clothes so that it was never far from her. Nails driven into the bedstead or an iron tool left beneath it or on the window sill were also sensible precautions. That said, it seems this remedy isn't completely foolproof. In one instance from Suffolk a mother awoke during the night to find the faeries in the act of undressing the baby before taking it away. They were carefully removing the pins in its swaddling clothes and laying them out head to head. Her intervention saved the babe and, after that, she took greater care to sleep with the infant between her and her husband and to ensure that its clothes were pinned to the pillow and sheets so as to make any attempted theft much harder;[350]

- use of milk from a cow that had grazed *mothan*. Dairy products made from this milk, if left on a table in the same room as the mother and baby, would be as powerful as iron in excluding the Fae;

- tying a red thread around the baby's neck. This was a simple and effective protection; so too were a man's shirt or the mother's bridal gown thrown over the cot;

- putting salt in a baby's mouth or marking its forehead with soot;

349. Stewart, *Ben Nevis*, 261; Grieve, *Colonsay and Oronsay*, 281.

350. *Printed Extracts, Suffolk*, 37.

- putting out cream and new baked cakes for the faeries. Providing a meal like this seems to be both an offering and a distraction to the faeries, hoping that if they're well fed they'll either decide not to take the family's child or they'll just forget why it was they were there in the first place;[351]

- blessing the mother and her new child and ensuring a prompt and early baptism. These were extremely important, but holy words and symbols provided defence in other ways. A page of scripture sewn into a baby's clothes would be efficacious, as would crossed sticks at the doorway or placing an open Bible on the newborn's pillow; and

Invoking faery aid against the faeries was even a possibility. In the next chapter we'll mention the faery called Elaby Gathen: midwives could invoke her to watch over and guard sleeping babies.

More actively offensive measures might be taken. A sprinkling of *maistir,* urine that's being saved for clothes washing, will repel the faeries. Perhaps on the same basis, carrying the mother over the drain from the cow shed is reckoned to be equally effective. Sprinkling the house with water in which an ember had been quenched is efficacious and, if one of the Good Folk is actually spotted in the vicinity, pelting them with burning peat is predictably good at driving them off.

As we've seen already, burning items to produce offensive smells is a common folk remedy for a range of ills and was judged effective in repelling changelings. Thus, a shoe burned on the fire can help protect a baby from abduction. Carrying a burning peat seven times sunwise around the new mother's bed, or around the outside of the house if space in the bedroom is restricted, is considered excellent protection in the far north of the Scottish mainland.

What Is a Changeling?

What differentiates the changeling phenomenon from other faery abductions is the element of exchange that is central to it. An infant is not just forcibly seized; some substitute is left in its place, only incidentally with a view to

---

351. Owen, *Welsh Folklore,* 70.

disguising the fact of the kidnapping—but more importantly, perhaps, because human care is desirable and appreciated.

What remained behind in the cradle might be a wax image—the "stock" as described in the last section—or it might be another living being, a faery substitute called a "changeling." The widespread conviction was that whoever was left would appear to have mental and physical disabilities—a "natural fool" or a lunatic as some writers put it. The child would be peevish and prone to weeping and by these characteristics would its true nature be disclosed. The Reverend Edmund Jones, writing in the 1780s, had personal experience of attempted and interrupted abductions and also met a changeling boy, elfin son of Edmund John William of Church Valley. The "idiot child" lived until he was ten or twelve years old (longer than was usual for his kind) and "was something diabolical in aspect" making disturbed motions and a disagreeable screaming sound. He was dark or tawny in complexion, unlike his family. Generally, Jones said, those exchanged were "of no growth, good appearance or sense."[352]

On Shetland the saying is that an "idiot" cannot ever sneeze. The belief relates to "oafs" or changelings and a newborn child was thought to be under the spell of the trows until it sneezed for the first time—at which point all danger was passed and it was proved not to be a changeling.

Despite the disagreeable looks of most changelings and their short life spans, they need not all be backward, repulsive, and crippled. Some changelings had preternatural knowledge: one Devonshire witness recalled an elderly female in his village who was said to have talked like a woman of fifty from the age of five and who spent all her time collecting wild honey. In another Dartmoor story, Jimmy Townsend swears that his sister Grace was changed by the pixies when he was a young boy. Nonetheless she grows into her twenties and is a healthy and marriageable young woman, whatever her brother had to say. In due course she marries, although Jimmy warns that the union is unlikely to be happy. At first his forecasts seem to be disproved, but then the new husband loses his cow, followed by his litter of pigs, and then his geese. He has to give up farming, but every other line of work he tries is

---

352. Hobbes, *Leviathan,* Part 4, 436; Scot, *Discourse,* Book II, chapter 4; Jones, *Appearance of Evil,* para. 66.

cursed with misfortune as well—a run of bad luck that locals take as proof that the man had chosen a pixie wife.[353]

So, the changed child was almost always disabled—an oaf or elf. This is the human perception, but that is the view of communities whose members have been stolen against their will, leaving substitutes that are unwanted and, in their eyes, unhealthy. Is this fair, though? The human perspective is only half the story and there's good reason to infer that the faeries see it rather differently. As we shall discover in the next section, they still care enough about those members of their society who have been left in the mortal world to protect them from any threat of harm and, as mentioned earlier, the infants taken seem to be well looked after. Harsh as their methods are, then, perhaps the faery motivations are in some way to do with care: the aim is ensuring that an elderly elf receives constant human attention and providing a good upbringing for a mortal infant. We know that humans are appreciated as wet nurses for faery offspring, in light of which changelings can be seen as being just another version of the practice.

Bearing these suggestions in mind, it's interesting to read an account from the Isle of Man in which the faeries replaced the human child moments after abducting it. A woman went to harvest corn in a field and laid her baby down whilst she worked. Seeing an opportunity, a faery snatched up the baby and set a changeling in its place. The elf child cried out and the human mother naturally made to pick up what she thought was still her infant. One of the men in the field prevented her and when it became apparent that the changeling was going to be being ignored, the faery replaced the human baby and departed. This account seems to confirm that the Good Folk are as concerned for the proper care of their own offspring as for any advantage they may gain by taking a human child.[354]

Exposing the Changeling

The consensus was that changelings were ugly and frail and prone to shrieking. That constituted the primary way in which they would be identified. Further proof might come by means of a ploy intended to expose the elf's great age.

---

353. Bowring, "Devonshire Pixies," *Once a Week,* vol. 16 (1867), 205; Crossing, *Tales of Dartmoor Pixies,* c. 5.

354. *Choice Notes & Queries,* 1859, 26.

For example, a conversation might be started about music and dancing; the suspected changeling might be involved and asked questions in the hope that it would be caught off guard and would reveal itself by joining in. The trick of pretending to brew beer in eggshells was a very popular way of getting the elf to exclaim upon the fact that, despite its age and worldly wisdom, it had never seen such a thing (incidentally confirming faeries' long life spans). Sometimes the changeling would blow its own cover, for example by asking for whisky or by performing some adult task such as playing the bagpipes or threshing grain. Once the problem had been diagnosed, there were then plentiful remedies available for reversing the situation.[355]

Expelling the Changeling

Changelings tend to have short life spans and it was said that, when the sickly infant does die, "the faeries have got their own." In other words, it's returned home to be with its own kind. Understandably, few parents could tolerate waiting for this dismal outcome and instead they sought to drive away the faery and get back their own offspring before it was too late.[356]

Desperate families have often resorted to desperate measures to recover their infants. One writer observed that parents were "apt to mischief" the elf child left behind. This is something of an understatement given the kind of mistreatment that was inflicted upon suspected changelings. Such ill treatment was intended to drive off the cuckoo infant and to force the faeries to return the abducted child. As will be seen, it was often ferocious and must have taken deep conviction and a resolute will to carry it through. Of course, it must have helped to tell yourself that the faeries had already acted violently and maliciously and that they were being repaid in the only terms they would understand and respect. It must have assisted, too, to know that this mistreatment had been found to get results, although any hesitation or mistake by the parents might lead to failure.

A range of escalating techniques was deployed by desperate families. At the end of all of these tortures, the expectation was that the changeling

---

355. Aitken, *Forgotten Heritage*, 9; Sutherland, *Folklore Gleanings*, 26.

356. Harland, *Lancashire Legends & Traditions*, 220.

would flee and the stolen infant would be deposited safe and sound by the faeries outside the home.

If you come across the faeries in the act of carrying off a baby, there is one foolproof means of rescue that relies upon their unshakeable belief in a fair bargain. The human instantly cries out "what's mine is yours and what's yours is mine" and throws to them some item, generally a small piece of clothing, in return for which the faeries are obliged to surrender the abducted child in their arms. Even blessing a cradle very shortly after an abduction could be enough to stop the faeries in their tracks. This might seem to be too late and to be a case of "bolting the stable door" but it seems to indicate that, until the child is actually taken within the faery dwelling, it is more easily recoverable.[357]

If it was too late for one of the moment-of-crisis remedies, one of the longer and more violent means of retrieval would have to be considered. On Shetland, if a child had been "taken from the ground," there was a special and lengthy ceremony to follow to protect it. This involved, first, collecting a bucket full of seawater from the breaking surf. This was boiled by throwing in three red-hot seashore pebbles and the suspect child was then bathed in the water, being turned three times in each direction. After this the baby was placed on a wet blanket and was passed through the flames of a peat fire before putting it to bed swaddled in the blanket. An effigy of the child was then burned. This remedy was laborious for the parents and possibly uncomfortable for the child, but it probably did no great harm. That was not always the case.[358]

Changelings could be driven away, forcing the faeries to return their infant captive, by exposing them to a range of unpleasant conditions. One of the mildest involved the stale urine mentioned earlier. A suspected changeling could be laid on top of the pot in which the liquid was being stored and, because the faeries object strongly to nasty smells, this might be enough to expel it.

Alternatively, the changeling might be exposed to the elements. In the Highlands, leaving the creature overnight at a faery well or at the junction of three shires or three rivers was recommended. A special receptacle for the

---

357. Crofton Croker, *Fairy Legends,* 43 & 39.

358. Spence, *The Fairy Tradition in Britain,* 147.

baby might exist for these purposes. Near the Moray Firth in the north of Scotland, there was once a stone trough at St. Benet's spring which was called the "faeries' cradle." Placing a suspected changeling in this overnight would recover the real baby from the Fae. Whether for good or ill, the trough was destroyed during the Jacobite Rebellion of 1745.[359]

On Shetland similar treatment was known to have worked. We have already seen the first part of this story in an earlier section: a man's quick action saved his newborn nephew from being taken, but his own family was then the subject of the faeries' reprisals. One of his children had cried for eight days and then slept for eight days, after which it seemed different. Convinced that the faeries had exchanged it, the father put the cradle outside— "beyond the shadow of the lintel." When he then looked at the baby in the cot, it was revealed to be just a lifeless image of the kidnapped child. Incidentally, this is not the only Scottish example of the protector being punished by the cheated faeries. A Perthshire herdsman saw a faery band approaching a cottage where he knew there to be a woman and newly delivered baby. He dashed to get there first and drew lines (circles) around the mother and child to protect them. This worked, but when he left the house, he was promptly carried off through the air for six or seven miles and back again before being dropped down through the smoke hole of his father's cottage.[360]

Another Highland cure was even more sinister. A shallow grave had to be dug in a field and the changeling was placed in it overnight in the expectation that the abducted infant would be returned by the next dawn. From the west of Scotland comes a detailed version of a related remedy. The baby had to be taken to a known faery haunt—a place where the wind is heard to sough in a peculiar way in the trees and one that is often near to a cairn, standing stone, green mound or dell, or a stone circle. Certain words were said and the child was left with an offering of food. After a wait of an hour or two, around midnight, the parent would return to find the food gone and the lost child restored.[361]

---

359. Grant Stewart, *Popular Superstitions*, 115.

360. Dalyell, *The Darker Superstitions of Scotland*, 538; Murray, *Tales from Highland Perthshire*, no. 204.

361. Browne, *History of the Highlands*, 115; Miller, *Scenes and Legends*, 105; Napier, *Folklore*, 42.

Direct physical violence intended to drive out the changeling was common. A Cornish remedy was to place the baby on the ash heap, beat it with a broom (with the help of neighbours) and then leave it naked under the church stile. Fortunately, merely suggesting harm to the changeling might succeed. In one case a Scottish mother was advised by the local wise woman to throw the "shargie" child in the river; it overheard the plan, took fright, and left of its own accord. Similarly, in Sutherland the practice was to take the changeling to the local smithy and lay it on the anvil. The blacksmith would then pick up his hammer and threaten to pound the baby to a jelly; this would be enough to drive off the elf. To be sure, once a changeling had fallen for such a trick and given itself away, very little compunction might then be shown over whipping the creature, casting it on the fire, or dropping it off a bridge.[362]

Violence might even be used against a faery mother. In one case from Rousay on Orkney, the advice to the mother of the taken child was to go to a well-known rock outcrop known to be haunted by the Fae. There the mother had to thrust a steel wedge into a prominent cleft in the rock until a door appeared and opened. Entering this, she would find a faery woman with a baby on her lap. Without uttering a word, the human mother was to strike the other three times in the face with a Bible. Leaving the rock and returning home, she would find her own child there, restored to her.[363]

Fire was often a key ingredient of any rescue attempt. Once again, the threat alone might work: in several Scottish cases a stock had been left and simply stoking the fire was sufficient to drive it away. In Cornwall one more elaborate cure required the parent to make a smoky fire with green ferns and, when the house had completely filled with fumes, to go outside and turn around three times.[364]

Heat was definitely seen as a key part of the process of expelling changelings. In a case from Scotland a wise woman advised the family that their child had been changed and what was in the cradle was really a "croupin," but a ready remedy existed. The fire had to be lit all night and all the requests

---

362. Courtney, *Cornish Feasts*, 126; Leather, *Folklore of Herefordshire*, 47; Sutherland, *Folklore Gleanings*, 26.

363. Marwick, *The Folklore of Orkney*, 83.

364. Grant Stewart, *Popular Superstitions*, 109; Courtney, *Cornish Feasts*, 126.

of the child had to be ignored. The first night this was tried the suspected changeling kept begging for water and was eventually given a drink. The parents thereby failed to break the faery spell. They succumbed too on a second attempt but on a third were deaf to all entreaties by the infant. Eventually it got out of bed, rolled around on the floor for a while and finally disappeared in a blue flame. To actually throw the changeling on the fire in the hearth or, at least, to hold it in the smoke and heat above the flames was the last resort, albeit one that was deemed highly effective. In one example from Dumfries and Galloway, a complex ritual led up to this. The parents had to sit on either side of their hearth, with a candle between them that had been lit using sparks from a hag stone. The suspected changeling was bound hand and foot with red cloth and then held in the smoke of a rowan fire. After considerable cursing, spitting, and screaming, the elf shot up out of the smoke hole in the roof.[365]

It may be a little comfort to know that it wasn't always the child that suffered. A remedy from North East Scotland recommended holding a black hen near to a very hot fire. The hen would naturally struggle to escape and would fly up the chimney, at which point the elf would also depart and the kidnapped baby would come back. This remedy aside, most traditional ways of expelling changelings did involve at least discomfort, if not peril, for the suspect baby. For this reason, they are now widely disapproved of and have fallen into disuse.[366]

The expectation behind all these remedies was that the stolen child would swiftly be returned. The faeries still care about and actively monitor the welfare of the changeling left behind and therefore will act promptly to prevent harm to it. If the changeling had been disposed of away from the house, on the parent's return home their infant would be found restored; if the oaf was held over the fire, the baby would immediately be heard outside.

We must admit, however, that even when the original child was restored, it might still be marked by its experiences. This may be because steps had already been taken by the faeries to make the stolen infant more like them-

---

365. Fergusson, *Rambling Sketches*, 127; Aitken, *Forgotten Heritage*, 12; Browning, *Dumfries & Galloway Folk Tales*, 53.

366. Gregor, *Notes on the Folklore*, 61; a comparable remedy involving roasting a black hen is reported from Wales: Jenkyn Thomas, *Welsh Fairy Book*, "The Llanfabon changeling."

selves, a process which may involve dipping the child in a magic well or anointing it with special ointment. An illustration of this comes from the Cornish story of the child beaten with brooms and exposed near the church. The abuse of the changeling meant that the woman's son came back to her from faeryland, but he never seemed right again: he spent his time alone tending animals and died at only thirty years old.[367]

It would be wrong, too, to present the faeries as entirely selfish and oblivious to the human parents' reactions. From Almscliffe Crag in West Yorkshire comes a mid-Victorian account of two children stolen from a woman whilst she was working in the fields at harvest. So great was her distress at their disappearance, and so prolonged her weeping, that the local faeries took pity on her and gave the children back. Even so, it's interesting to note the local belief that, despite their short time away, the kids were permanently affected by their experience and grew up distinctly smaller than others of their age.

Explaining Changelings

In previous centuries, murders of children obviously did occur during attempts to expel changelings.[368] Nowadays, plainly, child protection legislation is far more effective and none of this treatment should be possible. What's important though is the attitude that is revealed. The preparedness of parents to contemplate almost any steps to retrieve their lost child is predictable; their attitude to Faery is more surprising. Kidnapping was accepted as being a key characteristic of the Fae, something to be anticipated and fought against. It may be seen as another form of our traffic with the faeries—an extreme version that is involuntary and unbalanced, admittedly—but part of our constant dealings with them. This aspect of our relationship with the Good Folk, in particular, reinforces my frequent impression that they act toward us, in many respects, like a colonial power. For the Fae, humans can be a resource to be exploited; we are not to be treated as equals with rights, rather we are subjects; we are curious and amusing, but we only have any value insofar as we are useful to them.

Despite all the foregoing, we should acknowledge that the abuse of supposed changeling children might actually prove to be shortsighted. In one

---

367. Pegg, *Argyll Folk Tales*, 35; Bottrell, *Traditions and Hearthside Stories,* vol. 2, 199.

368. Dalyell, *The Darker Superstitions of Scotland,* 538.

Scottish story a nursing mother was approached by a faery woman asking her to care for her child as well. She agreed to this and looked after the baby so well that she was rewarded with cloth, faery medicines, and good fortune. From Suffolk we hear of a mother who accepted and cared for the changeling as her own, finding money left for her every morning as payment for her extra trouble. Happiest of all, in a case from Dartmoor the human mother who accepted the changeling and cared for it lovingly as her own so pleased the pixies that they returned her baby, which grew up endowed with good fortune.[369]

Finally, as the last story demonstrates, faery childcare is generally good. They like (perhaps even need) human children and they will usually care for them well and return them in good health. Even so, this is not universally the case: in one changeling story from Glengarry in the Highlands the elf was expelled by being thrown in a deep pool and the human child duly reappeared, but during its absence in Faery it had been underfed, neglected, and reduced to skin and bone.[370]

Elf-Addled

As I mentioned in chapter 2, our Anglo-Saxon forebears diagnosed a number of ailments which they ascribed to malign faery intervention, one of which was called *ælfadl* (which we may roughly translate as elf-addle today). Its nature is uncertain—it appears to have involved some degree of internal physical pain—but I have co-opted the name here to describe more broadly the health effects of contact with our faery neighbours. The more traditional term is "faery taken." This denotes not just the act of abduction but the medical consequences of this as well.

Physical Risks of Faeryland

It's pretty widely known that a visit to faeryland and any time spent "in the hill" can have serious physical consequences. Indeed, in the Scottish Northern Isles the adjective "trowie" (trow-like) was synonymous with sickly.

---

369. Aitken, *Forgotten Heritage*, 14; *Printed Extracts, Suffolk,* 37; Bray, *Description,* 177.
370. Sutherland, *Folklore Gleanings,* 26; MacDougall, *Folk Tales,* 117.

At the very least, the experience can be unpleasant and isolating. A Manx man was taken by the faeries for a space of four years. He said that, whilst he was away, he could still see his friends and family, but he could not be seen by them nor could he communicate with them in any way. When he returned to this world, he said it was like awaking from unconsciousness. This latter remark suggests some of the confusion and disorientation that the state of being elf-addled denotes. In another account from Perthshire in the Highlands, a man was working in his garden when the faeries came and abducted him for three days. When he was returned from the knoll he was in a dazed state and could hardly describe what had happened to him. He sickened and within two days was gone.[371]

Because time may pass more slowly in Faery, the returning visitor may discover that their few hours away were really years or centuries, so that they return to a land wholly unfamiliar to them and where they often crumble away to dust as soon as they have contact with the food or soil of the mortal world. For instance, a year and a day seem like a night, a few minutes are really twenty-three years, and what is experienced as a few hours turns out to be many decades. A vivid example of this temporal difference comes from Her-erefordshire. Some young people returning from a fair came across some faeries dancing in a ring. One man in the party joined them and only returned a year later, but the oranges and biscuits from the fair that were in his pockets were still fresh. He, however, quickly sickened and died. The time differences can be baffling and disorientating. In a story from Wales a boy was sent by his mother to fetch some barm (the froth of fermenting malt) from a neighbour's house. He was gone a year and a day, but when he reappeared, he was still holding the barm bottle his mother had given him and was under the impression he'd been absent barely minutes. In a related version of this story, the boy returns from his errand with the item he was sent to fetch in his hand; he had delayed on the way only a few minutes to listen to faery music but he comes home a very old man. Anticipating our next section, he then searches desperately for the way back into Faery, but is unable to find it.[372]

---

371. Murray, *Tales from Highland Perthshire*, no. 179.

372. Leather, *Folklore of Herefordshire*, 45–46; MacPherson, *Barra*, 173; Owen, *Welsh Folklore*, 48.

Closely related to these last cases is the condition of those who are taken in faery dances. Whilst they are with the faeries, they feel that almost no time has passed and they have hardly danced enough. Once rescued, they frequently collapse with exhaustion because they have in fact been dancing nonstop for a year and a day; they may also be reduced to starved skeletons because they have had no chance to eat during all that time.[373]

A sojourn of any duration in faeryland may change the body so that it cannot revert to its old life. This is the result of physical alterations caused by consumption of faery food. Though freed, the returning captive often dies soon afterward as a reaction to touching human food, which is now effectively poisonous.

The ill effects may be less drastic and more insidious than this, but nevertheless contact with the otherworld can lead to permanent physiological changes. On Shetland girls taken young by the trows were said to return strikingly beautiful, but they were also prone to die young.

Psychological Risks of Faery

Less well-reported are the psychological ill effects of a sojourn with the Fae. Abductees might be released from faeryland after a conventional captivity of seven years, but they can seldom settle again or feel like they fit in with human society. It is said that returnees often remember next to nothing of their time away, but they are nonetheless left blighted. A man called Iago ap Dewi of Llanllawddog in Mid Wales was taken for seven years by the tylwyth teg. When he finally returned, he never spoke a word about his experiences. Perhaps fear of betraying what he'd seen and heard was a part of this (and we know how highly discretion is valued by the faeries), but the disorientating and alienating effect of exposure to an otherworld must also be part of the explanation.[374]

We can piece together the mental ill effects of a visit to Faery from various sources across the centuries and the evidence we have is consistent: people who return from Faery are never the same again. There are many descriptions of this. In seventeenth-century England John Aubrey collected a story

---

373. Davies, *Folklore of West and Mid-Wales*,110; Owen, *Welsh Folklore*, 37.

374. Davies, *Folklore of West and Mid-Wales*, 110.

concerning a shepherd, employed by a Mr. Brown of Winterbourne Bassett in Wiltshire, who had seen the ground open and had been "brought to strange places underground" where music was played. As Aubrey observed of such visitors, once they had witnessed faery pleasures, they could "never any afterward enjoy themselves."[375]

Later the same century the Reverend Robert Kirk met a woman who had come back from Faery; she ate very little food and "is still prettie melanchollyous and silent, hardly seen ever to laugh. Her natural Heat and radical Moisture seem to be equally balanced, lyke an unextinguished Lamp, and going in a circle, not unlike the faint Lyfe of Bees and some Sort of Birds that sleep all the Winter over and revive in the *Spring*."[376]

The main symptoms seem to be a sense of bereavement and a longing to retrieve the joys of Faery. For example, those who returned home in Scotland "never again took kindly to the works and ways of their fellow men. They loved the sunny braes, glens and woods that lay far from the abodes of men ... With dreamy, longing eyes, gazing out for something that they could not reach, they pined away the rest of their days, beings apart."[377]

An identical description of the affliction comes from Cornwall. Those abducted were described as unhappy creatures who never again settled to work but "roamed about aimlessly, doing nothing, hoping and longing one day to be allowed to go back to the place from which they'd been banished."[378]

For returnees, mortal life becomes a pale substitute for what they have glimpsed and they can only linger on here, awaiting or hoping for escape. In James Hogg's famous poem "Kilmeny," the heroine suffers all these symptoms: "nae smile was seen on Kilmeny's face /... still was her look, and ... still was her e'e." Although she could not describe to her family where she'd been nor what she'd seen, her birthplace "wasna her hame, and she couldna remain." In bitter contrast to her parents' joy and relief at her return, she was desperate to leave "the world of sorrow and pain."

---

375. Briggs, *Fairies in Literature & Tradition*, 12.

376. Kirk, *Secret Commonwealth*, chapter 15.

377. Gregor, *Notes on the Folklore*, 62.

378. Courtney, *Cornish Feasts*, 121; see too the story of *Cherry of Zennor*.

Perhaps most upsetting and difficult for families and friends is the fact that those who've been taken seem unable to talk about their experiences. The Shetland trows would take children for a while but released them at puberty. Back with human society, they always maintained "an unbroken silence regarding the land of their captivity." Indeed, that silence could be physically enforced: in Ireland it was believed that "the wee folk puts a thing in their mouth that they can't speak." In modern terms, we might even see this as some sort of post-traumatic stress disorder: those at home can never understand what the returnee has been through.[379]

Irish poet W. B. Yeats was fascinated by the elf-addled condition and made a special study of it. He linked various physical symptoms to the distraction and sorrow suffered. A person who's been taken will have pale skin, a cold touch, and a low voice. They will suffer from fainting fits, fatigue, languor, long and heavy sleeping, and wasting. Being dazed and even trance-like, returnees seldom take care of themselves properly.[380]

Sometimes, of course, it's hard to determine whether the after-effects are primarily psychological or physiological (though one may lead to the other). All we can say for certain is that those who've been away are never the same again and that their return to this world is seldom the happy event that we might anticipate.

Cornish Case Studies

An example of being elf-addled comes from the well-known story of "The House on Selena Moor."[381] Pixie-led on Selena Moor in the far west of Cornwall, a Mr. Noy finds a farmhouse at which a celebration is taking place. As he approaches, he meets Grace, a former lover, whom he thought to have been dead, but who has actually been captured and enslaved by the faeries. She warns him not to touch the faery food and drink, as she had done, and tells him something of the faery life she now shares. The experience of seeing the faeries, and of knowing his lost love still to be alive in faeryland, deeply affected him:

---

379. Spence, *The Fairy Tradition in Britain*, 262.

380. Yeats, *Unpublished Prose*, vol. 1, 418 & vol. 2, 281; see too Jones, *The Appearance of Evil*, paragraphs 70, 68, 82, 56, 62, and 69.

381. Bottrell, *Traditions and Hearthside Stories*, vol. 1, 94–102.

From that night … he seemed to be a changed man; he talked of little else but what he saw and heard there … Often at dusk of eve and moonlight nights, he wandered round the moors in hopes to meet Grace, and when he found his search was all in vain, he became melancholy, neglected his farm, tired of hunting, and departed this life before the next harvest. Whether he truly died or passed into faery-land, no one knows.

Noy had had no physical contact with Grace nor had he partaken of the faery fruit and beer—otherwise he would never have been able to return home at all. Nevertheless, what he saw and heard was enough to take away his pleasure in the mortal life.

A very similar story from the same area is that of Richard Vingoe, who discovered Faery down a long passage under the cliffs near Land's End. He too met there a former lover who he believed had died but who had, in fact, been "changed into the faery state." She saved him from her fate and led him back to the surface, but nevertheless he was never as he had been before, took to drinking, and died young and unmarried.[382]

In both these cases the lot of the lover who's been abducted doesn't seem especially happy, but nevertheless the men pine to be reunited with them. Perhaps this was just love-sickness, but it seems too that the glimpse of another world beyond our own is part of the cause of their unhappiness.

Faery Haunting and Girdle Measuring

It isn't necessary to be abducted bodily to Faery to suffer the ill effects of faery contact. We've already looked at some of the other ways in which sickness can arise from proximity to the supernatural in this world. For example, in Wales the mere look of an elf was believed to be dangerous, and in Scotland it's been said that seeing a dwarf will mean that you'll fall ill within a year, whilst a faery's breath can instantly cause boils and sickness. As has also been mentioned, being pixy-led and travelling with the *sluagh* can both prove debilitating or fatal experiences.[383]

---

382. Bottrell, *Traditions and Hearthside Stories,* vol. 2, 102.

383. Crofton Croker, *Fairy Legends,* 116.

In fact, it appears that any prolonged physical exposure to the Good Folk could prove fatal. In one Scottish story a man awoke to find three little men gathered in front of his peat fire, enjoying the heat. As they warmed themselves, the three leaned back against his legs. The next morning his limbs felt heavy and he couldn't move them. As the days passed, they got more and more painful so that, within a week, he was dead.[384]

In addition, it has been widely accepted across the British Isles that faeries purposely can inflict harm upon humans, striking them with illness or disability whether by elf shot or by some mysterious "blast." This illness was so familiar in the past as to be known as "the faery," the symptoms of which might also be described as being "faery-taken" or "haunted by a faery."

On closer analysis, the situation turns out to be more complicated still. There are the straightforward cases of people who are made ill in this world by the faeries; secondly, there are those who continue to be present corporeally but whose soul is absent. It turns out that some visits to faeryland don't have to involve a physical journey: rather, the person's body remains behind, apparently struck down by sickness, while their spirit is transported. It is believed that part of their substance has been stolen, just as the nourishing part of food is abstracted. To friends and family at home, the absentee appears to have fallen into a dream or to be "as still as stones in the street." The patient who has been "taken" has been afflicted with a languishing disease termed "the phairie"—they are struck dumb and lose the use of their limbs. For example, on Shetland it was believed that the trows might steal part of a new mother, the part that remained at home seeming "pale and absent." W. B. Yeats described how Irish sufferers (especially women soon after childbirth) would take to their beds, perhaps for weeks and not uncommonly for years (frequently for the magically significant period of seven years, but sometimes for decades or even for the remainder of their lives), lying in a state of unconsciousness, as if in a trance. During this time, they were believed to be living in Faery.[385]

---

384. Murray, *Tales from Highland Perthshire*, no. 219.

385. William Browne, *Britannia's Pastorals*, Book I; Mr. S., *Gammer Gurton's Needle*, 1562, Act I, scene 2; Dalyell, *Darker Superstitions*, 538; Young & Houlbrook, *Magical Folk*, 132; Yeats, note 39 to Lady A. Gregory, *Visions and Beliefs in the West of Ireland*, Dublin (1920), 287–8.

Many mystery illnesses were blamed on faery influence in the past. In 1677, in his book *The Displaying of Supposed Witchcraft*, John Webster had this to say on the belief: "...the common people, if they have any sort of Epilepsie, Palsie, Convulsions and the like, do presently perswade themselves they are bewitched, fore-spoken, blasted, faery-taken or haunted with some evil spirit and the like..." A range of maladies and symptoms might be ascribed to supernatural causes and, this being the case, medical practitioners had to be able to respond with accurate diagnoses and effective cures.[386]

Furthermore, the condition of being taken was not necessarily just a one-off illness. Some individuals seem to have had multiple attacks or relapses. This explains a detail of the record of the accusations made against Isobel Sinclair, who was tried for witchcraft on Orkney in 1633. The court heard that she had been "six times controlled with the faery." In light of the above, we may conclude she had a half-dozen periods of illness when she was unconscious and was assumed by her family and neighbours to have been abducted to "Elfame."[387]

The coma-like state associated with "faery haunting" seems to have had consistent, recognisable symptoms, as a result of which healers felt confident that they could identify and treat cases of "taken" individuals. Very frequently this was done by means of "measuring." This was an ancient diagnostic practice worldwide, but in Western Europe it can be traced back at least to the time of Pliny. It was used in England until the late sixteenth century and in parts of Wales into the nineteenth century. A change in the size of a girdle or belt could indicate that a person had been invaded by a faery or evil spirit—clearly there are suggestions of demonic possession in this. Charms and prayers could exorcise the spirit and the belt might also be cut up as part of the cure. In Ireland headaches were treated by measuring the sufferer's head, whilst in Wales a range of conditions including depression, jaundice, nervous complaints, consumption, and being the subject of witchcraft were all detected by means of ritual measurement from the elbow to fingertip, or by tying a cloth or rope around the body or limbs. Suspected Scottish

---

386. Webster, 323.

387. See *The Survey of Scottish Witchcraft*, http://www.shca.ed.ac.uk/Research/witches/.

witch Bessie Dunlop, who learned her herbal medicine from the Fae, was also given a lace by them. She would tie this around a woman in childbirth to help ease the delivery.

Girdle measuring was explicitly used to identify and to help cure those who had been "taken" by the faeries. Here are a few examples: In 1438 Agnes Hancock in Somerset was found by the church authorities to be treating children afflicted with "feyry" by inspecting their girdles or shoes. In 1566 Elizabeth Mortlock of Pampisford, Cambridgeshire, was offering the same cure. She repeated a series of Catholic prayers and then measured the child's girdle from her elbow to her thumb, asking God to confirm if the girl was haunted with a faery. If the girdle or belt was shorter than usual, the nature of the affliction was clear. Mortlock claimed that she had assisted several children in this manner. In about 1570 another woman, Jennet Peterson, was accused of using witchcraft before the ecclesiastical court at Durham. According to Robert Duncan of Wallsend she had practised the "measuring of belts to preserve folks from the farye." Like Elizabeth Mortlock, Jennet seemed to have been making a good living by identifying and curing faery blights upon her neighbours. Lastly, Lady Gregory told a story of an Irish changeling child that had seemed to be thriving until a neighbour called into the house. The visitor proposed to measure both her own child and the changeling with the string from her apron. From that point on the infant did not thrive and was always screaming.[388]

I wonder if the process of girdle measuring is somehow concerned with gaining control over the faery's magic. In a story from Ardnamurchan in the Highlands, a man called Luran outwitted the faeries who had been reaping his crop at night by leaving a wise old man in the field. The faeries appeared from a knoll and started to harvest the crop; the guard then counted their number out loud and by this simple means banished them forever. There's certainly something magical and powerful about numbers, but usually the folklore works the other way around and in the faeries' favour. Staying in Scotland, the belief in the North East was that baked cakes should never be counted as the faeries will eat half of them or they will go off quickly. On

---

388. A. Gregory, *Visions and Beliefs in the West of Ireland*, 237, but see generally her chapter IV, "Away."

Shetland, counting any of your possessions—sheep, horses, fish, or chattels—was thought to attract bad luck. Presumably again, enumerating them put them in the faeries' power—a case perhaps of "counting your blessings."[389]

Summary

A visit to faeryland need not be harmful. Many travellers come and go unscathed. Some are even transformed for the better by the experience. As alluded to earlier, girls might be abducted by the Shetland trows but returned to their homes when they reached adulthood; they would be restored to their families "in maiden prime with a wild unearthly beauty and glamour on them." Nevertheless, we should recall that many are harmed in body or mind by the experience and that some people *never* return from Faery; they are abducted and are simply never seen again.[390]

The Good Folk weren't intentionally malicious when they stole people away. Rather, they were simply oblivious to the human consequences, as their needs were given complete priority. It may be significant that reports of faery abduction are very much reduced nowadays. Perhaps the Good Folk's opinion of us has changed as we have become more technically sophisticated; perhaps, instead, they prefer to try to work cooperatively with us now.

To close, time spent in Faery must *always* be viewed as potentially perilous. Even if the person is neither enslaved nor entrapped, they can still feel the effects of their adventure long-term.

---

389. J. G. Campbell, c. 2; Gregor, *Notes on the Folklore*, 65 & 157; *County Folklore*, vol. 3, 162.

390. Young & Houlbrook, *Magical Folk*, 132; Davies, *Folklore of West and Mid-Wales*, 122.

Chapter 13

FAERY MAGIC AND FAERY HEALING

The Good Folk are magical beings and this quality suffuses their relationship with mortals. Many faery activities are reliant upon their magical ability to manipulate their environment—or themselves. Inevitably, then, people have always sought to try to shape that relationship for their own benefit, attempting to gain control over the Fae through magic or to acquire some measure of their magical powers to obtain advantage in the material world.

Faery magic can be powerful, but it can also be quite "dark," in that it is most often wielded for the purposes of concealment and deception. The faeries have always used their abilities in the first instance to further their interests and to protect themselves from unwanted intrusions by humans. This isn't the whole story, nevertheless. Faery magic can be used to cure and to help both their own kind and their nearest neighbours. In this chapter I'll discuss some of these powers, primarily in the context of the Good Folk's relationship to people, and in particular I'll consider how magic powers might be obtained from the faeries by individuals and what they may be used for.

Faery Illusion

Faery magic powers have been summarised as including mist caps, rapid flight, prophecy, shapeshifting, and supernatural knowledge and abilities. We've already examined their power to change their size or shape and we'll consider soon their ability to see into the future. Our concern here will be their manipulation of the appearance of other objects and places.

The Good Folk are able to produce short-term, large-scale illusions as well as, rarely, long-term transformations. For example, they're known for passing off seashells, horse dung, or dead leaves as gold coins, and it's believed in Cornwall that if tin is placed in an ant's nest at the time of a new moon, the pixies will transmute it into silver. Such magical control of the elements is impressive, but given the contrary nature of the Fae, we have to remind ourselves that at the same time their powers seem curiously limited: they can't mend their own broken tools but they can perform alchemy.[391]

The use of glamour to create the appearance of places and things that don't exist is probably the most impressive of the Good Folk's magical displays. We have regular reports of this being done in two situations: in order to deceive midwives into believing they are attending births in rich mansions, and to trick travellers led astray. For the midwives, grand apartments and furnishings are really just caves scattered with rushes, a delusion perhaps created to encourage the women to stay and perform their work without any doubts over getting paid.[392]

In the case of travellers, the complex illusions that are conjured are harder to explain. Whole houses full of people and celebrations appear where no dwelling previously stood. The visitor will join in the feasting and dancing and will then be taken to a splendid chamber with soft bedding, only to awake the next morning lying out on the bare moor. In an example from Gloucestershire, the illusion lasted well into the following day. A man lost in the dark in deep snow on top of the Cotswolds near Dursley came across an inn where he found a room for the night. He slept well and found an excellent breakfast laid out for him the next morning. When he was ready to leave, he could not find any staff around so he placed two guineas in payment for his accommodation on the

---

391. Courtney, *Cornish Feasts,* 125.

392. Rhys, *Celtic Folklore,* 63, 213 & 247.

counter before continuing his journey. Arriving at his destination, he told his friends of his good fortune and they said there was no such inn in the place he described. Returning to the spot to settle the argument, he found no sign of the tavern, but his coins were lying in the snow.[393]

Faery glamour can be used to deceive, to reassure, to assist, and to protect humans. As with so many of the Good Folk's powers and abilities, how illusion may be applied in a particular case may often seem to be down to whim.

Spells for Summoning Fae

Before you can hope to receive magical powers from the Fae, you have to be in their presence. Some people are lucky enough to be endowed with the second sight and are born able to see faeries—although a child left sleeping on a faery knoll may also be imbued with the power and there is some evidence that children generally are more prone to see faeries than adults. Those with second sight are very few and far between and they must use their power circumspectly: talking too freely about what you have seen or heard may lose you your gift. On Shetland the belief is that, whilst it's good luck to hear the trows, it's unfortunate for most people to actually see them; the difference here may be that those with the second sight are imbued with a faery power and derive some protection from this.[394]

Other individuals, though lacking the second sight, may still be fortunate enough to be in the right place at the right time and encounter the Good Folk that way. These times are universally agreed to include the nighttime in moonlight, with the faeries regularly depicted as fleeing at cockcrow, but just after dawn on summer mornings and between dusk and dark in May and during the early summer are also reported to be fortuitous. If you are lucky enough to catch glimpse of a faery, it is important then that you don't move a muscle or an eyelash. So long as your eye is fixed upon them, they will not be able to disappear or to escape. Of course, the faeries are cunning and they will always find a way to distract you—that momentary lapse of attention will be enough for them to vanish. For instance, a Cornish tin miner who

---

393. Rhys, *Celtic Folklore*, 99, 115, 150 & 215; Palmer, *Gloucestershire*, 145.
394. Sutherland, *Folklore Gleanings*, 22; MacDougall, *Folk Tales*, 183; Saxby, *Shetland Traditional Lore*, 127 & 130.

broke through into a pixy tunnel discovered a group of knockers at work; they asked him for a candle and, as soon as he looked away to pick one up, they disappeared.[395]

Earlier in the book, I mentioned that your state of mind may play a role in seeing the faeries and that being a little "absent-minded" may make you more receptive. The Reverend Robert Hughes, a minister in North Wales in the early nineteenth century, saw some faeries riding on the road one morning. He found that if he "mastered his eyes" the vision would disappear, but would then return quite vividly. Letting rational thought intervene to exclude sensory experience seemed to be what made the difference here.[396]

Most of us are not going to be so lucky as to be granted—or to stumble upon—a faery vision and, this being the case, it may come as little surprise to discover that magic has long been deployed in order to try to summon and control faeries. Here I'll offer a small selection of practical faery-related magic for readers. The proper preparation for all of these is probably advisable: many of the older sources recommend fasting and cleansing for three or four days before any attempt to contact the otherworld. During this time, the magician would eat only bread and water and would avoid sex and other "pollutions" (presumably alcohol and tobacco). Immediately before the ceremony, he would bathe, put on clean clothes, and fumigate himself with incense. This sort of purification is advised because it shows proper respect for the magical beings. Secondly, some locations are more auspicious for establishing contact. Earlier I discussed preferred faery places: one magical source suggests that woods and mountains will be best for meeting faeries and nymphs.[397]

The first few spells for summoning faeries are relatively accessible to all. I've mentioned already that running around a faery ring will enable you to hear their music; running around a faery hill nine times in a left-handed direction on Halloween is likewise said to open the door of the faery dwelling to you. Similarly, if, on the first night of a new moon, you run nine times around a faery ring, the dancing faeries will be revealed to you.

---

395. Bottrell, *Traditions and Hearthside Stories*, vol. 1, 77.

396. Rhys, *Celtic Folklore*, 215.

397. Scot, *Discoverie of Witchcraft*, Book XV, chapter 4 & 1665 *Supplement* chapter 1.

Next, on a moonlit night when the catkin pollen is just ripened, you may take two of the branches and wave them gently singing this verse:

> Come in the stillness, come in the night;
> Come soon and bring delight.
> Beckoning, beckoning, left hand and right,
> Come now—Oh, come tonight.

This verse may appear very simple indeed, but Cornish girl Anne Jeffries, who was renowned for her faery gifts of healing and prophecy during the English Civil War, initially attracted the little people to her by singing equally unpretentious, almost childish, ditties whilst wandering amongst ferns and foxgloves. These were "Fairy fair and fairy bright / Come and be my chosen sprite," and "Moon shines bright, waters run clear / I am here, but where's my fairy dear?" These may be poor poetry, but they successfully conjured up the pixies for Anne.[398]

The last simple charm requires you merely to walk around a field in which cows are grazing. If you can complete the circuit and come back to your exact starting point at precisely midnight, the vision will be granted to you.[399]

The second set of spells demands a good deal more preparation. Sometimes you only need to acquire the correct materials: for example, if you can come by a cattle hide that has been pierced by a faery arrow, an elf shot, looking through the hole made in it will reveal the faeries to you. Sometimes a good deal more work than that is needed: in a manuscript that belonged to Elias Ashmole, and which is dated around 1600, there is a recipe for an unguent for eyes for use when you wish to summon faeries or when your vision of them is not perfect:

> Take one pint of salad oil and put it into a glass vial, but first
> wash [mix?] it with rose water and marigold water (the flowers
> to be gathered towards the east). Wash it till the oil comes white
> [i.e., an emulsion is made], then put it into the glass vial and

398. Simpson, *Sussex*, 59.

399. Graham, *Sketches Descriptive*, 103; Simpson, *Sussex*, 59; Palmer, *Shropshire*, 141.

put into it the buds of hollyhock and young hazel, the flowers of marigold and the tops or flowers of wild thyme. The thyme must be gathered near the side of a hill which faeries frequent. Add, too, some grass picked from a faery throne found there. All these put into the oil in the glass and set it to dissolve three days in the sun, and then keep it to thy use.[400]

Most of these ingredients are readily and cheaply available, but there are two catches: first, you need to be sure that the knoll where you pick your thyme is a favourite haunt of the faery folk. Sites that are traditionally believed to be such spots are plainly a safe bet, naturally; otherwise, your own experience and investigation may be required. Secondly, the hill must be a "faery throne." A common Scottish Gaelic name for faery hillocks is *cathair,* meaning "seat." The hill chosen ought therefore to be a place which the faeries inhabit as well as frequent. Poet William Browne mentions such a place: "A hillock rise, where oft the faery queen / At twilight sat, and did command her elves…" If your confirmed faery knoll is such a place, you're definitely in business.[401]

Another seventeenth century manuscript gives a charm for invisibility that appears very simple to prepare:

> Take water and pour it on an anthill and immediately look after it and you shall find a stone of divers colours sent from the faery. This bear in your right hand and you shall go invisible.

A further charm found in the same manuscript is a Latin and English invocation for summoning a faery. It depends upon magical words combined with the proper personal preparations (bodily and spiritual purification) and the creation of a chalk circle. Ashmole's manuscript, mentioned just now, contains similar very lengthy summoning charms in which named faeries, including Margaret Barrance and Elaby Gathen, are called upon for help. The right materials and the right preparations are essential to these and

---

400. J. Halliwell, *Illustrations of the Fairy Mythology of Midsummer Night's Dream* (London, Shakespeare Society, 1845), 62.

401. Dixon, *Gairloch,*159; *Britannia's Pastorals*, Book I, song 2.

they seem too to be effective only on Wednesdays and Fridays, days we have already seen to have particular faery significance.[402]

Circles drawn on the ground are frequently an important aspect of magic concerned with faeries: they usually help to protect the mortal from malign supernatural forces. For instance, if you are assailed by a malevolent faery you will be safe if you draw a circle around yourself, especially if this is done with an iron implement such as a knife or if religious powers are invoked at the same time. Perhaps the flipside of this is the magical quality of faery rings.[403]

Finally, a "magical miscellany" contained in a manuscript in the Bodleian Library in Oxford, and which is dated to the early seventeenth century, has a spell to conjure Oberon into a crystal seeing-stone, using Catholic prayers in Latin. It also has a spell to conjure other faeries which employs the "rime" found on a bowl of water which has been left out overnight for the faeries to bathe in. This again presupposes access to a key ingredient which—rather like four-leaf clover—is in the first place very hard to acquire. First get your faeries to come and bathe themselves and their children; then scrape off the tide mark that you hope they've left.

Readers should beware, nonetheless. Those who have attempted such spells have frequently failed in their resolution at the last minute because of fear or, upon succeeding, have either found the presence of the Fae over-whelming or have been punished for their temerity and want of proper preparation.[404]

These spells are all complex and serious matters. In everyday belief, invoking faery power and help has sometimes been diminished to something as simple as making a wish over a birthday cake, but the reality attested by those with long experience is that much greater dedication and application, as well as courage, will be required.[405]

---

402. Halliwell, *Illustrations of the Fairy Mythology*, 62–3.

403. Sutherland, *Folklore Gleanings*, 94; Murray, *Tales from Highland Perthshire*, nos. 167, 176 & 199.

404. W. Lilly, *Life of William Lilly*, 230–231.

405. Bennett in Narvaez, *Good People*, 112–113.

Spells for Getting Rid of Fae

Keen as many people are to contact the faeries, it is often found that their presence can be a nuisance, especially because of their constant mischief. Individuals who have lived with the Fae have found themselves worn down by the constant pranks and noise. As described earlier, it can often prove impossible to simply move away from the fairies, as they'll just move with you. It follows that, just as there are magical means of summoning them, there are charms for sending the faeries away again.

One of the easiest ways of banishing a faery is words—nothing complex is needed either. It has been said that their language contains "neither curses nor blessings" and this is a clue as to how to be rid of them. As I've suggested, many of the Good Folk seem to have an instinctive antipathy to Christian religion, and this means that a few simple holy words can be enough to expel them. A Shetland woman who awoke at night to see a small boy in a white cap sitting by her fire automatically blessed herself in surprise—and he was gone. A church minister lost at night on moorland came across a house where he was offered shelter. However, when supper was served, he instinctively began to say grace, only to find that the whole house disappeared around him. These were unintentional banishments, but it's said of another minister that he drove away one family's brownie by preaching his Sunday sermon at it; an attempt to baptise another brownie had the same effect.[406]

Godly words can repel the Fae, but so too, it seems, can swearing. In Cornwall the knockers in the tin mines are said to object to swearing and to whistling, and accordingly the cautious miners avoided both. A woman of Loch Aline in Scotland was caught by the Fae; she struggled to escape and was told it was useless to resist, at which she said she wished that it was an armful of dirt that the faery held. In saying this, according to the polite language of the published version, she uttered "a very coarse, unseemly word" and the faeries instantly abandoned their attempt. I think we can speculate as to what she said rather than "dirt."[407]

---

406. Edmondston, *A View of the Zetland Isles*, 211; Addy, *Household Tales*, 23; Aitken, *Forgotten Heritage*, 36; Hogg, "Odd Characters," 151.

407. Joseph Hammond, *A Cornish Parish—St. Austell*, 1897, 359; Campbell, *Superstitions*, 78.

In Wales it was said that the faeries most often come into homes in the winter. They can then become a nuisance with their demands for tidiness, food, and water, and their pranks. Mary Lewes recorded that, in such cases, the only way of getting rid of them was the pretty extreme measure of throwing iron at them. However, to do this you had to be able to actually see the faery and they were very adept at preventing this ever happening.[408]

I've mentioned that, at the end of Yule, the inhabitants of Shetland will drive the trows back under their knowes by lighting huge bonfires. A related custom at Stronsay on Orkney was the nightly "penning" of the local trows. Every sunset a circle of men and women would form around a local faery mound and would then advance inward, banging on milk pails and such like. This contained the "grey folk" for the night and protected the neighbouring homesteads.[409]

Various simple charms offer protection against nuisance faeries and are easily used. One is to mark any object to be protected with the sign of a heart between two crosses. The heart symbol used here seems to be particularly significant: in Herefordshire the faeries could be kept out of stables at night by twisting seven hairs from a grey mare's tail into a double heart and suspending it over the door. Crossing your fingers and, if you're wearing a hat, turning it back to front, will work too.[410]

The magical powers of metal can be used. In West Cornwall knobs of lead called "pixie feet" were put on farmhouse roofs to prevent the pixies dancing up there and to stop them souring the milk in the dairy. On Shetland the trows can be deprived of their power over a home by placing keys in all the locks, whilst leaving them unlocked. The metal plainly provides the main protection in these charms but, in the case of the keys, the iron's also put inside the keyholes, a traditional access route for the Good Folk, representing a physical as well as a spiritual obstacle.[411]

408. Lewes, *Stranger than Fiction,* 171; *Queer Side,* 119.

409. Marwick, *The Folklore of Orkney,* 37.

410. Tongue, *Somerset Folklore,* 111; Leather, *Folklore of Herefordshire,* 48.

411. Courtney, *Cornish Feasts,* 126; Deane & Shaw, *Folklore of Cornwall,* 91; *County Folklore,* vol. 3, 26. Of course, the faeries can be contrary: S. Baring-Gould, *A Book of Cornwall,* 1899, c. XVI, reports that around Helston these lead "pixy-pots" actually encouraged pixy dancing, which brought good luck.

There is also a procedure for "laying" faeries, just like ghosts. The ceremony seems to apply particularly to the boggarts of North West England and, it has to be said, the difference between boggarts and ghosts is not always clear-cut in the stories that are told in that region. Laying the boggart may involve as little as pronouncing a blessing or similar. At Dalswinton in South West Scotland a farmer and the local minister agreed that the farm hob should be baptised. He was surprised and holy water was thrown in his face, which was enough to drive him away forever. Sometimes, though, much more complex rituals are required. The boggart called Robin Red Cap at Spaldington Hall near Selby was laid by means of the simultaneous prayers of three churchmen; by their efforts he was confined to a local well—but that was only for a limited period of time. The combined prayers of an entire Lancashire village were required to lay the nuisance boggart called the Gatley Shouter. At Rowley Hall in the same county prayers alone were not enough; it was also necessary to set up a headstone at the junction of two streams. As I've just indicated, these exorcisms weren't always permanent resolutions. In the north of Scotland, the troublesome bogle of Auld-na-Beiste was laid by means of a religious service which consecrated the spot where he lurked. Even so, the ceremony had to be repeated annually until the bogle finally took the hint and gave up his haunting.[412]

In a few places macabre, even "black magic" methods were needed to lay a spirit. At Gristlehurst in the county of Lancashire a boggart was laid in a grave under an ash and a rowan tree and along with a staked cockerel. This combination of charms didn't work, though, as in 1857 the creature was still reported to be terrifying locals at night. At Hothersall Hall near Ribchester the boggart was laid under a laurel tree. Milk has still to be poured regularly on the tree roots, which is said to be both for the benefit of the tree and to prolong the spell. Just as we saw significant faery trees involved in the spell at Gristlehurst, the applications of milk at Hothersall remind us of the milk sacrificed or offered to many faery beings around Britain.

It was mentioned earlier on that some of the hobs and boggarts seem to be a little slow witted and this feature was exploited in a couple of the layings.

---

412. Bailey, *Lancashire Folk Tales*, 93; Browning, *Dumfries & Galloway Folk Tales*, 57; Roberts, *Folklore of Yorkshire*, 100; Sutherland, *Folklore Gleanings*, 93.

At Holden Clough in Lancashire the boggart was persuaded to promise not to return so long as there was ivy on the trees—the creature was evidently forgetting that it is an evergreen plant. A comparable trick was played at Hollins Hey Clough, where the boggart's undertaking was to stay away as long as there were green leaves growing in the clough. The "hollin" of the name is a holly tree and the valley is full of them and is green all year round.

As we've seen, it is often important that the spells are renewed periodically; equally, nothing should be done actively to break them. In Written Stone Lane, Dilworth, Lancashire, lies a slab of stone measuring nine feet by two feet by one foot, upon which is inscribed "Rauffe Radcliffe laid this stone to lye for ever, AD 1633." It's believed that this was done to trap a boggart who had haunted the lane and scared travellers. A local farmer later decided to ignore Radcliffe's wishes (and warning) and purloined the slab to use as a counter in his buttery. It took six horses several laborious hours to drag the rock to his farm and, after the stone was installed, nothing but misfortune followed. No pan or pot would ever stay upright upon it, which eventually persuaded the avaricious man to return the slab whence it came. It then took only one horse a short while to pull the rock back and once it was restored the disturbances promptly ceased. In County Durham Hob Headless, who haunted a highway, was laid under a large slab of stone for ninety-nine years and a day; rather as in the Dilworth case, it was said that the rock was never a safe place to sit and that weary travellers who paused to rest their feet would often find themselves tipped off.

Layings aren't necessarily permanent and they aren't always welcomed by the human community either. In Monmouthshire in Wales there was a domestic faery called the *pwcca* who, like all his kind, did many farm chores—feeding the cattle and cleaning out their sheds. Some busybody interfered and laid him for three generations, but his return was much anticipated by the locals, because it was believed that then their prosperity would resume.

Transferring Faery Magic by Touch

A little-known aspect of our Good Neighbours' magical powers is their ability to convey these by mere touch. The most significant consequence of this quality of their magic is that it demonstrates that their abilities seem not necessarily to be innate; they may be learned from grimoires or they may be transferred by supernatural means—they are capable of being passed simply and quickly from person to person. In this respect the situation resembles faery ointment, which will be discussed next. Magical ability is, we might say, a commodity to be acquired by anyone, regardless of birth or status.

The physical receipt of magic vision is demonstrated from several sources. Seers (those endowed with the second sight) can admit others to their visions by means of mere contact. The Reverend Kirk in chapter 12 of *The Secret Commonwealth* tells us about this:

> The usewall Method for a curious Person to get a transient Sight of this otherwise invisible Crew of Subterraneans, (if impotently and over rashly sought,) is to put his [left Foot under the Wizard's right] Foot, and the Seer's Hand is put on the Inquirer's Head, who is to look over the Wizard's right Shoulder, (which has ane ill Appearance, as if by this Ceremony ane implicit Surrender were made of all betwixt the Wizard's Foot and his Hand, ere the Person can be admitted a privado to the Airt;) then will he see a Multitude of Wights, like furious hardie Men, flocking to him haistily from all Quarters, as thick as Atoms in the Air...

Transference by touch was widely known in the past, as is shown in both literature, saints' legends and folklore, and it turns out that faery beings have the same power as those with second sight. In various Scottish ballads and poems, we hear of an identical process. In the "Ballad of Thomas the Rhymer" the hero meets the faery queen, who tells him

> Light down, light down, now, True Thomas,
> And lean your head upon my knee;
> Abide and rest a little space,
> And I will shew you ferlies [wonders] three.

The same is recounted in "Thomas of Erceldoune" and in "The Queen of Elfland's Nourice." Incidents recorded in folklore back up the literary accounts. A man at Papa Stour was told by his wife, who had the second sight, that the trows had emerged from their hill and were dancing by the seashore. He could see nothing until he either held her hand or placed his foot over hers. A farmer from Gwynedd in North Wales received the vision from one of the tylwyth teg. Every night he used to relieve himself just outside his cottage before going to bed. One night a strange man appeared, telling the farmer how much he and his family were annoyed by this habit. The farmer couldn't understand this, but the stranger replied that his house was just below where they stood. The farmer looked down and clearly saw that all his household slops went down the chimney of the other man's house, which stood far below in a street he had never seen before. The faery advised him to make a door in the other side of his house, and that if he did so his cattle would never suffer from disease. The farmer did as he was told, having his old door walled up and another opened on the other side of the house; ever after he was a most prosperous man in that part of the country.[413]

From the North West of England comes this snippet of information about the barguest (a kind of boggart which could only be seen by a limited number of people): "It is generally believed that the faculty of seeing this goblin was peculiar to certain individuals, but that the gift could be imparted to another at the time of the ghost's appearance by mere action of touching."[414]

Lastly, from Skye in the early twentieth century comes the case of three children taken by an old woman to see the faeries dancing in the twilight. She had the two boys and a girl hold her hand and, by that means, they were able to see tiny figures dressed in green dancing round a fire. Two of those children were the father and aunt of Katharine Briggs, renowned expert in faery lore, and it's clear that she completely accepted what they described to her.[415]

Faeries' magic power might be invested in items of clothing too, so that putting them on will transfer the "glamour" to the human wearer. In one story from the Scottish Lowlands a man was invited to attend a faery wedding. He was given a cap to wear during the celebration but at some time

---

413. Marwick, *The Folklore of Orkney*, 35; Rhys, *Celtic Folklore*, 230.

414. Halliwell, *Dictionary of Archaic and Provincial Words*, 1865—"barguest."

415. K. Briggs, "Some Late Accounts of the Fairies," *Folklore*, vol. 72 (1961), 514–5.

took it off—and found himself at home in his barn. A related but opposite account from North Yorkshire states that faeries are only visible when they take their magical caps off. Faery caps are also a means of conveying the faeries' magical capabilities to humans: in a Herefordshire account, a boy lost in woods at night is sheltered by two faery women and then joins them in their travels by purloining one of their caps.[416]

What can we conclude from all this? Well, the process of transference by touch certainly suggests the considerable power of the magic involved, yet at the same time it implies that magical ability is not unique. Anyone can acquire it, provided that they have the right materials (for example, to make ointment) or the right acquaintances. It suggests too that there may not be such a huge gulf between humans and faeries; we seem to be closely related and the narrow distance between us is easily bridged. All we need then is luck, the right contacts and/or determination and commitment (for example, to gather enough four-leaf clover to be able to produce a usable quantity of the magic ointment).

Faery Ointment

There are many stories about the effect of faery ointment in dispelling the glamour used by the faeries to disguise and hide themselves. The usual tale is of a human midwife or wet nurse who is called to assist with a faery birth and who is then asked to take care of the newborn baby, something which includes regularly anointing it—for an undisclosed reason. Despite stern warnings to guard against doing so, the woman accidentally touches one of her own eyes with some of the salve, thereby revealing to her the true nature of faerykind. When at a later date this regrettable slip is revealed (often when the woman spies one of the faeries thieving at a market), the unfortunate victim is blinded one way or another and the privileged view of Faery is ended. Here I examine why this ointment was needed by the faeries in the first place and how it's made.

As just mentioned, the typical story involving ointment involves a mortal caring for a faery newborn. Over and above the basic feeding and cleaning, an

---

416. Aitken, *Forgotten Heritage*, 19; Blakeborough, *Wit, Character, Folklore and Customs of the North Riding of Yorkshire,* 163; Leather, *Folklore of Herefordshire,* 176.

essential part of this care is anointing the child with special ointment and it is this task which gives rise to the revelation that all is not what it seems—that magic is being used to disguise the hovel in which the supernaturals actually live or to conceal their non-human nature. This cream clearly has an important function in the story relative to the human being; its significance to the faeries who provide it tends to be overlooked or taken for granted. Nevertheless, it is obviously even more vital to them than it is to the human helper: it's essential that a newly delivered baby receives this ointment regularly.

Why does the newly born infant need to have this treatment applied? We are never clearly told, but there seems to be a couple of likely explanations. First, it confers the faeries' magical powers: the ointment (or, sometimes, an oil) is most frequently applied to the eyes of the neonate—and of course it is an unintentional application to the human's eyes which leads to ejection from faeryland or blinding. This implies that the power to see through faery illusion or invisibility is what is being conveyed—that faery babies are born with non-faery vision. That said, from time to time the treatment prescribed is to rub the baby all over with the potion (there are examples from Wales and Cornwall of this). This obviously indicates that a more general alteration of the child's physical nature is intended and that not just a power to penetrate concealment or disguise but a range of other magical abilities—to fly, to transform objects and the like—are being passed on.

The faery ointment allows a person who has not been born with the second sight (called "pisky-eyed" in Cornwall) to see through the faery glamour, but it can bestow other benefits too. In the case of one Shetland midwife touching her eyes also gave her incredibly keen vision, so that she could see ships twenty miles out to sea and tell who each crew member was and what he was doing on board. Eventually, of course, she met a faery man who questioned how such an old woman had such good eyesight—and, learning the truth, instantly deprived her of it.[417]

Secondly, it appears that the ointment confers immortality and that, at birth, faery babies are much like human infants in terms of life span and need some intervention to bestow immortality or longevity upon them. There are a few brief mentions in verse and folklore of a faery practice of dipping

---

417. Edmondston, *A View of the Zetland Isles*, 211.

changelings in order to liberate them from human mortality. In the Welsh story of "Eilean of Garth Dolwen" it is notable that the heroine is a human captive in faeryland and that it is her half-human, half-faery child who has to be treated by the midwife, perhaps to free it of its maternally inherited human frailties. Comparable is the evidence of the faery story of "Childe Rowland," in which the King of Elfame uses a blood-red potion to revive two knights that he has slain. He achieves this by touching the corpses' eyes, ears, lips, nostrils, and fingertips with the liquid. In Milton's poem *Comus* a similar ritual is described. Delia has been enchanted and trapped by Comus; Sabrina, spirit of the River Severn, releases her from her captivity with drops from her "fountain pure" which are applied to Delia's breast, lips, and fingertips. In all these stories, then, a magical liquid confers life—either preventing death or reversing it.

Final confirmation of the need to transform faery children with ointment comes from a Northumbrian story concerning the fostering of a faery child by a couple from Netherwhitton. They are required by the faery parents to anoint the child's eyes daily with a never-ending supply of ointment. Predictably, the tale ends unhappily with the man blinded for abusing the magic ointment and the boy taken back to Faery, but it seems clear that the treatment has to be given to all faery infants, wherever they're raised.[418]

It might have been imagined that magic qualities are inherent in faery-kind, central to their non-human nature, but it seems not. These attributes need to be specifically conveyed, failing which—presumably—the child would be little different to any other. These magical powers can wash off too, so that even the water in which an anointed faery baby has been bathed will convey the second sight to the human nursemaid who splashes her eyes in the process.[419]

Pursuing this thought to its logical conclusion, it seems possible that a human who gets hold of the ointment (or who is able to manufacture it) should be able to apply it to their own body and thereby bestow upon themself quasi-supernatural powers. If this is right, we must ask what the ingredients of this ointment might be. The tale of "Cherry of Zennor" is one of

---

418. Grice, *Folk Tales*, c. 1.

419. Young & Houlbrook, *Magical Folk*, 127.

several stories that inform us that it is green in colour. Also from Cornwall, there's an account of a green faery salve made from certain herbs found on Kerris Moor, outside Paul, near Newlyn in the far west. It bestowed invisibility when rubbed on the eyes. Four-leaf clovers were renowned for their quality of dispelling faery spells and it seems very likely that this plant will form the main constituent of the salve, although others may be added to the mixture—likely candidates might include broom, ragwort, and cowslip, to name just a few. The herbal ointment on its own seems to have inherent magical properties, without any more ceremony (such as charms being said whilst the mixture is prepared) being needed.[420]

To summarise, the evidence presented seems to suggest that faerykind and humankind are not that different. Our closeness in physiology, and our ability to interbreed, would then be entirely understandable, given that what separates us is not any profound physical or mental differences but the application of an ointment that bestows magical powers. This may seem a surprising conclusion, but it is what we are driven to deduce from the stories. This may detract from the mysterious otherness of the Good Folk, but at the same time it puts Faery within tantalising reach: with the correct recipe for the salve, we could all aspire to pass into another dimension. Kerris Moor seems to be a good place to go; a bigger problem may be picking enough four-leaf clovers to make sufficient ointment…

Fern Seed

It is widely believed that fern seed has magical powers. On the continent it is used to disclose treasure; in Britain it brings love or conjures invisibility. It was used for concealment by both the faeries and humans; Ben Jonson, confident that his audience would understand the reference, referred to this in his play *The New Inn*: "I had / No medicine to go invisible / No fern seed in my pocket."[421]

The second use of fern seed is a little more prosaic. Samuel Bamford, witness of the Peterloo massacre in 1819, records a Lancashire tradition that the fern seed was used to obtain the heart of a loved one and he tells the tale

---

420. Evans-Wentz, *Fairy Faith*, 175.
421. Bamford, *Passages in the Life of a Radical*, cc. 20–22—see later; *New Inn*, Act 1, scene 6.

of an attempt to gather some in a highly melodramatic manner. In Michael Drayton's mock epic poem *Nimphidia* we also find the Fae, like mortals, using fern seed to win a loved one's affections.

Supernatural use of ferns is mentioned from time to time in faery literature. In one published version of the Cornish story "Cherry of Zennor," the young heroine is depicted pausing at a crossroads, uncertain which way to head. She idly picks and crushes some fern fronds, the effect of which is to conjure up a faery gentleman who becomes her employer and her suitor. The same book includes the poem "Mabel on Midsummer Day" by Mary Howitt. A girl is sent on an errand to her grandmother's, but is warned that it is Midsummer Day "when all the faery people / From elf-land come away." It's a dangerous time of year, then, and she must take care not to offend the Good Folk; for example, she should not "pluck the strawberry flower / Nor break the lady-fern."[422]

To add to the mystery of the process, the seed could only be seen and gathered at certain times of the year when it was shed from the plants' fronds: Midsummer's Eve was the main time, although midnight on Christmas Eve is also mentioned. Poet William Browne in "Britannia's Pastorals" referred to the "wondrous one-night seeding ferne." Midsummer Eve is also the eve of the feast of St. John the Baptist, and it was said that the fern seed fell at the precise moment of his birth.

The process of collection and the faery link were described more fully by Thomas Jackson in 1625:

> It was my happe since I undertook the Ministrie to question an ignorant soule … what he saw or heard when he watch't the falling of the Ferne-seed at an unseasonable and suspitious houre. Why (quoth he)… doe you think that the devil hath aught to do with that good seed? No: it is in the keeping of the King of Fayries and he, I know, will do me no harm: yet he had utterly forgotten this King's name until I remembered it unto him out of my reading of *Huon of Bordeaux*.[423]

---

422. See Frances Olcott, *The Book of Elves and Fairies*, 1918, c. VIII.

423. *A Treatise Concerning the Original of Unbelief*, 1625, 178–9.

Given these strong supernatural associations, it is not surprising that collecting the seeds was accompanied by some measure of risk, as told by Richard Bovet:

> Much discourse about the gathering of Fern-seed (which is looked upon as a Magical herb) on the night of Midsummer's Eve, and I remember I was told of one that went to gather it, and the Spirits whistlit by his ears like bullets and sometimes struck his Hat or other parts of his Body. In fine: though that he had gotten a quantity of it, and secured it in papers and a Box besides, when he came home, he found it all empty.[424]

Given these risks, great precautions had to be taken to protect the collector with charms and spells. Samuel Bamford's account describes the kind of ritual and incantations that would accompany an attempt to gather the seed and the ghastly retribution that might befall the seeker who erred in their supplications or who was deemed unsuitable by the spirits. The fern was to be found in Boggart, or Faery, Clough (gorge) and the collectors went there bearing items including an earthenware dish, a pewter platter, and a skull lined with moss and clay with a tress of the hair of the loved one attached to it. Various forms of words were recited whilst the seed was shaken onto the plates with a hazel rod.[425]

Fern seed seems to be a very powerful substance, then, but there's a substantial practical problem with it, in that collecting enough to produce a usable amount is likely to be extremely time-consuming and may demand a very large amount of luck. In other words, the offer of faery glamour is held out to us but, rather like a mirage, it is forever retreating before us.

Hand Charms

In an illustration to the "Story of Ciccu" in Andrew Lang's *Pink Fairy Book* of 1897, the artist Henry Justice Ford chose to depict a scene in which three sleeping brothers are magically endowed with gifts by three faery women

---

424. Bovet, *Pandaemonium*, 217.

425. see Sir Walter Scott, *Minstrelsy of the Borders*, II, 27; Bamford, *Passages from the Life of a Radical*.

who come upon them in a wood. The women are shown standing over the slumbering knights making curious hand gestures.

This illustration put me in mind of lines from Tennyson's poem "Merlin and Vivien," which forms part of his *Idylls of the King*. The young woman, Vivien / Nimue, wishes to learn the elderly magician's skills from him, especially one charm of "woven paces and waving hands." She slowly wears him down with promises of her love until he is "overtalked and overworn" and, against his better judgement, tells her the charm she wishes so much to know. Almost immediately she employs it to imprison him for eternity in an oak tree.

In both these examples we have faery women "waving hands" to cast spells. I know that various individual gestures and movements have magical or spiritual power. These are very often now labelled in Hindi "mudras" and "bandhas"—terms that have been borrowed from yoga practice when surely there must be native equivalents that we could use. It appears that the technique involves creating certain significant or powerful shapes, or tracing certain signs in the air. Mostly what I have encountered relates to static positions, rather than to the "waving of hands" described by Nimue, but it seems reasonable to suppose that a succession of gestures in the right order could enhance the power of any charm and could be another part of the faeries' magical arsenal.

In the Scottish ballad "Allison Gross" we hear of a witch turning round three times before waving her wand and pronouncing a spell. We've also seen turning used in magic procedures to get rid of changelings—whether it's the changeling baby being turned or the parent rotating. Movement is clearly integral to faery magic.

Spell Books

There is a scattering of evidence to the effect that faeries had their own spell books, although the references to these are tantalisingly few and far between. Spell books appear in ballads and romance for understandable dramatic reasons—for example, the poem "Lord Soulis" features a wizard and "lord of gramarye" who possesses a "black spae book" which is the source of his knowledge and power. These fictions probably did much to shape our expectations, but real spell books existed nonetheless.

In chapter 7 of Robert Kirk's *Secret Commonwealth* he informs us that

They are said to have many pleasant toyish Books; but the operation of these Pieces only appears in some Paroxysms of antic
corybantic Jollity, as if ravished and prompted by a new Spirit
entering into them at that Instant, lighter and merrier than
their own. Other Books they have of involved abstruse Sense,
much like the Rosicrucian Style. They have nothing of the
Bible, save collected Parcels for Charms and counter Charms;
not to defend themselves with, but to operate on other Animals, for they are a People invulnerable by our Weapons …

From this we can deduce that there seem to be three varieties of spell
book: one used to send the faeries into some sort of ecstatic dance; a second using scraps of Biblical verse for casting spells on others (rather like
local magicians offered to do in human communities); and a third that was
employed for more powerful conjuring—perhaps to contact other spirits
such as angels, a practice which was used by such magi as Queen Elizabeth's
own conjuror, John Dee.

A few named faery spell books are known to have existed. One is *The
Red Book of Menteith*: the story goes that a faery queen banished some troublesome elves from Cnoc-n'an-Bocan (Bogle-knowe, or Hobgoblin-hill) near
to Menteith into *The Red Book*. The condition was that they would only be
released when the laird of Menteith opened the volume. Eventually, this
happened by mistake and instantly the released faeries appeared before him
demanding work. To be freed of them, he had to set them various impossible tasks to complete. Scottish folklore also tells of a spell book owned by
the Wizard of Reay. This seems to have had powers very similar to those of
the *Red Book*. The wizard's young servant peeked inside the tome and was
instantly surrounded by little men demanding that he give them work to do.
Just as in the previous story he first asked them to make ropes of heather,
which they quickly did; then he asked for ropes of sand. When this proved
impossible, they deserted the wizard.[426]

The Red Book of Appin is another Scottish volume that seems to have
had power against both witch and faery spells. That said, its primary content

---

426. MacGregor, *The Peat Fire Flame*, 7.

is concerned with healing sick cattle and with maintaining the fertility of fields (although of course these may both be the subject of faery blights). The *Red Book* was therefore a local cunning man's book of incantations used for assisting small farmers with their common problems. The legend is that it came from a mysterious "fine gentleman," although it isn't clear whether or not he was of faery origin. When the book was obtained from him by devious magical means, he transformed into many shapes, implying that he was (at least) a wizard and maybe a demon. He was defeated, however, and the book came into more benign human hands.

Predicting the Future

Faeries have the ability to see into the future and, if they wish, to make this knowledge known to humans. For example, the Reverend Edmund Jones recorded that, in South Wales, the faeries were often heard talking and that the subject of their conversations seemed to be future events. The brownie who resided in Castle Lachlan near Stralachlan in Argyllshire was known for his prophetic powers.[427]

Although the last two examples indicate that the Good Folk may simply tell us what they have foreseen, in the majority of cases they prefer to rely instead upon their actions to convey meaning to us. Often, too, what they want to tell us is not good news.

There are several ways in which prognostications can be revealed to humankind. First, the foreknowledge might be disclosed to a family, a household or a community. For instance, the *glaistig* of Island House on Tiree was known to begin to work extra hard in advance of the arrival of unexpected visitors. This additional effort alerted the household to advent of likely guests.[428]

Another example of this kind of warning comes from those faeries whose actions would foretell a death or tragedy. The Scottish banshee and the related Caointeach (keener) and *bean-nighe* are known for this sort of prediction. By their howls or by washing winding sheets in rivers, they would signify imminent death, but they were not alone in having these powers. The

---

427. Jones, *Aberystruth*, 69; D. MacRitchie, *Testimony of Tradition*, 60.

428. MacGregor, *Peat Fire Flame*, 61.

Ell Maid of Dunstaffnage would cry out to warn of impending joy, or woe; on the Borders the *powrie* or *dunter* haunted the old fortified houses called pele towers and made a noise like the pounding of flax or grain. When this was louder than usual, or went on for longer, it was a sure sign of coming death or misfortune. In Lancashire the Walmsley family of Poulton had a boggart attached to the household who would make noise before a family member died.[429]

We have seen already that the faeries will conduct their own funerals. They also use these events as a way of conveying information to their human neighbours. In South Wales the Reverend Edmund Jones reported several such displays. A man in a field in Carmarthenshire saw a faery funeral procession pass by, singing psalms. Soon afterward a human funeral followed exactly the same route in the same manner. At Aberystruth in about 1770 two men mowing in a field saw a marriage company processing by; another man passing at the same time saw nothing even though he was actually seen to meet the faery wedding party. The event turned out to presage the death of the third man's employer and the marriage of his daughter.[430]

Elsewhere the Reverend Jones wrote that the faeries "infallibly knew when a person was going to die."[431] It follows from this that sometimes, rather than a general warning of a coming death, the faeries would appear to the victim him- or herself. Jones gives examples of this. A man was travelling near Abertillery when he heard people talking. He paused to listen, then heard the sound of a tree falling and a moan. It soon transpired that what he had witnessed was the faeries predicting his own death by a fall from a tree branch. In a very similar account, Jones described a young man at Hafod-y-dafal who saw a procession headed for the church. Walking with the faeries were a child and a young adult male who suddenly vanished. This proved to be a premonition: first the witness's child fell ill and died; then he too sickened and passed away.[432]

A very similar, but even more ghoulish, demonstration of this conduct comes from Lancashire. Two men encountered a faery funeral taking place

---

429. Macgregor, *Peat Fire Flame*, c. 5; Henderson, *Notes on the Folklore*, 255; Thornber, *Account of Blackpool*, 332.

430. Jones, *The Appearance of Evil*, paras 24 & 69.

431. Jones, *Aberystruth*, 72.

432. Jones, *The Appearance of Evil*, paras 56 & 62.

at the church of St. Mary near Penwortham Wood. The Fae were dressed in black and carrying a tiny coffin containing a doll-like corpse which looked exactly like one of the two witnesses. This man reached out to try to touch one of the mourners, causing the apparition instantly to vanish. Within a month, he fell from a haystack and was killed.[433]

These curious dumb shows might foretell not just death but disaster. At times of civil disturbance, faeries used to be seen on Mellor Moor in Lancashire, drilling in military formations. They were reported to have been particularly noticeable, for example, at the time of the Jacobite Rebellion of 1745.[434]

As well as predicting national crises and individuals' deaths, the Fae could more happily disclose their future spouses to lovers. The best example of this is the Borders brownie called Killmoulis. This being lived in mills by the grain kilns; on Halloween they would foretell love. If a person threw a ball of thread into a pot and then started to rewind it into another ball, a point would come near the end of the thread when Killmoulis would hold on and stop the winding. If you then asked "who holds?" the brownie would name your spouse to be. In East Yorkshire, some "faery stones" stood near Burdale and it was said that if a person visited these during the full moon, they would be granted a glimpse of their future partner.[435]

As with the second sight, the faery ability to see events yet to come can also be conveyed to humans. The Scottish *Leanan sidhe,* the faery lover, can endow her partners with knowledge of medicinal herbs and also of future events. There is too the story of a Scottish farmer from near Dingwall who was one day digging peat when he heard an unearthly voice in the air telling him to collect the white stones he would find on a green knoll because these would give him prophetic knowledge. This must have been a faery hill and the pebbles held faery power.[436]

Although rarely claimed in more recent times, this gift of prognostication was a faery favour often said to have been bestowed during the Middle Ages

433. Bowker, *Goblin Tales,* 83.

434. Bord, *Fairies,* 36.

435. Henderson, *Notes on the Folklore,* 252; Nicholson, *Folklore of East Yorkshire,* 85.

436. Browne, *History of the Highlands,* 112; Anon, *Folklore & legends,* 5.

and into Tudor and Stuart times. Marion Clerk of Great Ashfield in Suffolk admitted to a court in 1499 that "les Gracyousffayry" had given her the abilities both to heal and to predict the future. This benefit was granted to a significant number of other "cunning" men and women over the next hundred to one hundred fifty years, but seems since to have fallen from favour with the Good Folk.

"Make Three Wishes"

It may be a cliché of faery tales that the Good Folk can grant wishes, but it is a convention that has a good basis in folklore accounts of meetings with the Fae (and mermaids). It seems to be the case that making wishes come true is a boon that faeries will offer voluntarily. For example, the faery of Glen Tilt in the Highlands granted a man's wish to have a son after having several daughters; similarly, the faery of Baile Bhuidhe granted a man's desire to be able to do anything he put his hand to.[437]

A couple of words of warning must accompany this, though. First, as I mentioned in an earlier chapter, the faeries are always listening to us, for which reason we are well advised to be cautious in our words. A casual wish made in jest may be granted nonetheless—and we may not like what we get. Two men out hunting on a Scottish moor found themselves far from home as night drew in. They jokingly wished their girlfriends were with them and before too long two lovely girls in green appeared and sat beside them. The men were terrified of their intentions and had to sit up awake all night with the pair. The next morning the girls teasingly invited the men to meet them again the next night, presumably guessing that their tiredness would be too much for them by then. The men did not return, but the very likely result would have been death. Given the colour of the girls' dresses, and the fact that they had foxgloves in their hair, they were pretty clearly faeries and probably those of a description akin to vampires who prey on hapless men.[438]

Secondly, faeries may sometimes offer to grant wishes in situations where they have been annoyed or insulted by a human. In one Welsh case a woman lost her temper with faeries who kept coming to her house to borrow kitchen

---

437. Murray, *Tales from Highland Perthshire*, nos. 44 & 47.
438. Murray, *Tales from Highland Perthshire*, no. 190.

implements. She demanded that they grant her two wishes in return for the item they wanted. She asked that, when she awoke, the first item she touched would break (she wanted to get rid of a projecting stone in her wall) and the second would lengthen (she wanted to extend a roll of cloth she had). The faeries gave her exactly what she'd asked for—but the wishes didn't come true as the woman had planned: the next morning the first thing she touched was her ankle, the second her nose. The moral of this story is clear: if you're ever so fortunate as to be granted a wish by a faery, think very carefully indeed what you ask for, how you ask, and how you apply your gift.[439]

Faery Magical Healing

The Good Folk are quite often regarded as a source of healing knowledge and powers for favoured humans, despite their parallel reputation for blighting livestock and bringing ill fortune. The evidence of their healing abilities is, however, difficult to assess and can be puzzling in places.

Faeries with healing powers appear first in the medieval romances. The earliest example comes from Layamon's *Brut,* in which the elf queen Argante takes the wounded King Arthur to the Isle of Avalon to heal him—and the same history describes how elves bestowed upon Arthur the gifts of good luck and other qualities at his birth (acting as the original faery godmothers). In the French romance *Huon of Bordeaux* there is a reference to a healing horn that's presented to faery king Oberon by four faery "godmothers." Hearing a blast upon it will make the sickest man whole and sound instantly. In the later ballad "The Son of the Knight of Green Vesture" a cowherd is visited by a faery maid and is offered various magical objects, each in exchange for a cow. He swaps one of his kine for a jewel that heals sores.

There are a couple of much more recent stories from Shetland concerning the healing abilities of the trows. One of several similar accounts relates an incident when the "grey folk" were seen treating a jaundiced trow infant by pouring water over it—a human stole the bowl that was used for this and was able then to cure jaundice in humans. In another story, ointment is stolen from the trows which proves efficacious for healing any human injury. What is particularly notable about these accounts is that they are almost unique in

---

439. Jenkyn Thomas, *Welsh Fairy Book,* "A fairy borrowing."

describing faeries succumbing to illnesses and curing themselves. In a third Shetland story, a sick man lying in bed is visited by two trows with a "pig" (a stone bottle). They debate whether he would be cured by a drink from their bottle, but decide that time is too short and that they must leave before his wife returns home. He has the presence of mind to bless himself—and the bottle—which thereby falls into his possession. It contains a never-ending supply of liquid that cures him and any others needing it. In a comparable story from Argyll, faeries who left a farmhouse in a hurry when dawn over-took them left behind a small bag containing a tiny stone spade, a bowl, and some stone balls. The spade (which may actually have been a flint arrow-head), if placed under a sick person's pillow, would help predict their recov-ery depending upon whether or not a sweat broke out on the patient's fore-head. The stone balls, meanwhile, cured sick cattle if they were dipped in the beasts' drinking water.[440]

In these four cases the faeries possess healing materials, but they are only passed on to humans by mischance and against the faeries' will. The Good Folk's magical ability to cure might also be conveyed unintentionally and unwittingly: it seems that the healing touch might be transferred simply by proximity to the faeries. One Scottish blacksmith found himself caught up by the *sluagh* and carried over the countryside at night. On the way the faer-ies paused to cure a sick cow and, forever after that strange night, the smith found himself imbued with the same powers as well.[441]

In the Argyll case just recounted, the "faery spade" helped predict the outcome of sickness and it certainly looks as though the faeries' powers of predicting the future include giving prognoses on illnesses. A Glouces-tershire woman in the early eighteenth century was accused of witchcraft because she was able to tell whether a sick person would die or recover. She explained to the assizes that a "jury" of faeries would visit her at night and would consider the patient's situation amongst themselves. If at the end of this they looked cheerful, the person would get well; if they looked sad, the disease was fatal.[442]

---

440. Saxby, *Shetland Traditional Lore*, 151–2; J. Nicolson, *Some Folktales and Legends of Shet-land*, 38; Pegg, *Argyll Folk Tales*, 35.

441. Murray, *Tales from Highland Perthshire*, no. 191.

442. John Beaumont, *A Treatise of Spirits*, 1705, 104–5.

Magical healing powers are definitely an attribute of the Good Folk, as demonstrated by the sites around Britain that are associated more or less directly with faeries and healing—wells and standing stones and such like. For example, the "Hob Hole" on the North Yorkshire coast was said to be inhabited by a hobgoblin who could cure whooping cough if asked; the faeries' "dripping cave" at Craig-a-Chowie in Ross-shire could cure deafness. A particularly interesting story attaches to the Faeries' Well near Blackpool. The water of the well was known locally to be good for the treatment of weak eyes. A mother whose daughter's eyesight seemed to be failing went to the well to fill a bottle. There she met a small green man who gave her a box of ointment to apply to the child. Before treating her daughter, the cautious mother decided to test the safety of the substance on herself first and put some of the salve on her own eye, without ill effect. She therefore applied it to the girl, who was cured. So far, this is a happy tale of a benevolent faery bestowing his healing power out of pure goodwill. However, there is a familiar sequel. Sometime later, the mother saw the same little man at the market. She thanked him for the cure; he was angry and demanded to know with which eye she saw him. She was promptly blinded, as happens in all such stories of midwives and wet nurses. It appears, therefore, that her offence was to apply the curative ointment to anyone but the person for whom it was intended.[443]

Lastly, there are a few cases in which the Good Folk willingly and deliberately transmit their healing knowledge to humans. The first comes from Wales: the tale of the faery wife of Llyn y Fan Fach follows the usual course of all such stories of doomed human and faery marriage. The *gwraig annwn* is persuaded to marry a human male, but eventually he violates the conditions of their betrothal and she abandons him. However, in this particular instance, she still keeps in regular contact with her three sons, to whom she teaches healing skills. They became the renowned physicians of Myddfai. It may be worth pointing out that these recipients constitute a special case, as they are already half faery and may have been born with innate abilities anyway. Even so, on Shetland we hear of a faery wife who taught her human husband cures.

---

443. Spence, *The Fairy Tradition in Britain*, 156.

Healing ability may therefore be conveyed to relatives and loved ones; it may also be received as one of a person's "three wishes" as I have already implied. In the Cornish story of "The Old Man of Cury," the hero of the title rescues a mermaid stranded by the tide. In gratitude for carrying her back to the sea, the mermaid offers to give him any three things he cares to request. He asks not for wealth, but for the abilities to charm away sickness, to break the spells of witchcraft, and to discover thieves and restore stolen property. These are the classic faery powers that have always been claimed by local "cunning men" and women. Secondly, from Lowland Scotland, comes a similar story of a woman who won favour by nursing a faery child. She was rewarded with several gifts, amongst which were salves for restoring human health.[444]

Now, there's another body of evidence that describes faeries teaching healing skills to humans, but it's one I think we need to approach with great care. It's the records of British witch trials in the sixteenth and seventeenth centuries. First—and naturally most importantly—these people were on trial and facing torture and execution, so their testimonies are scarcely untainted. Secondly, they tended to claim that they'd been given three skills—to find lost property, to predict the future, and to diagnose and cure sickness. Foresight of matters to come and knowledge of hidden things are both conventional attributes of the Good Folk, as we've just seen. Also, as we saw in the earlier discussion of diagnosing illness using girdles, the malady that these individuals often claimed to be able to cure was "the feyry"—sickness inflicted by the faeries themselves. Quite a few cunning men and women alleged they had received from the faeries the ability to diagnose and heal mysterious and magical illnesses. In the case of Joan Willimot, who was accused of witchcraft in 1619, she said that a wizard had blown a faery into her mouth and that this spirit then emerged "in the shape and form of a woman" who used to help her identify those who'd been cursed.

It's curious, to say the least, that what the faeries should confer is the ability to undo their own spells. This leads me to suspect these prisoners may have been trying to show their inquisitors that theirs was really "white magic" and not malign at all, with a desperate (and doomed) hope of deflecting

---

444. Aitken, *Forgotten Heritage*, 14; Dalyell, *The Darker Superstitions of Scotland*, 28.

the accusations. Given too that many of the folk remedies they seem to have been using are very similar to the Anglo-Saxon diagnoses and cures mentioned at the start of this book, it seems inescapable that this healing knowledge will have been passing from generation to generation for centuries. When the men and women accused of witchcraft said they'd got their wisdom from faeries, it could well have been a way of deflecting suspicion from relatives and neighbours, who were the real source of their skills.

Certainly, the remedies recommended by faeries all tend to be simple, traditional herbal cures, such as using nettles, gathered before sunrise on three successive mornings, to treat "trembling fevers." There is one story from East Yorkshire that tells of a medicinal "white powder" provided by the fairy queen, but the preference for salves made from herbs seems to be supported by the story from Dartmoor of an unknown plant used by the faeries to heal a maid whom they'd previously lamed for refusing to leave them water at night. Comparable to this is an incident in John Lyly's play "Endymion," in which the character Corsites is first pinched black and blue by the faeries and is then cured by them, using the plant "lunary." This is common moonwort (*Botrychium lunaria*), a fern used by alchemists that is said to have the power to open locks and to unshoe horses. Scottish witchcraft suspect Alison Peirson told her trial that she had seen the Good Neighbours preparing their balms and ointments in pans over fires, using herbs gathered before dawn. Another suspected witch, Bessie Dunlop, said she too was taught herbal cures by a faery man, although the only recipe of hers we know of involved ginger, liquorice, cloves, and aniseed—all of which are a good deal more exotic and expensive than nettles.[445]

Undoubtedly, the Good Folk can have an effect on human health, but that's generally negative, whether it's through the deliberate blights they inflict or because a person becomes "elf-addled" by faery contact. Healing ability is seldom voluntarily and freely conveyed to humans but, where it is, the recipient is highly favoured.

Finally, we should note once again the contrary nature of faery abilities. They may have their cures and magical vessels, but they will still sometimes need human aid. We know that childbirth is a process in which a human midwife's intervention can be deemed essential. Equally, in a story from Somer-

---

445. *County Folklore*, vol. 6, 55; John Lyly, *Endymion* (1591), Act IV, scene 3.

set, an old woman with healing skills and medicinal knowledge was called away to attend a pixy's wife when their own remedies had been exhausted and it seemed that nothing more could be done for her. The woman looked after the pixy wife morning and evening for a long period until she was completely recovered, and she was well paid for her dedication.[446]

Conclusion

For those in regular contact with the Good Folk, "everyday magic" is part of the fabric of daily life. Acts like carrying pins or turning your pockets become habitual protections against faery influence. These instinctive safeguards are something that many of us have today forgotten. Charms for attracting the Good Folk can be just as simple, although harder to come by.

It's worth closing this section with a brief summary of the Good Folk's likes and dislikes, a list of what attracts and repels them. They will be drawn to anyone who is clean, neat, and respectful; who offers bread, cheese, and other dairy products; and who improves their home or themselves with perfumes and with the flowers and greenery of certain plants. They will be driven away by powerful stinks or fumes, by holy words (whether spoken or written), by iron in almost any form, by salt (and this seems to include seawater and items associated with the sea), by certain plants and flowers, and by particular shapes and numbers. Many of these charms were, in fact, efficacious against a range of supernatural threats; their specific manner of use is what may distinguish them when directed toward faeries.

At the same time, faery magic is strangely accessible, as it will frequently only require possession of the right ingredients or words, most of which are commonplace. Many years ago, faery lore expert Katharine Briggs remarked that the "faeries owe their powers to spells and not their own natures." As I have tried to demonstrate in this chapter, this seems to be perfectly correct and what separates us is not so great a gulf as some may imagine.[447]

---

446. Mathews, *Blackdown Borderland,* 59.
447. Briggs, "English Fairies," 277.

Section 5
MODERN TIMES

Chapter 14

ELVES AND
FAERIES YET?

Poet Dora Owen urged children never to forget that "there are elves and faeries yet." She encouraged them to hold on to their beliefs in the face of apparent fact that the faeries have always been leaving the human world, never to be seen by us again. And yet—they have never finally and completely gone. In "Farewell to the Faeries," the final chapter of her book *Strange and Secret People,* Carole Silver comments on this: "The faeries have been leaving England since the fourteenth century but have never quite left despite the rise of the towns, science, factories and changes of religion."[448]

Two processes have been believed to be working in parallel. There is an active departure on the part of the elves, a permanent withdrawal to a separate and possibly distant faeryland, united at the same time with a growing disbelief amongst the human population. Combined, these factors have convinced observers again and again that our Good Neighbours had deserted us. Despite these repeated protestations, though, they still linger. Neither they, nor we, can ever quite separate.

---

448. Dora Owen, "Children, children, don't forget"; Silver, *Strange & Secret People,* 185.

Always Leaving, Never Left

Poet Geoffrey Chaucer was the first to declare that the Fae had disappeared, as early as the closing decades of the 1300s, and there has been a chorus of lamenting voices ever since. These were strengthened from the mid-sixteenth century onward by a belief that it was the Reformation which had driven out the supernaturals.[449]

By the late sixteenth century Reginald Scot felt able to declare that "Robin Goodfellow ceaseth now to be much feared." Elsewhere in his book *The Discovery of Witchcraft* he noted that "By this time all Kentish men know (a few fooles excepted) that Robin Goodfellow is a knave." There wasn't just disbelief, there was growing contempt for anything deemed childish or credulous. In 1591 George Chapman had a character in a play query whether "faeries haunt the holy greene, as ever mine auncesters have thought." The faery faith was increasingly seen nostalgically, as a thing of the past, or at the very least as a matter for an older generation and for less well educated and more superstitious folk. Writing in 1639, Richard Willis described how "within a few daies after my birth … I was taken out of the bed from [my mother's] side and by my sudden and fierce crying recovered again, being found sticking between the beds-head and the wall and, if I had not cried in that manner as I did, our gossips had a conceit that I had been carried away by the Faeries …"[450]

These early sources would suggest that faery belief was a matter only of some imprecise "olden times" and was over and done with by the start of the seventeenth century—except for a few silly old women. That was far from being the case. As late as 1669, it seems, a spirit called "Ly Erg" still haunted Glen Moor in the Highlands. Describing the Hebrides in 1716, Martin Martin averred that "it is not long since every Family of any considerable Substance in these Islands was haunted by a Spirit they called Browny …" The domestic faeries had survived into the late seventeenth century, apparently,

<hr />

449. See for example Jones, *Aberystruth,* 85 or James Hogg, *The Queen's Wake,* 1813, 380; & *A Queer Book,* 1831, 168.

450. Scot, *Discovery,* "To the Reader" and Book XVI, chapter 7; Chapman, *A Humorous Day's Mirth*; R. Willis, *Mount Tabor—or Private Exercises of a Penitent Sinner,* 92–93.

despite confident predictions to the contrary at least one hundred years before.[451]

Nevertheless, describing Northumberland in 1729 the Reverend John Horsley felt that "stories of faeries now seem to be much worn, both out of date and out of credit." Fifty years later in 1779 the Reverend Edmund Jones alleged that, in the parish of Aberystruth, the apparitions of faeries had "very much ceased," although the tylwyth teg had once been very familiar to the local people.[452] In other words, there had been belief but it had been dwindling during the course of the eighteenth century, or had died out entirely.

The faery faith was still apparently on the wane, or only just faded, as the next century began. This was particularly believed to be the case in Scotland. Shepherd poet James Hogg described the experiences of William Laidlaw, also called Will O'Phaup, who had been born in 1691 and who was "the last man of this wild region who heard, saw and conversed with the faeries; and that not once but at sundry times and seasons." Will lived on the edge of Ettrick Forest, which was "the last retreat of the spirits of the glen, before taking their final leave of the land of their love ..." The Fae's departure was a regular theme for Hogg. For example, in 1818 in *The Queen's Wake* he claimed that "The faeries have now totally disappeared ... There are only a very few now remaining alive who have ever seen them." Two years later Sir Walter Scott also confidently announced that "The faeries have abandoned their moonlight turf." Writing of the Tay basin in 1831, James Knox agreed that "during the last century the faery superstition lost ground rapidly and, even by the ignorant, elves are no longer regarded, though they are the subject of a winter evening's tale." In a description of the Highlands in 1823 it was (again) said that brownies had by then become rare, but that once every family of rank had had one. Likewise, Alan Cunningham, a Lowland Scot, said that in Nithsdale and Galloway "there are few old people who have not a powerful belief in the influence and dominion of the faeries ..." Once again, belief was

---

451. M. Martin, *A Description of the Western Isles*, 391.

452. Dalyell, *Darker Superstitions*, 541; Martin, *A Description of the Western Isles*, 391; Horsley, *Materials for a History of Northumberland*, 1730, cited in *Denham Tracts*, 136; Jones, *Aberystruth*, 84.

said to be fading, except amongst the elderly and ill-educated rural poor, and even for them it was degrading to nothing more than a bedtime story.[453]

Simultaneously, the faeries of the Lake District were pronounced extinct and, at the opposite end of the country, Fortescue Hitchins mourned that in Cornwall "the age of the piskays, like that of chivalry, is gone. There is perhaps hardly a house they are reputed to visit … The fields and lanes are forsaken."[454]

Several eyewitness accounts of the faeries' departure from the Scottish Highlands can be dated to about 1790, so that by the nineteenth century the days of Faery seemed conclusively to be over. And yet a lingering faith persisted with some into the middle of the century. In 1850 a Galloway road-mender refused to fell a local faery thorn, for example. Of Northamptonshire in 1851 it was said that "the faery faith still lingers, but is in the last stages of decay." More than that, there were pockets of resistance. In 1867 John Harland could write that "the elves or hill folk yet live among the rural people of Lancashire." Researching Devon folklore in the same year, Sir John Bowring interviewed four old peasants on Dartmoor who assured him that "the piskies had all gone now, although there had been many formerly." Despite this, he was simultaneously told a version of the common story of pixies caught stealing grain from a barn, something that had apparently happened as recently as three years before. Describing the same region a few decades later, John Page claimed that "Faith in the elfin race is growing weaker by the day … The pixies are departing from Dartmoor." Clearly it depended on whom you spoke to.[455]

Rehearsing what was by then a very familiar lament, John Brand declared of Shetland in 1883 that "not above forty or fifty years ago every family had an evil spirit called a Browny which served them." This was the third time

---

453. Hogg, "Odd Characters" in *The Shepherds Calendar*, vol. 2, 150; *The Queen's Wake*, 1813, 380; Knox, *Topography of the Basin of the Tay*, 111; W. Grant Stewart, *Popular Superstitions*, 139; A. Cunningham, *Remains of Nithsdale and Galloway Song*, 236.

454. Craig Gibson, "Ancient Customs," 108; Hitchens, *A History of Cornwall from the Earliest Records*, 1824.

455. Aitken, *A Forgotten Heritage*, c. VI; Sternberg, *Dialect and Folklore*, 131; *Lancashire Folklore*, 110; J. Bowring, "Devon Folklore Illustrated," *Transactions of the Devonshire Association*, vol. II (1867) 70; Crossing agreed—*Tales of Dartmoor Pixies* cc. 1 & 4; Page, *Dartmoor*, 40.

that the brownies' recent departure had been recorded. In light of this, when that same year Menzies Fergusson said of the same islands that the "credulous times are long, long gone by and we can see no more of the flitting sea trow … Civilisation has crept in upon all the faery strongholds and disenchanted the many fair scenes in which they were wont to hold their fair courts," we may be inclined to doubt his confident assertion.[456]

The valedictory tone persisted, nevertheless. Speaking of his youth in the first half of the century, Charles Hardwick stated that faeries had then been "as plentiful as blackberries" but this no longer seemed to be the case in the Lancashire of the 1870s. Recounting Cornish folk belief in 1893 Bottrell cited a verse to the effect that "The faeries from their haunts have gone." Entering the next century, in 1912 a Mrs. Leather of Cusop near Hay-on-Wye recalled faeries being seen dancing under foxgloves in Cusop Dingle: a vision that was within the memory of people still living, she recorded.[457]

Repeatedly, from the sixteenth to the nineteenth centuries, faeries were said to have only recently departed and the faery faith was felt to be in the process of dying out in the face of progress and rationalism. The faeries were always "yesterday," it seemed—they were the property of a generation that was itself dwindling. They were remembered, but they were no longer encountered.

Modern Disbelief

Predictably, perhaps, twentieth-century writers echoed their predecessors—perhaps even more forcibly, given the accelerated urbanisation and mechanisation of our world.

In 1923, folklorist Mary Lewes recorded a "practically universal belief among the Welsh country folk into the middle of the last century [which] is scarcely yet forgotten." She blamed education and newspapers for having quenched the people's spirits: "Mortal eyes in Cambria will no more behold the Fair Folk at their revels." She lamented that "even the conception of faeries seems to have been lost in the present generation." A couple of years later,

---

456. Brand, *Zetland,* 169; Fergusson, *Rambling sketches,* 121.

457. Hardwick, *Traditions, Superstitions and Folklore,* 124; Bowker, *Goblin Tales,* Introduction; Brand, *Description of Zetland,*169; Fergusson, *Rambling Sketches,* 121; *Traditions and Hearthside Stories of Cornwall,* 2nd series, 112.

reflecting on western Argyll as it had been in the 1850s, another writer rem-
inisced over the "dreamland" people had inhabited before "the fierce eye of
bespectacled modern omniscience" had dispelled belief. "These were the
days of elemental spirits, of sights and sounds relegated by present day sceptics to the realm of superstition or imagination." Adopting a similar tone, and
whilst maintaining that belief in the Cornish piskies was not entirely extinct,
Bottrell nonetheless condemned the "love of unpoetical facts [that] had come
into fashion, until they were frightened away." By the 1920s, it was really only
old people who recalled the wealth of the Cornish folktales. The faery faith
was also felt to be going or gone by this time from Herefordshire, Shropshire,
and from the Lake District.[458]

Times changed, but the refrain didn't. Toward the end of last century,
describing Sussex folk belief, Jacqueline Simpson made a familiar declaration
to the effect that "although it is most improbable that a belief in faeries is
seriously entertained by any adult of the present generation, it was a different matter in the nineteenth century … Even one generation ago, it was not
utterly extinct." Of the Dartmoor pixies, another writer of the same period
was of two minds whether true belief persisted into the 1960s. On the one
hand she felt it was only incomers who liked to keep the stories alive, and
that genuine faith had died out centuries before; on the other hand, she still
heard from time to time of sightings and of respectful conduct maintained.[459]

"The Faeries Travel Yet"

Continually, then, it has seemed to investigators to be the case that faery
belief had been strong until only a generation or so before they wrote, but
had since expired. This has been asserted every few decades over several centuries. For this reason, when Robin Gwyndaf alleged as recently as 1997 that
"faery belief persisted in Wales until the late 1940s or early 1950s," how confident should we be in the red line he seeks to draw? As we've seen, plenty of
writers have done the same before, and have found themselves subsequently

---

458. Lewes, *Queer Side*, 111, 113 & 139; Grant, *Myth, Tradition & Story*, 1 & 3; Bottrell, *Traditions and Hearthside Stories*, vol.1, 75; Leather, *Folklore of Herefordshire*, 43; Palmer,
Shropshire, 141; Rowling, *Folklore of the Lake District*, 28.

459. Simpson, *Folklore of Sussex*, 52; St. Leger Gordon, *The Witchcraft and Folklore of Dartmoor*, 16 & 21.

contradicted (or repeated). The demise of the faeries has rolled forward every generation; it is always—apparently—just passed out of sight, just over the horizon. Equally, there have been stubborn writers who have not been so ready to pronounce the faeries' obituary.[460]

As already noted, the faeries were declared dead and gone from the Lake District in both 1825 and the early twentieth century. Another observer was not so pessimistic. "The shyness of the British faery in modern times has given rise to a widespread belief that the whole genus must be regarded as extinct," wrote a Mrs. Hodgson in 1901, yet she felt confident specimens could still be found in remote Cumberland and Westmorland neighbourhoods. On the Welsh borders in the 1870s Francis Kilvert was told by David Price of Capel-y-ffin that "we don't see them now because we have more faith in the Lord and don't think of them. But I believe the faeries travel yet." In 1873 William Bottrell confidently wrote that, in West Cornwall, "belief in the faeries is far from being extinct.[461]

In assessing the true state of faery belief, it seems that it all depends on who does the asking and whom they're talking to. The evidence of the recent *Fairy Census*, and of Marjorie Johnson's collection of sightings in *Seeing Fairies*, suggests that—contrary to all reports—the faeries are still present and active. It's only with a little retrospect, when we've had a chance to pull together the evidence, that we can truly judge the state of the faery faith at a given point in time. Our perspective on the present can be narrow, but with hindsight we can better assess the scale and continuity of sightings and belief. When disparate references are combined, it seems often to turn out that the Good Folk are as alive and well as they ever were.

New Faery Forms

People continue to see faeries and they see them too in new shapes and doing new things. Earlier, I mentioned the surprising new forms of faeries that have been identified during the last century or so: the furry faeries, faeries like trees, and faeries like points of light. What we see when we hear the word "faery" seems to be under constant challenge and revision.

---

460. Gwyndaf, in Narvaez, *The Good People,* 155.

461. Hodgson, "On Some Surviving Fairies," 116; Simpson, *Welsh Border,* 72; Bottrell, *Traditions and Hearthside Stories,* vol. 2, 245.

There's more to this transformation than just outward physical description tion though. Our conceptions of the *purpose* of faeries has been evolving over the last hundred years as well. This last section very briefly sketches some of the newer ideas that have emerged.

The impact of Rosicrucian and Theosophist thinking has grown steadily since the seventeenth century and, over the last 150 years, has become particularly strong in faery lore. As a result of this influence, it has become conventional to view faeries as nature spirits, part of a natural hierarchy that can range from nearly invisible "elementals" all the way up to angels, and whose purpose is to stimulate and even guide the growth of plants. Out of this, in the last few decades, has emerged a broader concept of faeries as guardians of the entire planet and its environment. In contrast, as the foregoing description of traditional faery functions and behaviours will suggest, the folklore record for these beings is quite limited.

These newer perceptions have expanded the scope of faery for us and have identified new members of the faery family. However, this had led to some confusion over the nature and purpose of those beings already known. The "nature spirit" concept can have the tendency to reduce all of the Good Folk to tiny cogs in the natural machine and to deprive them of their individuality and free will. Elementals and elves ought not to be equated—they're different beings with different functions.

Secondly, the importation of external ideas, inherent in Theosophy, has also had a complicating effect on faery lore. The roster of native British faeries, sketched out at the start of this book, has been very freely swelled with categories of supernaturals from many other lands and cultures. Dwarves, vilas, peris, and devas—not to mention entirely made-up beings such as gnomes—have all been divorced from their roots and assimilated, with writers often struggling as a result to find some relationship between them where little (or none) may exist. Confusion and uncertainty can result when attempts are made to identify and classify beings; furthermore, people's preconceptions about what they see can be affected, which can make it difficult to assess what they have actually witnessed. Avoiding the risk of this confusion was part of my deliberate focus on British faery types alone in this book.

The second strong element in recent faery thinking is not unrelated to the last. It might be called the "Faery Faith" and it has involved a reassessment of the faeries' relationship to us in spiritual rather than physical terms. In fact, the two new visions of Faery are very far from separate, but the Faery Faith conceives of itself as a reversion to an older interaction with the Fae. They are seen as powerful semi-deities whom humans can contact through worship and magic. The faeries may use their supernatural abilities to assist those who show them the proper respect. Once again, this view of Faery draws upon authentic themes in the traditional materials and combines them with elements from witchcraft and goddess worship. This spiritual awareness of nature, combined with reconstructed magical ceremonies, reconfigures the entire dynamic that exists between the Good Folk and ourselves whilst preserving the power of the Fae and the sense of awe with which they should be approached.

The result of these combinations of ideas has been, especially in North America, the emergence of a tradition of witchcraft that places great emphasis on contacts with Faery for wisdom and magical power. Since the 1960s diverse pathways have been formulated by numerous teachers and groups that are distinct from the British Wicca inspired by Gardner and Alex Sanders. Whilst traditional witchcraft may be distinguished by its focus on medieval lore and practice, and its sense of being a craft rather than being a Neopagan religion, a core element of the diverse new approaches has been the incorporation of faery folklore and beliefs into personal practice. Methods used include contacting faeries, journeying to the otherworld, and honouring the particular faeries who feature in the path's mythology.

Amongst the paths followed are *Feri* or *Vicia*, as developed by Victor and Cora Anderson in the late 1940s; *Faery Wicca*—a Celtic pathway working with the *Tuatha Dé Danann*; and the *Faerie Faith*, a Neopagan practice that has branched off from the "Old Dianic" tradition developed by Mark Roberts and Morgan McFarland in Texas in the 1970s. The *Faith* believe in a symbiotic relationship with the faery folk, in the spiritual reality lying behind nature, and in a reverence for the earth. The joy and spontaneity of the faery realm is used as a focus for dynamic spiritual connection with the inner Fae. Lastly, *heritage witchcraft*—as exemplified by the teachings of Ari Devi and Grayson Magnus—seeks to collaborate with faery beings for initiation into the faery mysteries, self-realisation, and higher awareness. This is achieved through a romantic courtship between the mystic and a faery lover.

Many of these new perceptions are difficult to accommodate with the testimony of folklore experience which this book has laid out. In this more traditional view, there is very limited evidence of any faery concern for our spiritual or moral development—or, for that matter, for their own, given that the faeries might most often be regarded as amoral, if not sometimes immoral. Equally, the sources provide only scattered indications of any wish on their part to collaborate with or assist us in material or personal improvement. The older views are clearly more pessimistic about faery motivations and moods. A new openness and receptiveness on our part—and perhaps a new urgency in our need to reconnect with natural forces—may very well have changed the ways in which we interact with the supernatural, revealing aspects and interests formerly concealed from us by the Fae. For example, in the last example given, of faery consorts, we may identify a positive development of our relationship away from the often possessive and dangerous *lhiannan shee* to something far more mutual and spiritual.

Final Thoughts

It's impossible to be didactic about the Good Folk, especially when the subject is beings who are invisible and secretive. Contacts with them are rare and fleeting, so any impressions formed will always be uncertain and unconfirmed. As I've suggested, the lack of consistency throughout the reports may seem to give excellent grounds for rejecting them all as fictions. What is odd, though, is that these tales derive from a period when there was a genuine and widespread belief in (and fear of) faeries. This being so, you might expect the folk stories to provide listeners with consistent and coherent statements about the supernaturals, so that audiences might be forewarned and forearmed. The lack of correspondence between accounts might then be argued to be an indicator of authenticity.

Experience is ultimately the key—and people still have faery encounters, probably just as often as they ever did. Whilst belief may not be so widespread as once it was, our interactions with Faery carry on and, in many respects, seem more intense than ever. We continue to be amazed—and we continue to learn.

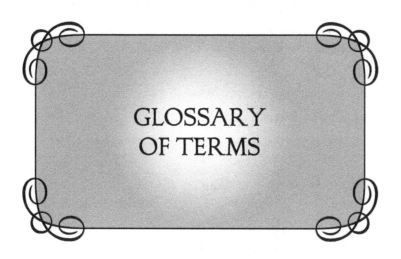

GLOSSARY
OF TERMS

adder stone: a stone pierced through by a natural hole

asrai: a water sprite of the English Midlands

banshee / bean-sidhe: an Irish and Scottish female faery particularly tied to certain families

boggart: a brownie gone bad, who only plays pranks and does harm

bogle (also bogie or bug): a mischievous or dangerous spirit

brownie: a domestic faery of the East and North of England and Lowland Scotland

bwca / bucca: a Welsh / Cornish faery, related to "Puck"

Caointeach (pronounced "koniuch"): a Highland banshee; her name means "keener"

ceol sidhe (pronounced "kyolshee"): the Irish Gaelic for "faery music"

changeling: the faery left behind for a stolen human child

derrick: a pixy of the South Coast of England (Dorset and Hampshire)

Doonie: a Scottish wild faery who appears as a horse or as an old woman

dwarf: not a British being; a German and Scandinavian goblin

elf: the Old English/Anglo-Saxon name for the being we now tend to call a faery

Elfame / Elphame: the Scots English word for the faery kingdom under the hills

elf bolt / elf shot: flint arrows fired by the elves

ellyllon: simply the Welsh for "elves."

Faery: used in the book to mean faeryland, but the word is just a variant of faery

faery: the more modern word for an elf. Fae, fay, and fairy are all variants and all denote a supernatural being of some kind. It's used in the book as a very general term

ferisher: the word for faeries used in the North West of England (Lancashire). *Feorin* is another such term from this region

fenodyree / phynoderee: the Manx equivalent of the brownie

foison / foyson: the nutritional essence of food that's stolen by the Fae

frairy: the dialect word for faeries in East Anglia

Gean-Cannah: a male faery who seduces women

glaistig: a hairy female faery of the Scottish Highlands

gnome: an invented word, meaning a small, dwarfish being

goblin: a type of bad faery

grey folk: a Shetland euphemism for the trows

gruagach: a hairy Scottish Highland being, rather like a brownie

Gwragedd Annwn: Welsh faery women who live under lakes; the singular is *gwraig annwn*

Gyre-Carlin: the faery queen in Fife who has links to spinning

Habetrot: a faery woman especially linked to spinning thread

hag stone: another word for an adder stone

hobgoblin: hobs and lobs are a general class of beings in England that include the Pucks and the brownies

hyter sprite: a type of tiny faery from East Anglia

kelpie: a water monster of the Scottish Highlands

knocker: a type of goblin who lives in mines, especially in Cornwall or in Wales (where they're called *koblynnau*—goblins).

leanan sidhe / lhiannan shee: an Irish or Manx name for a female faery who seduces and haunts men

Loireag (pronounced "loryack"): she is a water sprite of the Scottish Highlands, associated with spinning

Mab: the faery queen and a common personal name for faery women

nursery sprites: a modern term used to describe faeries whose main function seems to be to scare children away from dangerous places, such as rivers and ponds

pharisee: the word for faery in the English county of Suffolk

pixy / pisgy / pisky: a small faery being from the South West of England (the counties of Cornwall, Devon, and Somerset)

pixy-led: the experience of being mischievously enchanted and led astray by faeries, especially pixies

pobel vean: the Cornish name of the pixies, meaning "the little people."

portunes: a medieval name for tiny brownie-like creatures found in eastern England

Puck: an old English name for a hobgoblin

rade: some faeries are known for "trooping" in procession on horseback, a parade called the "faery rade"

Red Cap: a malevolent goblin of the Scottish Borders

seelie: the Scots English name for the good faeries

sidh / sith (pronounced "shee"): respectively the Irish and Scottish Gaelic words for "faery"

sithbruaich (pronounced "shee-brooack"): a faery hill

sithean (pronounced "shee-an"): a faery hill

sluagh (pronounced "slooa"): the faery host that rides through the skies at night

spriggan: a sort of pixy—but perhaps more malevolent

Tiddy Men / Tiddy Ones: a type of faery unique to the fenland country of East Anglia in England

toradh: the Gaelic word equivalent to "foison"

tylwyth teg (pronounced "terlooethtayg"): the "fair family" of faeries in Wales

unseelie: the Scots English name for the bad faeries

urisk: a brownie-like being of the Scottish Highlands

witch stone: see "adder stone"

Yarthkin: another name for the "Tiddy Men" or "Tiddy Ones"

BIBLIOGRAPHY

Addy, Sidney. *Household Tales.* London: Nutt, 1895.

Aitken, Hannah. *A Forgotten Heritage: Original Folk Tales of Lowland Scotland.* Scottish Academic Press, 1973.

Allies, Jabez. *On the Ancient British, Roman and Saxon Antiquities of Worcestershire.* Worcester, 1840.

Anon. *Folklore and Legends: Scotland.* W. W. Gibbings, 1889.

Atkinson, John. *Forty Years in a Moorland Parish.* London: MacMillan & Sons, 1891.

Bailey, Jennie. *Lancashire Folk Tales.* Stroud, UK: The History Press, 2014.

Barbour, John. *Unique Traditions, Chiefly of the West and South of Scotland.* Hamilton, Adams & Co, 1886.

Barton, Ingrid. *North Yorkshire Folk Tales.* Stroud, UK: The History Press, 2014.

Beaumont, John. *A Treatise of Spirits.* London: D. Browne, 1705.

Berry, Claude. *Cornwall.* Robert Hale Ltd., 1949.

Besant, Annie, and Charles Webster Leadbeater. *Thought-Forms.* London: The Theosophical Society, 1905.

Bett, Henry. *English Myths and Traditions.* Batsford Ltd., 1952.

Billingsley, John. *West Yorkshire Folk Tales*. Stroud, UK: The History Press, 2010.

Blakeborough, Richard. *Wit, Character, Folklore and Customs of the North Riding of Yorkshire*. London: H. Frowde, 1898.

Bord, Janet. *Fairies: Real Encounters with Little People*. New York: Carroll & Graf, 1997.

Bottrell, William. *Traditions and Hearthside Stories of West Cornwall*. Penzance, vol. 1, 1870; vol. 2, 1873.

Bovet, Richard. *Pandaemonium*, 1684.

Bowker, James. *Goblin Tales of Lancashire*. London: Swan Sonnenschein, 1878.

Bowring, John. "Devon Folklore Illustrated." *Transactions of the Devonshire Association for the Advancement of Science and Literature*, vol. 2 (1867–68), 70.

Brand, John. *A Description of Zetland*. Edinburgh: W. Brown, 1883.

Bray, Anna. *A Description of the Part of Devonshire Bordering the Tamar and the Tavy*. London: W. Kent & Co., vol. 1, 1886.

———. *Peeps on Pixies*. London: Grant and Griffith, 1854.

Briggs, John. *Remains of John Briggs*. Kirkby Lonsdale: A. Foster, 1825.

Briggs, Katharine Mary. "English fairies," *Folklore*, vol. 68.

———. "The Fairies and the Realms of the Dead," *Folklore*, vol. 81, 1970.

———. *The Fairies in Tradition and Literature*. London: Routledge & Kegan Paul, 1967.

———. "The Fairy Economy: As It May Be Deduced from a Group of Folk Tales," *Folklore*, vol. 70, 1959.

———. "Some Late Accounts of the Fairies," *Folklore*, vol. 72, 1961.

Browne, James. *History of the Highlands*. Glasgow: A. Fullerton & Co., vol. 1, 1838.

Browning, T. *Dumfries and Galloway Folk Tales*. Stroud, UK: The History Press, 2016.

Burne, Charlotte. *Shropshire Folklore: A Sheaf of Gleanings*. London: Trubner & Co., Part I, 1883; Part III, 1886.

Campbell, James. *More West Highland Tales*. Edinburgh: Oliver & Boyd, vol. 1, 1940.

Campbell, John. *Popular Tales of the West Highlands.* Edinburgh: Edmonston & Douglas, vol. 2, 1860.

———. *Waifs and Strays of Celtic Tradition* (Argyllshire Series, vol. 5). London: Nutt, 1895.

Carmichael, Alexander. *Carmina Gadelica.* Edinburgh: Oliver & Boyd, vol. 2, 1900.

Chambers, Robert. *Popular Rhymes of Scotland.* London: W. Chambers,1905.

County Folklore, vol. 2–8. London: The Folklore Society, 1901–1965.

Courtney, Margaret. *Cornish Feasts and Folklore.* Penzance: Beare & Son, 1890.

Cowper, Henry. *Hawkshead.* London: Bemrose & Sons, 1899.

Coxhead, J. *Devon Traditions and Fairy Tales.* Exmouth: Deiderfield & Sons, 1959.

Craig Gibson, A. "Ancient Customs and Superstitions of Cumberland," *Transactions of the Historical Society of Lancashire and Cheshire,* vol. 10, 1858.

Cririe, James. *Scottish Scenery.* London: T. Cadell, 1803.

Crofton Croker, Thomas. *Fairy Legends and Traditions.* London: John Murray, vol. 3, 1828.

Crombie, R. Ogilvie. *Encounters with Nature Spirits.* Rochester, VT: Inner Traditions—Bear & Company, 2018.

Crossing, William. *Tales of Dartmoor Pixies.* Newcastle upon Tyne: F. Graham, 1890.

Cumming, Joseph. *A Guide to the Isle of Man.* London: E. Stanford, 1861.

Cunningham, Allan.*Remains of Nithsdale and Galloway Song.* London: T. Cadell, 1810.

Daimler, Morgan. *Fairies: A Guide to the Celtic Fair Folk.* Alresford, UK: John Hunt Publishing, 2017.

Davies, Jonathan. *Folklore of West and Mid-Wales.* Aberystwyth, 1911.

Dalyell, John. *The Darker Superstitions of Scotland.* Edinburgh: Waugh & Innes, 1834.

Dathen, Jon. *Somerset Fairies and Pixies.* Milverton: Capall Bann, 2010.

Deane, Tony, and Tony Shaw. *Folklore of Cornwall.* Stroud, UK: The History Press, 2009.

"Denham Tracts" *Folklore Society,* vol. 35, London, 1895.

Dixon, John. *Gairloch in North West Ross-shire.* Edinburgh: Co-operative Printing Co., 1886.

Doyle, Arthur Conan. *The Coming of the Fairies.* London: Hodder & Stoughton Ltd., 1922.

Edmondston, Arthur. *A View of the Ancient and Present State of the Zetland Isles.* Edinburgh: Ballantyne & Co., vol. 2, 1809.

Edmonston, Biot, and Jessie Saxby. *The Home of a Naturalist.* London: J. Nisbet, 1888.

Edmonston, Eliza. *Sketches and Tales of Shetland.* Edinburgh: Sutherland & Knox, 1856.

Edwards, Gillian. *Hobgoblin and Sweet Puck, Fairy Names and Natures.* London: Bles, 1974.

Evans-Wentz, Walter. *The Fairy Faith in Celtic Countries.* Oxford: Oxford University Press, 1911.

Fairy Census (see S. Young).

Fergusson, Robert. *Rambling Sketches in the Far North and Orcadian Musings.* London: Simpkin, Marshall & Co., 1883.

Firth, John. *Reminiscences of an Orkney Parish.* Stromness: Orkney Natural History Society, 1974.

Gascoigne, George. *The Buggbears* (play), 1565.

Gill, Walter. *A Manx Scrapbook.* London: Arrowsmith, 2 volumes, 1929 & 1932.

Gordon Cumming, Constance. *In the Hebrides.* London: Chatto & Windus, 1883.

Graham, Patrick. *Sketches Descriptive of Picturesque Scenery in Perthshire.* Edinburgh: Ballantyne & Co., 1810.

Grant, Katharine. *Myth, Tradition and Story from Western Argyll.* Oban: Oban Times Press, 1925.

Grant Stewart, William. *The Popular Superstitions and Festive Amusements of the Highlanders of Scotland.* London: Aylott & Jones, 1823.

Gregor, Walter. *Notes on the Folklore of the North East of Scotland.* London: Folklore Society, 1881.

Gregory, A. *Visions & Beliefs in the West of Ireland*. Dublin, 1920.

Grice, Frederick. *Folk Tales of the North Country: Drawn from Northumberland and Durham*. London: Nelson & Sons, 1944.

Grieve, Symington. *A Book of Colonsay and Oronsay*. Edinburgh: Oliver & Boyd, vol. 2, 1923.

Halliwell, James. *Illustrations of the Fairy Mythology of Midsummer Night's Dream*. London: Shakespeare Society, 1845.

———. *Popular Rhymes and Nursery Tales*. London: J. R. Smith, 1849.

Hardwick, Charles. *Traditions, Superstitions and Folklore (Chiefly of Lancashire and the North of England)*. Manchester: Ireland & Co, 1872.

Harland, John. *Lancashire Legends and Traditions*. London: Routledge, 1873; *Lancashire folklore*. London: Warne & Co., 1867.

Harris, Henry. *Cornish Saints and Sinners*. London: Clowes & Sons, 1907.

Harte, Jeremy. *Explore Fairy Traditions*. Avebury: Heart of Albion, 2004.

Hawker, Robert. *Footprints of Former Men in Far Cornwall* (chapter titled "Old Trevarten"). London: John Lane, 1893.

Hayward, L. "Shropshire Folklore of Yesterday and Today." *Folklore*, vol. 49, 1938.

Henderson, George. *Survivals of Belief Amongst the Celts*. London: Macmillan, 1861.

Henderson, William. *Notes on the Folklore of the Northern Counties of England and the Borders*. London: Folklore Society, 1879.

Herbert, Agnes. *The Isle of Man*. London: John Lane, 1909.

Hewett, Sarah. *Nummits and Crummits: Devonshire Customs, Characteristics and Folklore*. London: T. Burleigh, 1900.

Hibbert, Samuel. *A description of the Shetland Isles*. Lerwick: T. Manson, 1891.

Hill, Paul. *Folklore of Northamptonshire*. Stroud: The History Press, 2005.

Hobbes, Thomas. *Leviathan*, 1651.

Hodgson, Mrs. "On Some Surviving Fairies." *Transactions of the Cumberland and Westmorland Antiquarian and Archaeological Society*, vol. 1, 1901.

Hodson, Geoffrey. *Fairies at Work and Play*. Theosophical Publishing House, 1925.

———. *The Kingdom of Faerie*, 1927.

Hogg, James. "Odd characters" in *Shepherd's Calendar*. London: T. Cadell, vol. 2, 1829.

———. *A Queer Book*. Edinburgh: Blackwood, 1831.

Hunt, Robert. *Popular Romances of the West of England*. London: Chatto & Windus, vol. 1, 1903.

Hutton, Ronald. *The Witch*. New Haven: Yale University Press, 2017.

Jackson, Thomas. *A Treatise Concerning the Original of Unbelief*, 1625.

Jenkinson, Henry. *A Practical Guide to the Isle of Man*. London: E. Stanford, 1874.

Jenkyn Thomas, William. *Welsh Fairy Book*. New York: F. A. Stokes, 1908.

Johnson, Marjorie. *Seeing Fairies*. San Antonio: Anomalist Books, 2014.

Jones, Edmund. *The Appearance of Evil: Apparitions of Spirits in Wales*. Cardiff: University of Wales Press, 2003.

———. *A geographical, historical and religious account of the parish of Aberystruth*. Trevecka, 1779.

———. *A Relation of the Apparition of Spirits in the County of Monmouth*. Newport: E. Lewis, 1813.

Keightley, Thomas. *The Fairy Mythology*. London: G. Bell, 1850.

Knox, James. *Topography of the Basin of the Tay*. Edinburgh: J. Anderson, 1831.

Kruse, John. *British Fairies*. Street: Green Magic Publishing, 2017.

Leather, Ella. *Folklore of Herefordshire*. Hereford: Jakeman & Carver, 1912.

Leney, I. *Shadowland in Ellan Vannin*. London: E. Stock, 1880.

Lewes, Mary. *Stranger Than Fiction*. London: Rider & Son, 1911.

———. *The Queer Side of Things*. London: Selwyn & Blount, 1923.

Licauco, Jaime. *Dwarves and Other Nature Spirits*. Quezon City: Rex Book Store, 2005.

Lilly, William. *Life of William Lilly*. London, 1681.

MacDougall, James, and George Calder. *Folk Tales and Fairy Lore in Gaelic and English*. Edinburgh: John Grant, 1910.

Macgregor, Alasdair. *The Peat Fire Flame: Folk Tales and Traditions of the Highlands and Islands*. Edinburgh: Moray Press, 1937.

MacKenzie, Donald. *Scottish Folklore and Folk Life*. London: Blackie & Sons, 1935.

———. *Wonder Tales From Scottish Myths*. London: Blackie & Sons, 1917.

Mackinlay, James. *Folklore of Scottish Lochs and Springs*. Glasgow: W. Hodge, 1893.

MacPhail, Malcolm. "Folklore from the Hebrides I." *Folklore*, vol. 7, 1896.

———. "Folklore from the Hebrides II." *Folklore*, vol. 8, 1897.

MacPherson, John. *Tales of Barra, told by the Coddy*. Edinburgh: W. Johnstone, 1960.

MacRitchie, David. *The Testimony of Tradition*. London, Kegan Paul, 1890.

Martin, Martin. *A Description of the Western Isles of Scotland*. London: A. Bell, 1716.

Marwick, Ernest. *The Folklore of Orkney and Shetland*. Edinburgh: Birlinn Ltd, 2011.

Mathews, F. *Tales of the Blackdown Borderland*. Taunton: Somerset Folk Press, 1923.

McDougall, James. "Craignish Tales." *Waifs and Strays of Celtic Tradition*. London: A. Nutt, vol. 1.

McPherson, Joseph. *Primitive Beliefs in the North East of Scotland*. London: Longmans, 1929.

Miller, Hugh. *Scenes and Legends of the North of Scotland*. Edinburgh: Johnstone & Hunter, 1835.

Moore, Arthur. *Folklore of the Isle of Man*. London: D. Nutt, 1891.

Morrison, Sophia. *Manx Fairy Tales*. London: D. Nutt, 1911.

Murray, Lady Evelyn. "Gaelic texts no. 7." *Tales from Highland Perthshire*. Edinburgh: Scottish Gaelic Texts Society, 2009.

Napier, James. *Folklore or Superstitious Beliefs in the West of Scotland Within this Century*. Paisley: A. Gardner, 1879.

Narvaez, Peter, ed. *The Good People: New Fairylore Essays*. Lexington: University of Kentucky Press, 1997.

Nicholson, Edward. *Golspie: Contributions to its Folklore.* London: D. Nutt, 1897.

Nicholson, John. *Folklore of East Yorkshire.* London: Simpkin & Co., 1890.

———. *Some Folktales and Legends of Shetland.* Edinburgh: T. Allen, 1920.

Norway, Arthur. *Highways and Byways of Yorkshire.* London: Macmillan, 1899.

O'Neill, Susanna. *Folklore of Lincolnshire.* Stroud: History Press, 2012.

Owen, Elias. "Rambles over the Denbighshire Hills," *Archaeologia Cambrensis,* vol. 3, 5th series, no. 9, 1886.

———. *Welsh Folklore.* Oswestry: Woodall, Minshall & Co., 1896.

Page, John. *An Exploration of Dartmoor and its Antiquities.* London: Seeley & Co., 1892.

Palmer, Kingsley. *Folklore of Somerset.* London: Batsford, 1976.

Palmer, Roy. *Folklore of Hereford and Worcester.* Hereford: Logaston Press, 1992.

———. *Folklore of Leicestershire and Rutland.* Stroud: History Press, 2002.

———. *Folklore of Radnorshire.* Hereford: Logaston Press, 2001.

———. *Folklore of Shropshire.* Hereford: Logaston Press, 2004.

———. *Folklore of Warwickshire.* Stroud: History Press, 2004.

———. *Folklore of Worcestershire.* Hereford: Logaston Press, 2005.

Pegg, Bob. *Argyll Folk Tales.* Stroud: History Press, 2015.

Pennant, Thomas. *The History of the Parishes of Whiteford & Holywell.* London: B. White, 1796.

———. *A Tour in Scotland.* London: B. White, 1769.

———. *A Tour in Scotland and a Voyage to the Hebrides.* Chester: John Monk, 1771.

Pike, Signe. *Faery Tale.* London: Hay House, 2010.

Plot, Robert. *The Natural History of Staffordshire.* Oxford, 1686.

Poole, Charles. *The Customs, Superstitions and Legends of the County of Stafford.* London: Rowney & Co., 1875.

———. *The Customs, Superstitions & Legends of the County of Somerset.* London: Sampson Low, 1877.

Purkiss, Diane. *Troublesome Things: A History of Fairies and Fairy Stories.* London: Penguin Books, 2000.

Rabuzzi, Daniel. "In Pursuit of Norfolk's Hyter Sprites." *Folklore,* vol. 95, 1984.

Rhys, John. *Celtic Folklore.* Oxford: Clarendon Press, 1901.

———. *Manx Folklore and Superstition.* Isle of Man: Chiollagh Books, 1994.

Richardson, Moses. *Local Historian's Table Book.* Newcastle upon Tyne: M. Richardson, 1844.

Riche, David, and Brian Froud. *Art of Faery.* London: Paper Tiger, 2003.

Roberts, Kai. *Folklore of Yorkshire.* Stroud: History Press, 2013.

Roeder, Charles. *Manx Folk Tales.* Isle of Man: Chiollagh Books, 1993.

Rowling, Marjorie. *Folklore of the Lake District.* London: Harper Collins, 1976.

St. Leger Gordon, Ruth. *The Witchcraft and Folklore of Dartmoor.* London: Robert Hale, 1965.

Saxby, Jessie. *Shetland Traditional Lore.* Edinburgh: Grant & Murray, 1932.

Scot, Reginald. *The Discoverie of Witchcraft* (1584). London: Elliot Stock, 1886.

Sikes, Wirt. *British Goblins.* London: Sampson Low, 1880.

Simpson, Evelyn. *Folklore in Lowland Scotland.* London: J. M. Dent, 1908.

Simpson, Jacqueline. *Folklore of Sussex.* Stroud: History Press, 1973.

———. *Folklore of the Welsh Border.* London: Harper Collins, 1976.

Spence, John. *Shetland Folklore.* Lerwick: Johnson & Greig, 1899.

Spence, Lewis. *The Fairy Tradition in Britain.* London: Rider & Co, 1948.

Stanley, W. "Folklore superstition in Anglesey." *Notes and Queries,* 4th series, vol. 9, 1871.

Sternberg, Thomas. *Dialect and Folklore of Northamptonshire.* London: J. R. Smith, 1851.

Stewart, Alexander. *'Twixt Ben Nevis and Glencoe.* Edinburgh: W. Patterson, 1885.

"Stories of Fairies from Scotland" *Folk-Lore Journal,* vol. 1, 1883.

Sutherland, George. *Folklore Gleanings & Character Sketches from the Far North.* Wick: John O'Groats Journal, 1937.

Taylor, Lea, and Sylvia Troon. *Midlothian Folk Tales.* Stroud: History Press, 2018.

Terrell, Henry. *The Wee Folk of Menteith*. London: Houghton Publishing, 1935.

Thomas, Taffy. *Cumbrian Folk Tales*. Stroud: History Press, 2012.

Thornber, William. *A Historical and Descriptive Account of Blackpool and its Neighbourhood*. Blackpool: Smith, 1837.

Tongue, Ruth. *Somerset Folklore*. London: Folklore Society, 1965.

Tregarthen, Enys. *North Cornwall Fairies and Legends*. London: Wells Gardner, 1906.

———. *Pixie Folklore & Legends*. New York: Gramercy Books, 1996.

Udal, John. *Dorsetshire Folklore*. Hertford, 1922.

Waldron, George. *A Description of the Isle of Man*. Douglas: Manx Society, 1731.

Watson, Rosamund Marriott. *The Poems of Rosamund Marriott Watson*. London: John Lane, 1912.

Waugh, Edwin. *Sketches of Lancashire Life & Localities*. London: Simpkin & Co., 1855.

Willis, Richard. *Mount Tabor, or Private Exercises of a Penitent Sinner*, 1639.

Wilson, William. *Folklore and Genealogies of Uppermost Nithsdale*. Dumfries: J. M. Laing, 1904.

Wimberley, Lowry. *Folklore in the English and Scottish Ballads*. New York: Frederick Ungar Co., 1928.

Worthy, Charles. *Devonshire Parishes*. Devon: W. Pollard & Co., 1887.

Wright, Mary. *Rustic Speech and Folklore*. London: H. Milford, 1913.

Wright, William. *Picturesque South Devonshire*. Dundee: Valentine & Co., 1905.

Yeats, William Butler. *Faery and Folk Tales of the Irish Peasantry*. London: W. Scott, 1888.

Yn Lioar Manninagh, 1895–1901.

Young, Ella. *At the Gates of Dawn: A Collection of Writings of Ella Young*. Edited by J Matthews & D. Sallee. Cheltenham: Skylight Press, 2011.

Young, Simon, ed. *Fairy Census 2017*. Fairy Investigation Society, 2018.

Young, Simon, and Ceri Houlbrook. *Magical Folk*. London: Gibson Square Books, 2018.

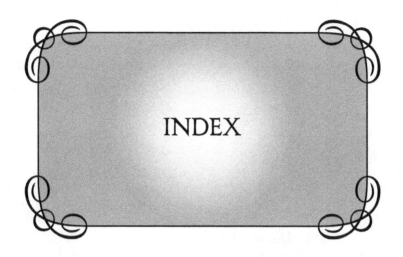

INDEX